W9-AZK-786

KINGDOM OF THE SUN GOD

January: earthing up the potatoes with hoes.

KINGDOM
OF THE
SUN GOD

A History of the Andes and their People

Ian Cameron

Facts On File

New York • Oxford • Sydney

Text Copyright © 1990 by Ian Cameron
Maps copyright © Random Century 1990

Facts On File, Inc.
460 Park Avenue South
New York NY 10016

Library of Congress Cataloging in Publication Data

ISBN 0-8160-2581-9

Facts On File books are available at special discounts when purchased in bulk quantities for businesses, associations, institutions or sales promotions. Please call our Special Sales Department in New York at 212/683-2244 (dial 800/322-8755 except in NY, AK or HI).

Text and jacket design by Behram Kapadia/Maps by Ian Sandom

Composition by SX Composing Ltd, Rayleigh, Essex

Color separation by Colorlito, Milan

Printed and bound in Spain by Graficas Estella, SA

Contents

CARTAGENA
CARACAS
TRINIDAD
PANAMA
Lake
Maracaibo
CUMANA
LLANOS
Orinoco
GUYANA
BOGOTA
VENEZUELA
SURINAM
COLOMBIA
FRENCH
GUIANA
ESMERALDES
Negro
QUITO*
ECUADOR
Amazon
Chimborazo
TUMBES*
Napo
Solimoes
PERU
CAJAMARCA*
AMAZON
BASIN
CHANCHAN*
HUANUCO*
CHAVIN DE
CALLAO
HUANTAR*
MACHU
BRAZIL
PICCHU*
LIMA
CUZCO*
NAZCA*
BOLIVA
Lake
Titicaca
LA PAZ
Lake Poopo
PARAGUAY
ANTOFAGASTA
Licancabur
CHILE
Parana
Mercedario
URUGUAY
VALPARAISO
Aconcagua
MONTEVIDEO
MENDOZA
SANTIAGO
PAMPAS
BUENOS
AIRES
HUMBOLDT
CURRENT
CONCEPCION
ARGENTINA
ATLANTIC
OCEAN
VALDIVIA
PACIFIC
OCEAN
PUNTA
ARENAS

(* INCA OR PRE INCA TOWNS)

The Legend of El Dorado

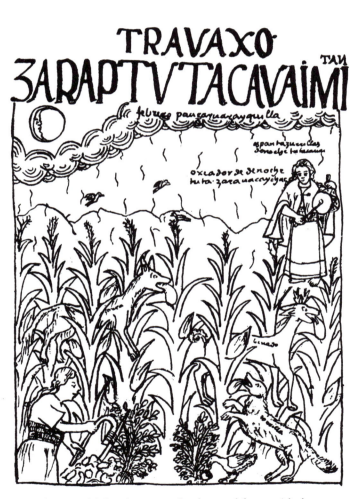

February: frightening away the deer and foxes with drums.

It was dawn in the foothills of the Andes. One by one, touched by the light of the rising sun, the great peaks were transformed from granite-grey to flamingo-pink; but the lake remained in shadow, for it lay in the crater of an extinct volcano. The lake was not beautiful, nor was it in any way sinister or mysterious; it seemed a very ordinary circle of water. Very ordinary, that is, until the first rays of sunlight burst over the rim of the crater and spotlit, at the water's edge, the figure of the man. He stood, arms outstretched, in the path of the sun. He wore no clothing; yet he could hardly be described as naked, because he was covered from head to foot in gold.

In a diurnal ritual of propitiation the golden man walked slowly into the lake, immersing himself in the water until every particle of gold-dust had been washed from his body.

This is one of the many versions of the legend of El Dorado, the gilded (or golden) man: a legend which encapsulates the image that the rest of the world has for a long time had of South America.

According to this particular version of the legend, El Dorado was the chief of the Chibcha Indians. His wife had been unfaithful and in remorse had drowned herself in Lake Guatavita, which lies in the crater of an extinct volcano about 30 miles north-east of Bogota. Here, the legend has it, her spirit liaised with a monster which lived in the depths of the lake, and the pair of them proceeded to terrify and devour the local fisherfolk. It was to appease these creatures that the chief of the Chibcha made his daily offering in gold, first annointing his body with a mixture of oil and *achote* (resin), then getting his servants to coat him in gold-dust which had been mined from alluvial deposits on the upper reaches of the Magdalena River. 'This powdered gold,' writes the Spanish historian Fernandez de Oviedo, 'adhered to the oil and *achote* until his entire body was covered from the soles of his feet to the top of his head, and he looked resplendant as a golden artefact worked by the hand of a great artist . . .'

In another version of the legend, four chiefs, again coated in gold-dust, embark on a raft with a cargo of emeralds and *objects d'art*. To the accompaniment of chanting and music from the shore they cast their tribute into the lake. 'From this ceremony,' writes the historian Juan Rodrigues Fresle, 'was taken that famous name "El Dorado", which has cost so many men their lives and fortunes.' Another contemporary Spanish historian records yet another version: that a young man was chosen by lot, killed, opened up, salted with gold-dust and cast as a sacrifice in the lake – 'hence they call him El Dorado, the golden one'.

Here, one might be forgiven for thinking, are different renderings of a traditional Indian legend. The truth, however, is that the legend of El Dorado has its roots not in Indian folklore but in Spanish greed. The golden man was an invention of the consquistadors.

The legend originated in Ecuador soon after the crushing of the first of the Inca rebellions against the Spaniards. John Hemming, in his book *The Search for El Dorado*, makes this point very clearly: 'All sources show that it [the legend] started in Quito; and contemporary sources leave no doubt that it took shape there in late 1540. The story seems to have been brought back by the Spaniards returning from Bogota. It was the creation of the Spaniards themselves and not of [the] Indians.' The whole thing seems to have been based on a misconception. The Yalcones Indians, who live in the foothills of the Andes between present-day Quito and Bogota, defended their territory with particular desperation and skill. This convinced the Spaniards that they were defending an area of particular value. Nothing, to Spanish eyes, was as valuable as gold; hence the idea that hidden in these remote and inaccessible foothills of the Andes was an area of fabulous wealth, an El Dorado.

How did such a misconception become legend, and how did the legend gain credence until it came to affect – and indeed still affects today – the attitude of the rest of the world to South America?

The European exploration of South America was initiated and sustained by lust for gold. Columbus, the first European to sight the continent, brought back glowing reports of 'rivers of gold nuggets of such quality it was a marvel'. Balboa, the first European to cross America and sight the Pacific, reported that 'on the shores of the new-found ocean even cooking pots are made of gold', and the first Europeans to explore the mainland have been likened by John Hemming to 'packs of hounds roaming the interior to pick up a scent of gold'. In the words of their contemporary, Oviedo, 'They had come only to get gold and wealth . . . and to this end they subordinated honour, morality and honesty.' These early explorers of the mainland had no need of a mythical El Dorado to spur them on; they had the reality of finding gold or the promise of gold in almost every other village they came to. The most fabulous riches fell to Francisco Pizarro in Peru, where a room measuring 22 feet by 17 feet was filled with gold ornaments to a height of 7 feet and the contents handed over to him; but Quesada in Colombia and Dalfinger in Venezuela were almost equally successful in amassing plunder. It was only gradually, as the obvious sources of gold were one by one discovered and ransacked, that the conquistadors began to feel the need for a specific goal to aim for in order to justify further exploration in terrain that was as difficult to travel through as any in the habitable world. This need for a specific goal became more pressing as Spain assumed increasingly effective control over her New World dominions. Soon it was no longer possible for groups of adventurers simply to strike out on pillaging forays into the unknown; expeditions had to have an authorized leader, a royal licence 'to conquer and settle' and an approved target. It therefore suited the conquistadors very well to claim that they were searching for some definite objective such as the Golden City of Manoa (said to lie in the headwaters of the Amazon), the River of Silver (supposedly in Argentina), the Enchanted Palace of the Caesars (supposedly in Chile) or El Dorado (described by *The Oxford Dictionary* as 'an area abounding in gold believed by early explorers to exist in the Andes'.)

Of these myths, that of El Dorado was to prove the most enduring, and almost every year from 1541 to the present day has seen at least one expedition combing the Andes or draining Lake Guatavita in search of the elusive golden man.

The first of these expeditions was led by Gonzalo Pizarro – younger and crueller brother of the better-known Francisco – and it set an unhappy precedent. It consisted of 220 Spanish adventurers, each carrying only his weapons and a small bag of emergency food, together with 4,000 press-ganged mountain Indians, each carrying a heavy load of food and equipment; also taking part were horses, llamas, 2,000 live swine and a pack of hunting dogs specially trained to savage recalcitrant Indians. The expedition left Quito in March 1541, and almost at once had to climb a high spur of the Andes where some 500 of the Indians died of cold, exposure and exhaustion. They then plunged into the humid and precipitous rain forest where, a contemporary writer tells us, 'both the Spaniards and their horses became quite exhausted from the great hardships they had to endure, climbing and descending the mountains, and building bridges over the many rivers'. Pizarro halted and asked the local Indians how long it would be before his expedition reached the open gold-bearing country for which he was searching. The Indians told him they had no knowledge of such a country, but Pizarro refused to believe them. He ordered bamboo barbecues to be built and had the Indians tied to them, tortured and burned to death. 'Other Indians,' writes Cieza de León, 'he ordered to be thrown to the dogs who tore them limb from limb and devoured them. It is said that there were women among those both burned to death and eaten.'

The expedition then moved on, hacking its way with increasing frustration through the rain forest. There were more interrogations, and more charred and mutilated bodies left in the Spaniards' wake. Each time they came to a new tribe they captured the chief, tortured him to make him disclose the way to El Dorado, then forced him to accompany the expedition in chains. A contemporary writer tells us what, inevitably, happened next. 'On the banks of a broad river [probably the Napo] a local chief named Delicola, having heard of the great cruelty of the Spaniards, decided to get rid of them by telling them that a land of many people and much gold lay only a little farther to the east . . . and Pizarro and his followers were delighted, believing this to be true.'

So a new twist was added to the legend. El Dorado had been invented by the Spaniards, but now, it seemed, the Indians were confirming that it did indeed exist and were holding out hope that the longed-for crock of gold lay only just across the next river or beyond the next range of hills. Many Spaniards, writing in the cool of their *haciendas*, appreciated in retrospect that the Indians were simply telling them what they knew they wanted to hear – 'Indians,' wrote Oviedo, 'ever promise Christians that which they realize is dearest to their hearts: namely gold.' However, in the steaming heat of the rain forest or the bitter cold of the Andean snows it wasn't easy to be dispassionate. The consquistadors had journeyed far and suffered much; they weren't going to give up easily. It was only natural that they should go on hoping against hope that each new promise would turn out, at last, to be the truth.

Buoyed up by such a hope, Pizarro struggled on, leaving in his wake a trail of misery and terror. At the end of six months not one of his 4,000 Indian porters was left. Those who could had fled; those who couldn't had died. In the course of the next year some of the Spaniards were whirled willy-nilly down the Amazon, looting and murdering en route. The remainder, soaked by torrential rains, squelched their way through the swamps to the east of the Andes, ever seeking but never finding the elusive El Dorado. No one will ever know how many Indians died as a result of their frenzied searching, but 2,000 would probably be too conservative an estimate. After 15 months of almost unbelieveable cruelty, hardship and suffering, the expedition staggered back to Quito, according to de León, 'with no horse or other thing, bereft of all but their swords and a staff to lean on'. Bereft, too, of gold.

Subsequent expeditions often followed a similar pattern, setting out with high hope which, in the heat and humidity of the jungle, turned to frustration; frustration then turned to disillusion, and disillusion to reprisal, with the Indians being massacred sometimes literally by the thousand.

There are many well-documented examples of this brutal treatment of the people of the Andes:

There is known to have been much ill-treatment of the Indians. There have been murders and the cutting off of limbs and members, so that some villages have become altogether depopulated. (Jiménez de Quesada).

It is known that Juan de Arévalo sacked the town of Cota because its chief did not give him enough gold. He destroyed that town utterly, killing many Indians, cutting hands or noses off some, cutting the breasts off the women and the noses off the small children . . . This resulted in the death of three or four thousand souls. It was said openly that Herod's cruelty against the Israelites was no greater than the cruelty of Arévalo against these innocent people. (Jeronimo Lebrón).

Martin Pujol set his hunting dogs on the Indians of Guasca and Suba, defending his action by saying that the Indians had refused to disclose the source of their gold, and that they had, in any case, been baptized before they were killed and eaten. (Miguel de Armandáriz).

Lope de Lugo wrote that he

favoured the impaling of recalcitrant Indians, because they do not fear being hanged or beheaded, but they fear very much death by impaling, this being done by inserting a stake from between the legs to emerge at the head.

The records of Spanish South American courts during the late sixteenth and early seventeenth centuries are full of cases of rape, pederasty, sodomy and bestiality. Cases of hanging Indians upside-down over a fire, burning them to death with hot oil, and killing babies so that their mothers could carry heavier loads are commonplace.

Although the atrocities perpetrated by the conquistadors are not typical of the Spanish regime as a whole, nevertheless the treatment initially meted out to the people of the Andes by their conquerors is a sickening story of indifference and cruelty.

This treatment of the Indians has helped to bring about what might be called the El Dorado syndrome, a widely-held and still prevalent belief that the treasure of the Andes and the people of the Andes are there simply to be exploited, are 'up for grabs'. This attitude is nicely summed up in a recent geography text book, *Lands of the Americas* by Allen and Anderson: 'The fabled land of El Dorado no longer appears on our maps. However, from the Spanish conquest to the present day men have continued to act on the idea that great wealth may be obtained [from South America] without a great deal of investment and labour.'

This El Dorado mentality epitomizes what might be called the dark face of the Andes. There is also, happily, a brighter and, indeed, an inspiring face: the Indians' success in establishing prosperous farming communities on the world's highest habitable plateaux, the agricultural and organizational expertise of the Incas, the dedication of the early European scientists, the fervour of the revolutionary armies, the exploits of mountaineers, and the concern of missionaries and, in our own day, of conservationists. It all adds up to a story with hardly a dull moment. Yet at the heart of it is a dichotomy.

The Andes are the greatest mountain range on earth – twice the length of the North American Rockies and nearly three times the length of the Himalayas. They are rich in both mineral resources and scenic beauty. They are uniquely varied, encompassing the world's driest desert, the most active belt of volcanoes, the highest peaks in the southern hemisphere, and the hottest and densest rain forest and the coldest and most storm-lashed deciduous forest. Their indigenous people are patient, kind and physically and mentally resilient. Yet for the last 500 years these people have had virtually no control over their own future or that of their mountains. Their land, which in happier times they cared for with great skill, has been taken or is being taken from them. The conquistadors turned them into slaves. The modern Andean republics are turning them into second-class citizens with no votes, no rights and little future.

Yet, in the story of the Andes, these descendants of once-great people are always in the background, ever watching and waiting; the ruins of their magnificent cities, roads and irrigation channels a mute condemnation of their conquerors, their herds of llama and vicuña abiding testimony to a way of life that was already old when the first of the Inca princes was enthroned in Cuzco. They are a phlegmatic, long-suffering people, and great survivors. There was a time, a couple of generations after the conquest, when there was real danger they might *not* survive, that the diseases and demands of their European conquerors might decimate them utterly; their numbers slumped from something over 12 million in 1500 to something under 3 million in 1600. But that crisis passed. Today they are still there.

The Andes are their mountains. They were the first of its explorers, and the greatest. It may well be that long after the myth of El Dorado has been forgotten, Indian herdsmen will still be driving their vicuña to pasture in a ritual half as old as time and twice as enduring as the ritual of the golden man which may or may not have taken place on the shore of Lake Guatavita.

CHAPTER I

The Forming of the Mountains

March: birds attack the crops.

He stood alone on a spur of the Andes, and so clear was the air that from a distance of 26 miles he could see the masts of his ship at anchor in Valparaiso harbour. Before him lay the coastal plain of Chile, spread out as though on a map; behind him, their summits wreathed in cloud, lay the towering cordillera of the Andes. 'I could not help wondering,' wrote the young Charles Darwin, 'what forces had fashioned such a fine chaos of mountains.'

Darwin was one of the first people to ask himself how the Andes had been formed. Before he cast his inquiring eyes on the cordillera, the people who lived in South America – the Indians, the conquistadors and the early European settlers – had accepted the fact that the mountains were there and left it at that.

The Indians of the Andes had never worshipped their great peaks with the single-minded devotion that the people of the Himalayas worshipped peaks like Kailas or Annapurna. Pantheism among the South American tribes embraced not only mountains but almost the entire range of natural phenomena – the sun, the moon, the stars, forests, rivers and, in particular, lakes; their navel of the world was not Chimborazo, Cotopaxi or Aconcagua but Lake Titicaca. It is true that the mythology of some tribes identified a particular peak with a particular deity; this, however, was the exception rather than the rule. For most of the Indians most of the time the mountains were ageless, inanimate and indifferent to the affairs of mere mortals.

The conquistadors had a more definite attitude to the Andes. They hated and feared them, regarding them as obstacles to conquest and the hiding place of unsubmissive Indians. Dalfinger, when he crossed the cordillera in 1532, lost several hundred men and wrote, 'we thought we should all die of cold in these abominable mountains, and indeed many of us were badly frostbitten and frozen near-solid.' A few years later and some thousand miles to the south, Almagro found himself in even deeper trouble: 'Many men and horses froze to death in the high passes, for neither clothes nor armour could protect them from the piercing wind. Many of those who died remained standing, frozen solid to the rocks as they leaned against them.' It is not surprising that the conquistadors viewed the Andes with a jaundiced eye.

The early settlers also eyed the cordillera without enthusiasm. The idea that mountains are one of the splendours of nature and meet-to-be-admired had few advocates before the last decade of the eighteenth century when romantic poets began to extol the wonders of the natural world. Prior to that, people still clung to the traditional view that mountains were useless and dangerous, the abode of demons and dragons, a view supported by Christian dogma – witness Milton:

> Through many a dark and dreary vale
> They passed, and many a region dolorous,
> O'er many a Frozen, many a Fiery Alp.
> Rocks, caves, lakes, fens, bogs, and shades of death,
> A Universe of death, which God by curse
> Created evil.

Those who lived in or visited the Andes prior to 1800 were therefore unimpressed by the mountains' spectacular desolation; nor did they ask themselves *why* the great peaks were so spectacular and desolate. That, to their way of thinking, was the way God had created them, and nothing more need be said.

So when a young British botanist, Charles Darwin, set off on a series of journeys through the Andes making notes and collecting rock samples, his behaviour was considered at best eccentric and at worst sacrilegious. 'I don't like it,' wrote a respected Valparaiso lawyer. 'No country is so rich that it would send out people to pick up such rubbish. Something fishy is going on!'

Darwin is best known today for his theory on the origin of species, but he also made a sizeable contribution to modern geology, for he was one of the first people to suggest that mountain ranges were not 'eternal hills' which had remained unaltered since the biblical creation, but were ever-changing structures still in the process of being created. He formed this view while serving as botanist aboard HMS *Beagle*; for while *Beagle* surveyed the Pacific coast of South America, Darwin had the opportunity to spend long spells ashore, and the Andes became both his playground and his workshop. He loved the mountains. 'Never,' he wrote after a particularly gruelling expedition, 'did I more deeply enjoy an equal space of time.' The invigorating air, the physical challenge and the vast open spaces must indeed have been a welcome change from the claustrophobic quarters of a ten-gun brig. However, there was more to his love affair with the Andes than physical exhilaration. There was mental exhilaration too. He made important discoveries. At 7,000 feet in the cordillera east of Valparaiso he found a cluster of petrified pine trees embedded in marine rock, and a few weeks later at 12,000 feet he found a strata of fossilized seashells. How, he asked himself, could these marine deposits have arrived several hundred miles inland at a height of many thousand feet? He discussed the possibilities with his commanding officer, Captain Robert FitzRoy of the *Beagle*. FitzRoy fell back on the Bible: this, he said, was how God had created the mountains, and that was explanation enough. It wasn't explanation enough for Darwin.

Darwin was a committed Christian; but he was also a committed scientist, and the more scientific evidence he collected the more convinced he became that the mountains of South America had been created not in the biblical six days but over a span of many million years, and were indeed still in the throes of creation. Early in 1835, as though to prove his point, South America suffered one of the most devastating earth tremors of modern times.

On 20 February *Beagle* was anchored off Valdivia in southern Chile. Darwin had just gone ashore with his assistant Covington, and the two of them were resting in an apple orchard when a sudden wind swept through the trees and the ground started to tremble. They leapt to their feet, feeling sick and giddy. Darwin wrote afterwards, 'The world, the very emblem of all that is solid, moved beneath our feet like crust over a fluid.'

Valdivia was only on the fringe of the earthquake. Over the next few days, as *Beagle* stood north, Darwin was able to see for himself the whole horror of what had taken place. From Osorno in the south to Aconcagua in the north a whole chain of volcanoes had almost simultaneously erupted. Concepcion and its port Talcahuano were close to the epicentre, and survivors described to Darwin the terrifying sequence of events. In the early hours of the morning huge formations of sea birds were seen flying inland, and the dogs in the coastal settlements took to the hills. A little before midday the shock waves started. At first they were little more than a subterranean trembling, but within minutes they built up to a terrifying crescendo. The ground heaved and split open. Fissures reeking with the stench of sulphur zigzagged through woodland, field and city. The sea drained out of Talcahuano harbour then with an appalling roar swept back in a succession of tidal waves. Ships were tossed ashore like flotsam. Whole houses were picked up, carried inland, then sucked out to sea to disappear in a series of sulphurous whirlpools. The town of Concepcion was demolished in six seconds. When, a couple of days later, FitzRoy and Darwin rode through it, not one building was standing; instead of streets there were lines of rubble. No one has ever been able to estimate how many were killed.

At the time, people could think of only two possible reasons for what had happened. The educated and intelligent believed that the earthquake was caused by the wrath of God, a punishment for human wickedness. The uneducated and superstitious believed it was caused by an old Indian woman, a witch, who had been insulted by the people of Concepcion and had taken her revenge by climbing the Andes and plugging up the vents of the volcanoes. Darwin had other ideas. It seemed to him that the earth – like the plants and creatures that lived on it – was in a state of continuous evolution. 'We can scarcely avoid the conclusion,' he wrote, 'that a vast lake of melted matter is spread out beneath a mere crust of solid land. Nothing, not even the wind, is so unstable as the crust of the earth . . . and this crust is being restructured by volcanic activity.' As evidence of this he was able to point to the results of *Beagle's* survey of the Chilean coast both before the earthquake and after. In the second survey it was found that vast reaches of rocks along the shoreline had been raised out of the sea, sometimes by as much as six feet. Darwin remembered the marine deposits he had found high in the cordillera. Here, he suggested, was an explanation of how they had got there. The mountains must have been raised by volcanic activity out of the sea.

If one reduces the evolution of the Andes to the simplest possible terms, Darwin had got it right. An important first step had been taken towards understanding how the range was formed.

Almost a hundred years were to pass before another equally important step was taken. In 1915 the German meteorologist Alfred Wegener published his famous book *The Genesis of Continents and Oceans*.

Wegener was intrigued by the fact that many parts of the world which are now tropical contain evidence of previous glaciation. To explain this he reassembled the continents in a huge conglomerate around the South Pole, and suggested that over a period of hundreds of millions of years the conglomerate broke up, and its component parts drifted slowly into their present positions under the influence of thermal currents welling up from the core of the earth. He named his conglomerate Pangaea (the Greek for 'All Earth'), and his theory became known as the theory of continental drift.

Wegener's theory provided a logical explanation for many of the world's phenomena. It explained why the continents resemble the bits of a jigsaw puzzle and if you compress them they slot together – the bulge of Africa, for example, dovetails almost exactly into the bight of the Caribbean. It also explains how many of the great mountain ranges could have been formed by the collision of continents; the Himalaya, for example, were obviously squeezed up – like toothpaste between the contracting walls of its tube – as the subcontinent of India crashed into the underbelly of Eurasia. However, some mountain ranges, including the Andes, were clearly *not* formed this way, since scientists are agreed that no continental landmass ever came into collision with the Pacific coast of South America. Wegener was too far ahead of his time, and throughout the first half of the twentieth century geologists were reluctant to admit that a mere meteorologist could have come up with so revolutionary a theory and be right. 'Unfortunately for Wegener's daring hypothesis,' stated the Time-Life Nature Library as recently as 1964, 'there are no known forces strong enough to move the continents around the earth, let alone split them into fragments. For these reasons the theory of continental drift has been abandoned by nearly all geologists.'

For several decades it looked as though Wegener's supporters had been led into a scientific cul-de-sac. Then came a discovery which not only established the concept of continental drift on a firm scientific basis, but also provided an explanation of how ranges such as the Andes could have been formed: the discovery of plate tectonics.

Over the last twenty years many scientists have contributed to our understanding of plate tectonics, but the basic concept stems from the research work of Harry H. Hess into the mechanics of seafloor spreading.

It has long been apparent that volcanic activity doesn't occur at random anywhere in the world but takes place again and again in the same narrow and well-defined zones, the most obvious of these being the 'ring of fire' which virtually encircles the Pacific. Figure 1 shows the distribution of earthquakes world-wide, over a period of six years. It has been established that nearly all earthquakes coincide with lines of fracture in the crust of the earth, and that the lines of fracture coincide with the boundaries between plates. It is now known that the earth's crust consists of six or seven major plates (Eurasia, Africa, India/Australasia, the Pacific, Antarctica and North and South America), and about the same

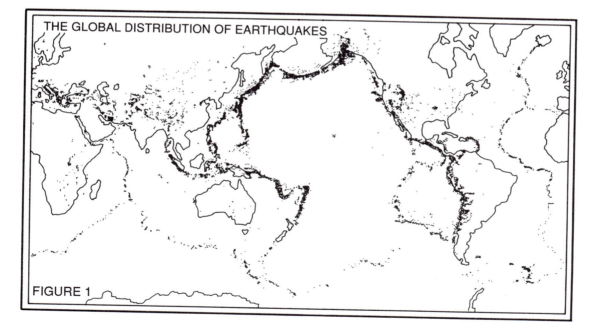

THE GLOBAL DISTRIBUTION OF EARTHQUAKES

FIGURE 1

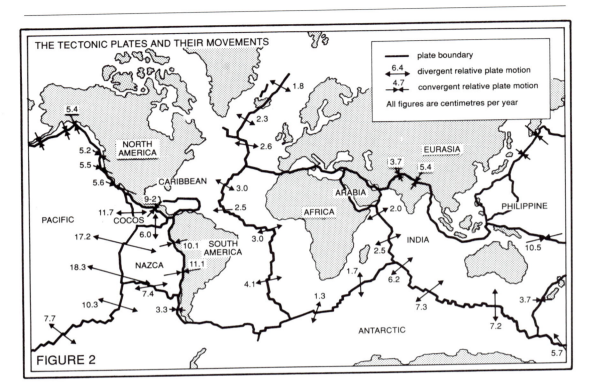

FIGURE 2

number of minor ones (Arabia, Caribbean, Cocos, Nazca, Philippines and Scotia.) Some of these plates are continental and have a crust that is relatively thick, some are oceanic and have a crust that is relatively thin, and all of them rest on the asthenosphere which is a layer of semi-molten matter sandwiched between the earth's cold and solid outer crust and its hot and liquid core. The essence of plate tectonics is that the asthenosphere forms a viscous surface across which the plates are being fractionally but continuously moved by convection currents welling up along the fracture lines. This might be described as a corollary to Wegener's theory of continental drift. Instead of visualizing the surface of the earth as a series of continents ploughing their way like ships through passive seas, we should visualize it as a series of plates, both continental and oceanic, all continually on the move, and all being continually prised apart or ground together. Figure 2 shows the present position of the plates and the direction in which they are moving, some as slowly as 1 centimetre a year and some as quickly as 18 centimetres. It can be seen from this diagram that the major oceans – the Atlantic, the Pacific and the Indian – are all bisected by a continuous extensional fracture-line: that is to say a fracture-line along which the plates are being forced apart; and it is here that there takes place a process for which Hess coined the phrase 'seafloor spreading'.

Along these extensional fracture-lines the ocean floor is ruptured, and magma from the asthenosphere comes welling up in a gentle and continuous outpouring; this magma is deposited in ridges along either side of the fracture-line, and as the outpouring continues so the ridges are built up and are pushed farther and farther apart. The perfect example of this is the Mid-Atlantic Ridge which runs almost exactly down the centre of the ocean from Spitzbergen in the north to the Scotia Arc in the south. Along such extensional mid-ocean fracture-lines the earth's crust is being continuously created.

It is a very different story along fracture-lines that are not extensional but are either compressional or transform, that is to say where the adjoining plates are meeting head on or are sliding past one another. Here volcanic activity is not gentle and continuous but violent and spasmodic, and the earth's crust is being not created but consumed. It is along such a compressional fracture-line that the Andes have been created.

Over the last 200 million years the heavy plate of South America has been continuously forced westward by seafloor spreading out of the Mid-Atlantic Ridge, while at the same time the light oceanic plate of Nazca has been continually forced eastward by seafloor spreading out of the East Pacific Rise. As the two plates have met head-on off the Pacific coast of South America, the heavy continental plate has been buckled to form mountains, and the light oceanic plate has been subducted, that is, broken up and pushed down into the asthenosphere to form a deepsea trench and a line of frequently erupting volcanoes. The Scientific-American publication *Planet Earth* sums it up in a single sentence: 'The history of the Andes can be understood in terms of the consumption of a plate of the earth's crust plunging under South America.'

This points to a far more lengthy and far more complex process of mountain-building than anything envisaged by Darwin, or indeed by Wegener: just how lengthy and complex can be seen from the diagrams in Figure 3.

Diagram 1 shows a cross-section of what is now the Andes (along the latitude of Lake Titicaca) about 250 million years ago. The Nazca and South American plates have only recently started to press together, creating no more than a slight bulge in the offshore sea-bed. There are no mountains.

Diagram 2 shows the same cross-section about 175 million years ago. The Nazca and South American plates are now in violent collision, and the light oceanic plate has been pushed down beneath its heavy continental neighbour into the asthenosphere. This subduction has resulted in (a) the forming of a deepsea trench and an arc of offshore volcanoes which have been created where the Nazca plate has broken up and overheated as it plunged into the molten core of the earth; and (b) the buckling of the South American plate to form the original Jurassic cordillera of the Andes.

Diagram 3 shows this cross-section about 75 million years ago. The arc of offshore volcanoes has now built up by accretion into a continental cordillera. To the east of this cordillera upthrusting magma has pushed aside the old sedimentary Jurassic rocks to form a new range rising out of the debris of the old. Material from both these ranges has begun to pour into the altiplano, a valley-like depression, beaded with lakes, which lies between the cordillera.

Diagram 4 shows the cross-section as it is today. Seismic activity has progressed steadily inland, and huge deposits of silicic ash from the erupting volcanoes have covered the mountains to a depth of anything up to 1,600 feet. This outpouring of ash was followed by a more recent outpouring of lava which has solidified into the present day volcanoes of the east and west cordillera. The altiplano has become so choked with eroded debris that the only trace of the great sheets of water which once covered its floor is the fast-dwindling remnant of Lake Titicaca.

THE EVOLUTION OF THE ANDES

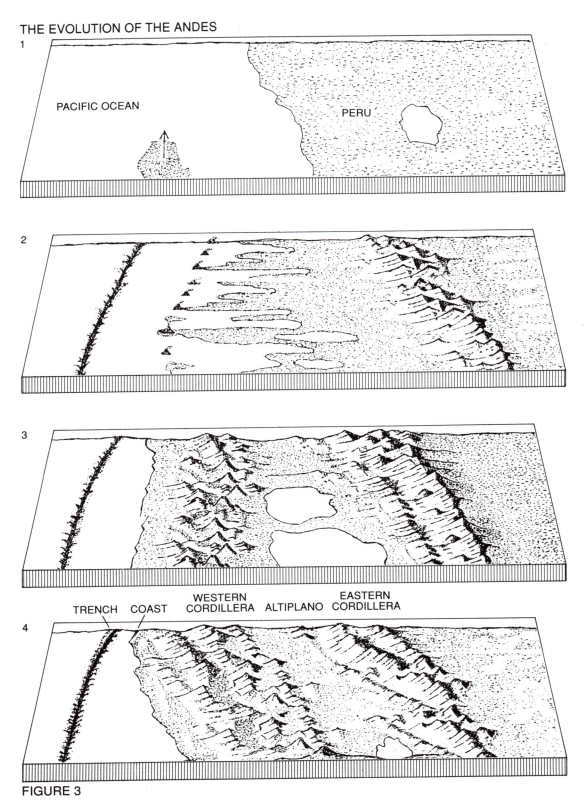

FIGURE 3

This long and complex gestation is one reason for the amazing diversity of the Andes; some of its rocks are 200 million years old and some have been thrust up within living memory. This diversity is accentuated by extremes of climate. In the tropical north, in the rain forest of Peru, the average annual temperature is over 80°F; in the sub-Antarctic south, in the Hielo Continental of Chile, it is below zero. In the east, the Colombian town of Tutuendo is the wettest place on earth, with an annual rainfall of 463 inches; in the west, Calama in the Atacama Desert is the driest, with an official annual rainfall of nil.

As a result of this varied structure and these extremes of heat and cold, flood and drought, the Andes include just about every known variety of terrain: lifeless desert and insect-teeming rain forest, precipitous valleys and featureless plains, glaciers at sea-level and snowfields on the equator, cloud-woodland where the trees suck moisture not from the ground but from the air, forests so thick it is impossible to set foot on the ground, vast saltpans, mineral-impregnated lakes that are sometimes turquoise-blue, sometimes emerald-green and even on occasions salmon-pink, and the world's most active belt of volcanoes.

Perhaps the best way to appreciate this diversity is to take a look at the different terrain we would pass through if we walked the length of the Andes from north to south.

The Andes are part of that great chain of mountains which stretch from Alaska to Cape Horn, and are all formed by the compacting of adjoining plates. In the centre of the chain the land has sunk almost to sea-level to form the Isthmus of Panama; and our obvious starting-point would seem to be here, where the low-lying isthmus of Central America gives way to the coastal cordillera of South America. However, the obvious starting-point is not in this case the right one, for in their northern reaches the Andes are fragmented into three separate ranges; of these, the Cordillera Occidental runs in much the same direction as the rest of the chain, but the Sierra de Perija and the Cordillera de Mérida have been so forced out of alignment (by pressure from the Caribbean and Cocos plates) that instead of running north-and-south parallel to the Pacific, they have been swivelled round until they run very nearly east-and-west, parallel to the Atlantic. Our walk therefore begins in an apparently unlikely spot: the island of Trinidad, where the last remnants of the Andes' Jurassic rocks plunge into the waters of the Atlantic.

Most people equate the Andes with the Pacific; yet for almost 1,000 miles the range borders the Caribbean-cum-Atlantic. This is a beautiful coast. In some places the mountains rise near-sheer from the sea to over 10,000 feet, white sands and tropical palms at their feet, glaciers and snowfields on their summits. In other places lush swampland, subject to tidal flooding, stretches inland for anything up to 100 miles, while overhead gather fantastic cloud-formations, as moisture-laden winds from the Caribbean impinge on the cordillera. It is, however, a coast more pleasant to look at than to live in, for the soil is poor, lush jungle clings to the slopes of the mountains, the swamps are miasmic and the climate unhealthy – this is the notorious 'fever coast', where in places like Cartagena the early Spanish settlers died in their thousands of malaria and yellow fever. There was nowhere here where early humans could put down roots for long enough to build up a civilization, and most of the pre-European inhabitants were hunter-gatherers who lived peripatetic lives in the rain forest. As we head west from Trinidad, the rainfall decreases: over 150 inches a year in the humid rain forest of Venezuela, under 15 inches a year in the arid thornscrub of Colombia. In the Atlantic Andes this change from lush east to barren west is gradual. It is a different story in the Pacific Andes.

Running south from the Isthmus of Panama is another coast that might be described as difficult: difficult both to traverse and to live in. The climate is enervating, with long spells of breathless calm shattered by sudden and violent thunderstorms. The terrain has been described by Pizarro, one of the first white men to see it, as 'swamp, jungle and savage hills ... there are few people and less food'. There are also few harbours – a characteristic of almost the whole Pacific coast of South America, which is one reason why the exploration of this part of the world proved so difficult. At first the Andes can't be seen from the sea; but a little north of the equator they appear out of the near-perpetual mist, usually veiled with white festoons of cloud that cling to their slopes like mildew. The rainfall here is heavy, and the approaches to the cordillera are barred by deep ravines, near-impenetrable jungle and completely impenetrable swamps. Writers have described this part of the coast as a 'green hell'; and certainly the early European explorers, harassed by venemous insects and poisoned arrows, found it little to their liking. However, as one heads south the rainfall decreases, and surprisingly, although we are astride the equator, the temperature falls.

The reason for this apparent paradox is the phenomenon which dictates the pattern of life throughout most of the west face of the Andes: the Humboldt (or Peru-Chile) Current. It would be difficult to overstate the influence of this gargantuan mass of cold-water which wells up off the sub-Antarctic coast of Chile and runs parallel to the continent for more than 3,000 miles. For, most unusually, the air temperature over the Humboldt is lower than the air temperature over the adjacent land; so winds as they blow inland do not deposit moisture on to the ground as rain, but suck moisture out of the ground as mist. This current brings life to the sea, for its mineral-rich waters sustain huge shoals of plankton, krill and fish, and these in turn sustain huge flocks of sea-birds; but it brings death to the land, its winds sucking dry what would otherwise be pastureland and transforming it to the most arid desert on earth – there are parts of the Atacama, which runs parallel to the coast of Chile, where it *never* rains.

So the west face of this central section of the Andes is essentially a desert face, with vegetation, and hence early human settlement, restricted to the occasional river-valley and river-mouth. These river-mouths were the site of the earliest South American civilization – the Mochica, Nazca and Chimu – brilliant but idiosyncratic and inward-looking races who developed in isolation from one another, because the desert which lay between their valleys proved a formidable obstacle to people who lacked both transport animals and the wheel.

The east face of the central Andes, in contrast, is a forest face; for winds coming in from the Atlantic rise as they meet the mountains and void enormous quantities of moisture. Here are the world's wettest and most extensive rain forests and swamps, the home of a shy, peripatetic people who have survived by turning themselves into part of the life cycle of the rain forest.

The dividing line between these very different worlds is the narrow summit-ridge of the Andes. To the west of the peaks lies arid desert, to the east, little more than 100 miles away, lies teaming rain forest. No other range affords such a dramatic contrast.

24

Running parallel to and indeed merging into the Atacama Desert are some of the highest, driest and coldest mountains in the world. It is so dry in the desert that naturalists have come across the mummified remains of Stone Age hunters, their hand-plaited ropes still perfect as the day they were made. It is so cold in the mountains that neither flora nor fauna can live. Nor can humans. The Jesuit Alonso de Orvalle describes the fate of Spanish troops who tried to cross the mountains:

De Almagro and his men suffered greatly. Some became blind, others lame. Many were frozen to death, and with them their horses; and several months later other Spaniards attempting to cross the mountains found these same horses so fresh and well-preserved that they were able to eat them . . . And six years later others going this way found one of Almagro's Negro followers who during the crossing had been frozen to death, and they found him still leaning against an outcrop of rock, leading his horse, the reins in his outstretched hand, all perfectly preserved.

However, round about the 31st parallel there takes place another of those dramatic changes which are typical of the Andes. The desert is metamorphosed to beautiful and fertile coastal plains: a world of rich soil, warm sun and gentle rain that was known to the early Spanish settlers as the Vales of Paradise – hence the name Valparaiso. The reason for this sudden transformation is that as one heads south the continental landmass becomes steadily cooler; the temperature difference between the cold sea and the hot land diminishes, until there comes a time when condensation which impoverishes the land is superseded by rainfall which enriches it. Orvalle extols the wonders of this Chilean heartland:

The opinion of all is that the soil and climate of this country surpasses all others, and it fully deserves the praise heaped upon it by all travellers . . . It receives cooling breezes both from the sea and from the prodigiously high mountains, so that the heat of the sun is never in any way troublesome. It is free of poisonous creatures such as vipers, snakes, scorpions and toads; there are no tigers, panthers or other mischievous animals; nor will the climate suffer poisonous insects or bugs . . . The fields are full of such an abundance of flowers that they look as though they had been painted; and it is difficult to credit the vigour with which the earth brings forth all types of vegetation.

Soon, however, there is another, albeit this time a gradual, transformation. As we head south, the Vales of Paradise turn increasingly chilly, windswept and rainsodden, until we come at last to what has been dubbed the utmost end of the earth: the heavily-forested fjordland where the Andes disappear into the storm-lashed approaches of the Antarctic. This, to quote one of the region's most eloquent explorers, Eric Shipton, is 'a stark inhospitable land, most of it rugged and uninhabitable. The climate is sub-Antarctic, and the terrain unusually difficult, the forests often presenting an impenetrable barrier.' Darwin also testifies to the 'impossible nature of the forests'. When he and the *Beagle's* ship's company tried to explore the island of Chiloe, they became ensnared in a tangle of undergrowth, creepers and fallen trees so thick it was impossible to set foot on the ground. They had to crawl on hands and knees along the branches, often 15-20 feet above ground level, the seamen jokingly calling out 'soundings' as they inched forward. Having covered only 200 yards in 24 hours, they very prudently gave up. This remote and inaccessible land has been the bane of explorers, whose frustration is perpetuated by the names they inked-in on their charts – Isle of Desolation, Port Famine, Anxious Point, East and West Furies, Cape Disappointment, Useless Bay – yet for all its hazards it has a brooding beauty: the beauty of million upon million acres of virgin forest, great glaciers sweeping down to the sea, and the weather-eroded pinnacles of the cordillera rising ghost-like out of a near-perpetual canopy of cloud.

Here our journey ends, in terrain so different from the swamps of Venezuela or the sands of the Atacama that we might be on another planet.

The story goes that as God was resting on the seventh day after creating the world He noticed some bits and pieces had been left over, so He told His angels to sweep them up and hide them behind a high wall; this is how Chile came into being. The story that is told of Chile could be told equally well of the Andes.

This was the world which hunter-gatherers from North America first entered roughly 12,000 years ago: a world that was complex, diverse and daunting but potentially rewarding.

CHAPTER 2

The Discoverers

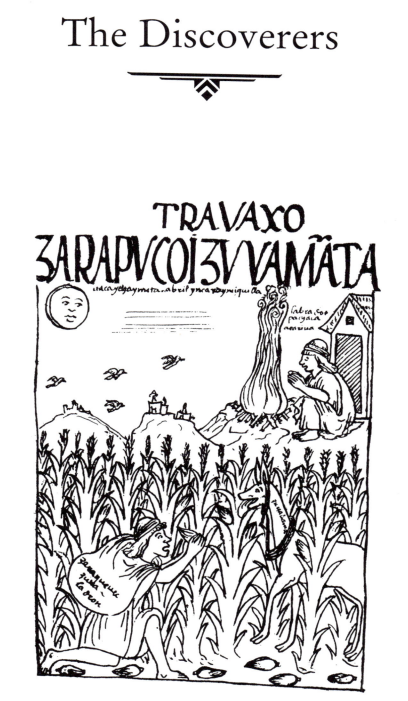

April: picking fruit.

The desert lay silent under the moon, apparently deserted; but in the chain of oases where a stream meandered down from the Andes there was movement and life, a group of primates at play in the cool of the Palaeolithic night. There were about two dozen of the primates, shy and huge-eyed douroucouli monkeys, splashing about in the water and swinging from branch to branch by their prehensile tails. Being nocturnal, the douroucouli had little fear of predators and were taking no special precautions to safeguard their young. This was a mistake. For the desert was not as empty as it seemed. Crouched behind the rocks which bordered the stream were newcomers to the oasis, a species which had never been seen there before, a pair of *Homo erectus* hunters. It was several days since the *Homo erectus* had eaten. Their mouths were salivating. Their hands grasped clubs of sharpened stone.

A sudden dash, a flurry of blows, and a baby douroucouli was dead. The primates, screaming with rage and terror, were fleeing in great swinging loops through the trees, and the hunters were left triumphant over their kill. The oasis, by right of conquest, was theirs.

Such episodes were the cornerstone on which all subsequent discoveries were based. When a Stone Age hunter stood gazing at some lake, river or mountain which no human being had before set eyes on, these were the truly great moments in the story of exploration. Until recently we could only speculate on how and when such events took place; but modern techniques of carbon dating and computer analysis help us to recreate these first discoveries if not in detail at least with a degree of accuracy.

Until comparatively recently, theories about early humans had to conform to a biblical framework; in other words, they had to fit in with the concept that we were all descended from Adam and Eve, and that Adam and Eve were conceived in a moment of time in the Garden of Eden – an event which theologians usually placed about 4,000 BC. This led to difficulties. How, for example, was one to account for the indigenous inhabitants of the New World? There was no way they could have migrated there from Eurasia *since* 4,000 BC. An obvious solution was to place the Garden of Eden in South America, a valley in central Bolivia being the most popular location, and this idea found considerable favour first with Spanish theologians and then with South American nationalists. Another solution was to fall back on the flood: to suggest that it was Noah's son Shem who, after the deluge, fathered the entire population of the Americas – the genetic impossibility of this being conveniently overlooked. Yet another idea was that the people of America might have come from Africa at a time when the two continents were joined together. Such ideas were often supported by a wealth of esoteric scholarship, but they were all scientifically flawed. So how and when *did* the first *Homo erectus* hunters arrive in the Andes?

Scientists now agree that humans evolved from the primates something like 1½ million years ago on the plains of Africa. The theory that our species may have developed more or less simultaneously in different parts of the world – say in Java or China as well as in Africa – is no longer generally regarded as tenable. Human beings seem to have first emerged and then prospered in the great rift valleys of present-day Kenya, their initial success being due to good eyesight, intelligence and the ability to communicate and act as a group. These early *Homo erectus* were creatures of the tropics, ill-equipped to withstand cold; it was not until they had learned to control fire, build shelters and make clothing that they were able to move out of their natal environment. They seem to have acquired these skills by about 300,000 BC, and there then began a series of sustained migrations into the temperate plains of Eurasia. It is best not to be too dogmatic in dating the events of prehistory: but humans don't seem to have penetrated into the New World before about 30,000 BC, for no human remains have been found in the Americas which can with certainty be dated prior to this. When one remembers that human bones have been found in Africa, China and Indonesia which are 200,000 years old, the New World seems aptly named.

We know that 30,000 years ago the earth was in the grip of a mini ice age, the seas were far lower than they are today, and Asia and North America were joined by a landbridge over what is now the Bering Strait. It was via this bridge, probably a little after 30,000 BC, that groups of Mongoloid hunter-gatherers first crossed from Asia to America. Soon they were pushing south, ever seeking better sources of food and a better environment. They were the first Americans.

To start with their progress would have been slow, hampered by ice-sheets; but about 18,000 years ago the earth's climate began to improve, and a corridor is known to have opened up to the east of the Rockies between the ice-caps. Through this corridor the hunter-gatherers came streaming south into the American heartland; and what a cornucopia they found awaiting them: great plains teeming with herds of bison, casteroides, musk ox, mastodons and mammoths – a hunter's El Dorado. Yet within a thousand years of the hunters' arrival these herds had been decimated and many species had been hunted to extinction. There is plenty of evidence that this was due in large part to human predators – the great creatures' fossilized bones shattered by blows from weapons, and cave paintings depicting hunters stampeding the herds into swamps or over cliffs – and it was partly due to this overkill that our ancestors didn't settle in large numbers in the plains of North America, but continued to head south into the more arid territory of present-day Texas and Mexico. By about 10,000 BC they were at the approaches to South America.

The diminution of their meat supplies must have posed serious problems for our ancestors. A mastodon weighed nearly 1½ tons – enough to feed a fair-sized tribe for several weeks – and with the extermination of a whole genera of these enormous creatures, new sources of sustenance had to be found. It was fortunate for the human race that temperatures were now rising all over the world, the ice-caps were in retreat, and potentially fertile valleys were being laid bare to the warmth of the sun. For the first time humans had both ability and the opportunity to domesticate animals and cultivate plants.

From this moment evolution has tended to progress to the beat of a different drum. Slowly but surely, in a process still going on today, hunting gave way to harvesting; crops began to replace meat as the staple diet; people began to settle into permanent and static communities, and implicit in this change were the seeds of what we call civilization.

We have come today to regard civilization as being almost synonymous with urbanization – the most civilized of all societies, scholars assure us, were the Greek city states – and it is true that many of the greatest discoveries have stemmed from the desires and pressures of people living together in a static community. However, as regards geographical discovery it has not been the most highly civilized peoples who have been the great explorers. The great explorers of the world have been not the Egyptians, Chinese, Greeks, Romans or Hapsburgs, but the Polynesians, Phoenicians, Vikings and Portuguese: small, mobile populations living in bleak lands and occupying a relatively low position in what might be called the culture charts. What has been true throughout history was probably also true in prehistory. So the first people to set foot in South America are likely to have been not 'civilized' agriculturalists, but 'uncivilized' hunter-gathers: foraging parties forcing their way through the Panama rain forest, or fisherfolk cast up by storm in their *canoa* on some Caribbean shore. The date of their arrival is unlikely to have been much before 10,000 BC, because no human remains have been found in or at the approaches to South America which can be reliably dated earlier; and it can't have been after 8,000 BC because human remains *have* been found in South America which are more than 10,000 years old, and these skeletons, moreover, were unearthed in the extreme south, in Patagonia, which would have been one of the last parts of the continent into which our ancestors penetrated.

So, over a period of not much more than a thousand years, hunter-gatherers fanned out from their bridgehead at Panama to populate the whole of South America.

This great feat of exploration was sustained and given impetus by the fact that South America would have offered these first explorers little incentive to put down roots; for the continent had few fertile river-valleys (like the Nile or Euphrates) and few well-stocked grasslands (like the plains of Africa) which could act as cradles for a civilization. It offered instead a mosaic of difficult environments: near-impenetrable rain forest divided from near-uninhabitable desert by near-unclimbable mountains. Hunters would have had good reason to keep on the move.

The first Stone Age people to penetrate South America would have found a plentiful and exotic supply of meat; for the continent's fauna was far more extensive and varied in those days than it is now. From the evidence of fossils it is possible to discover the sort of game that was hunted. Because South America had for long been cut off from the rest of the world – the present isthmus of Panama being a strait – a unique community of mammals had evolved in the continent, all stemming from ancient genera and all developing in isolation from the rest of their species. When, late in the Pleistocene era, a landbridge formed between the Americas, many competing types of fauna came pouring in from the north. Some of the ancient South America species adapted and survived – the monkeys, opossums, sloths and armadillos. Others, less adaptable, found themselves under threat, and for many of these threatened species the coming of humans proved the last straw. Like the mastodons and the mammoths of the north they were hunted to extinction. Among the creatures which fell victim to the first hunters were the hairless and semiaquatic *toxodon*, distant cousin of the hippopotamus; the huge and loose-jointed *macrauchenia*, forerunner of the guanaco; and the even huger *mylodon*, a giant sloth more than 15 feet in length, with paws as thick as a man's torso; also the three-toed *prototheres*, an early type of horse. (It is often said that the horse was introduced to America by sixteenth-century Europeans. This isn't strictly so; for horses were once abundant in both North and South America, but were exterminated by Stone Age man; they were later reintroduced by the conquistadors.) It is strange to think that only a few thousand years ago – yesterday in terms of world evolution – these prehistoric creatures were being hunted by Stone Age people in South America. Indeed, some, like the *mylodons*, were obviously kept for food, for their remains have been found walled up at the back of caves like cattle awaiting slaughter.

When our ancestors had hunted such creatures to extinction they were obliged to seek other sources of food. Some retreated deep into the rain forest; here small groups were able to sustain a peripatetic existence by selective hunting-and-gathering over a wide area. Others, realizing that the sea was more bountiful than the land, settled along the coast; here, according to the evidence of excavated middens, they lived almost exclusively on a diet of fish, shellfish, sea-birds and seals. Yet others took to pastoral farming, some settling in the valleys of present-day Peru and some in the altiplano. It was from these static agricultural communities that, about 6,000 years ago, the first South American civilizations began to emerge.

CHAPTER 3

The Early Civilizations

May: harvesting the corn.

The idea that civilization in the Andes began with the conquistadors is absurd. Almost equally absurd is the idea that it began with the Incas; for the Incas were no more than the unifying force which fused into one empire a conglomeration of already existing cultures, some of which were as old and in many ways as remarkable as those of Greece or Rome.

The first of these ancient civilizations began to emerge about 4,000 years ago on the coast of Peru.

The coast of Peru seems, on the face of it, an unlikely cradle for civilization, since almost 99 per cent of it is desert with an annual rainfall of less than 5 inches a year. However, the remaining 1 per cent consists of fertile land around the mouths of the dozen or so rivers which cut through the desert between the mountains and the sea. These rivers have a steep fall and their volume is unusally consistent throughout the year. This makes them ideal for irrigation, and it was on the bedrock of their irrigation systems that the early settlements were based. (In this, South America conformed to a global pattern; most of the world's earliest and greatest civilizations evolved in semidesert regions which were enriched by irrigation projects – the Sumerian on the banks of the Euphrates, the Egyptian on the banks of the Nile, the Harappan on the banks of the Indus, and the Maya in the arid valleys of Mexico.)

Archaeologists tell us that by about 2,500 BC small villages had sprung up around the mouth of the Chicama, Chilloa, Moche, Nazca, Paracas and Viru rivers. We know from the excavation of middens that the inhabitants of these villages lived mainly on seafood and to a lesser degree on potatoes and beans. Potatoes and beans grow wild in the Andes, and it would have been in their wild state that these vegetables were first gathered. However, as soon as families became established in permanent settlements they would have discovered the benefit of planting seeds and tubers close to their homes; they would soon have discovered too the benefit of weeding, fertilizing and selective propagation. Quite a lot is known about the lifestyle of these early villagers. They lived in small, semi-subterranean dwellings whose walls were made of boulders or bricks of adobe, and whose roofs usually consisted of a mixture of timber and whalebone. They went fishing in *balsas* of inflated sealskin and in *cabillitus* of lashed-together reeds. They grew cotton (the 26-chromosome variety, *Gossypium barbense*) with which they wove undecorated cloth; and they used small hot stones for cooking, often dropping these together with their food into water-containers, very much as the North American Indians were doing only a couple of hundred years ago. 'The overall picture,' writes Alden Mason in his excellent work, *The Ancient Civilizations of Peru*, 'is of a sedentary, simple and peaceful people, living in small cultivable oases by the sea, fishing, raising a few food crops, living in crude non-masonry houses, and making the objects necessary for their economic and household life, with scant attention to art.'

All this hardly adds up to civilization, but it was the womb from which civilization was soon to emerge. And here, as in several other parts of the world, the catalyst which precipitated birth was the introduction of a staple annual crop: in this case corn.

Corn appears to have been brought to the coastal valleys of Peru *circa* 1,350 BC, almost certainly by a people emigrating south from central America via the highlands of the Andes. The corn would have been of a primitive type – a small-eared popcorn – but it would have had the same characteristics as the crops of today in that it would have depended on a careful programme of sowing, harvesting and seed retention. In return for such a programme the corn would have yielded a nutritious and easily-preserved source of food which was not only more reliable than the spoils of hunting or fishing, but which was capable of improvement and increment. Corn was therefore the stabilizing factor which helped to bring an orderly way of life to a whole plethora of communities which came to depend for their well-being on the cultivation of a specific area of land.

From these communities stemmed the pre-Inca civilizations.

Hunter-gatherers have no fixed home since they are often obliged to follow migrating game; also, they have no source of food which can be increased by their own skills. They therefore usually lack both the leisure and the incentive to improve their lot. Agriculturalists, on the other hand, have permanent homes and, once they have established a staple crop, they find themselves with both the leisure-time and the incentive to improve the world they live in. This encourages them to indulge in those activities, like making pottery, decorating cloth and building places of worship, which are generally regarded as manifestations of culture.

All the world's ancient civilizations mirror, to a certain extent, the terrain in which they evolved. The terrain of the Andes is rugged, arid, and often too demanding for an individual farmer to cope with by his own efforts. Not only is a communal effort called for, but it often takes the whole of a community the whole of its time to wring a livelihood out of the unyielding mountains. This utter absorption with community-style farming accounts not only for the lifestyle of the people of the early South American civilizations; it accounts also for their character and achievements.

Their lifestyle revolved round their *ayllus*. The west slopes of the Andes are often little more than desert; the peaks are a lunar world of rock and snowfield; and although it is true that the east slopes often support luxuriant rain forests, these (as we are learning today to our cost) exist on their recycled detritus. The soil from which they spring is poor and shallow and if the trees are cut down the land is metamorphosed to wilderness. Such a terrain compares unfavourably with that of, say, Iraq, India, China and most of the other early centres of civilization, where rich soil, warm sun and a plentiful supply of water ensure that almost every plant that is pushed into the ground will flourish. The Andes offer no such easy returns. They can be brought under human control only by large-scale communal projects, usually involving terracing and irrigation, and it was to facilitate such projects that the South Americans developed their *ayllus*.

An *ayllu* has been variously described as 'a village community', 'an extended family group' and 'a clan', and the first of these definitions fits the earliest *ayllus* well enough. They began to take shape about 3,000 years ago, as soon as the people of the corn-producing, llama-owning villages began to realize that their crops and flocks could be improved more easily by communal than by individual effort. One family, for example, would be hard-pressed to terrace a worthwhile area of hillside and divert and regulate a river to water it, whereas for several dozen families the task would be feasible. Communally owned flocks grazing common pastureland could be cared for more easily than individual animals roaming different segments of a mountain. It must soon have become apparent that if two or three villages pooled their resources they could sometimes achieve more by working together than by themselves; so the concept of the *ayllu* gradually expanded to embrace little clusters of villages. For these larger communities 'a clan' is probably the best definition, for each was ruled by an extended patrilineal family, each had its exclusive territory of communally owned and communally farmed land, and each strove to be self-sufficient and was mistrustful of outsiders. All this added up to a way of life that was tied to the earth. It is not therefore surprising that the gods of the *ayllus* were down-to-earth gods – 'Their deities,' Garcilaso de la Vega tells us, 'were trees, rocks, caves, hills, rivers and lakes' – nor is it surprising that over the centuries the people of the *ayllus* became not only utterly dependent on their land but utterly devoted to it.

From this rapport with the soil stem both the Indians' physique and their character.

The physical appearance of a race changes little over the millennia, so the *ayllu*-dwellers of 1,000 BC must have looked very similar to the Andean Indians of today: short and barrel-chested, with copper-coloured skin and little body hair. It has been estimated that the average height of the men was a little over 5 feet, and of the women a little under 5 feet. They were a brachycephalic (broad-headed) people, with prominent cheekbones, arched, rather broad noses, low foreheads and chestnut-brown eyes which were nothing like as deeply-set as those of their Mongoloid ancestors. Their outstanding characteristic – then as now – was the size of their upper torso; this was unusually well-developed to accommodate a heart and lungs which were considerably larger than average. This enlargement was due to the altitude at which they lived. The earliest South American civilization may have originated on the coast, but subsequent development centred around the altiplano, the great inland plateau between the east and west cordillera. This is the highest inhabited part of the earth – higher even than the so-called 'Roof of the World' in the mountains of central Asia – for few of its villages are below 12,000 feet and several are as high as 17,000. The average person begins to suffer from lack of oxygen at roughly 10,000 feet; so the Andean Indians needed to develop special characteristics to enable them to make the best use of what little oxygen their environment allowed them. Their hearts were 20 per cent larger than normal; their bodies had 15 per cent more blood than normal, and this blood contained an above-average quota of red corpuscles and haemoglobin; their lung sacs, which transfer oxygen from air to blood, were not only larger than normal but were kept permanently dilated to provide the maximum surface for transferring oxygen. No wonder doctors have commented on 'their remarkable thoracic development . . . and the very high capacity of their lungs.' Corresponding to the size of their torso, their shoulders and hips were well-developed, and this tended to give their forearms and thighs the appearance of being foreshortened. Their heartbeat was slow; and because those who rush things at altitude get out of breath, their gait, speech and behaviour were also slow. It would be wrong to describe them as slow on the uptake, and even more wrong to describe them as slow-witted; but they had (and still have) an aura of passivity which those used to a more hectic way of life have at times mistaken for dullness.

Physiognomists would claim that the Indians' character is writ plain in their appearance. They are a hardy, earthbound people, tied by bonds both physical and mental to their family, their *ayllu* and their particular patch of land; from the strength of these bonds stem both their virtues and vices. Most visitors to the Andes would agree that

South American Indians are not the easiest people to get to know, for they have a deep-rooted mistrust of *gringos*. However, once their friendship is won, they are likely to prove friends for life: kindly, patient, unselfish and at times quixotically brave and generous. For the whole basis of life in the *ayllu* was that a person's individual needs should be subordinated to the needs of the community, and this encouraged hard work, kindness, loyalty and unselfishness. These traits were the hallmark of the South American Indians a couple of thousand years ago, and they are their hallmark today. However, there is a less commendable side to their character. An *ayllu* was not only close knit and self-sufficient, it was also close-fisted and self-centred; it was mistrustful of strangers. So not only do the Indians of the Andes mistrust *gringos*, they mistrust one another; those who live in the next valley are regarded as strangers, while those who live in another part of the mountains are regarded almost as creatures from another planet! They are not (like the Afghans) congenitally warlike; but they are congenitally fragmented – a fragmentation sustained both by their *ayllu*-mentality and by an isolated and dramatically changing terrain. Only once in their history have the people of the Andes been united – by the agricultural despotism of the Incas – for they have a penchant for parochial independence which makes political or economic integration virtually impossible.

So the early Andean civilizations tended to evolve in isolation, each developing its own idiosyncratic skills. Thus the Chavin became famous for its stone carvings, the Mochica for its realistic pottery, the Nazca for its linear patterns cut into the altiplano, the Tiahuanaco for its monolithic sculptures, and the Chimu for its geometrically laid-out cities. However, they did have one thing in common – they all depended on agriculture and in particular on irrigation, and their network of canals, aqueducts and runnels which brought their semidesert environment to life must be regarded as their greatest achievement. On this their existence depended.

The first primitive irrigation channels were probably dug in the coastal valleys of north Peru at least as early as 1,300 BC. The site that has been examined most thoroughly is the flood plain of the River Moche. This has been the scene of careful archaeological research, and by reconstructing what happened in this valley we can visualize what is likely to have happened in other parts of the Andes.

The River Moche rises in the Cordillera Blanca and flows westward for about 70 miles to enter the Pacific not far from the 8th parallel south. It has a drainage area of some 580 square miles, a steep slope and a reasonably constant flow of water throughout the year. In its upper reaches it is entombed between steep-sided walls of rock, but about 15 miles from the sea it emerges into an alluvial flood-plain. It was here that the first settlements and subsequently the first irrigation works were sited.

The original people to settle beside the Moche lived almost entirely by fishing; but over the centuries crops such as manioc, potatoes, beans and pepinos gradually replaced fish as their staple diet. Most of these crops would have been grown on the upper slopes of the flood plain, where the soil was fertile and free from salinization, and the vegetation less dense than along the riverbanks. At first there can have been no shortage of cultivable land. However, the introduction of corn posed a problem. Corn is not a robust crop; it requires a fair amount of water and a reasonable soil. The upper slopes of the flood-plain

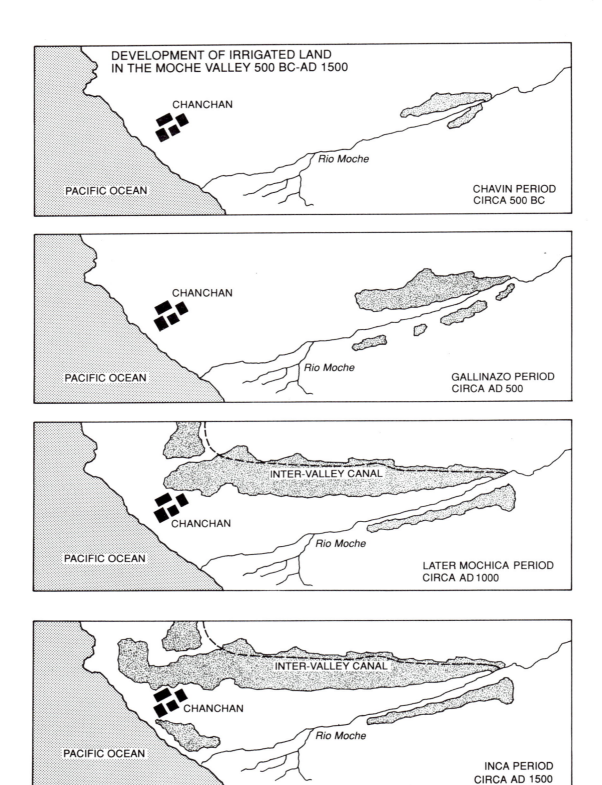

DEVELOPMENT OF IRRIGATED LAND
IN THE MOCHE VALLEY 500 BC-AD 1500

CHANCHAN

Rio Moche

PACIFIC OCEAN

CHAVIN PERIOD
CIRCA 500 BC

CHANCHAN

Rio Moche

PACIFIC OCEAN

GALLINAZO PERIOD
CIRCA AD 500

INTER-VALLEY CANAL

CHANCHAN

Rio Moche

PACIFIC OCEAN

LATER MOCHICA PERIOD
CIRCA AD 1000

INTER-VALLEY CANAL

CHANCHAN

Rio Moche

PACIFIC OCEAN

INCA PERIOD
CIRCA AD 1500

FIGURE 4

 Land brought under cultivation by irrigation

(where the rainfall averaged no more than 4 inches a year) were too dry for it, and along the river-banks the soil was too waterlogged. So, round about 1,300 BC, the villagers began to dig small canals to channel surplus water to the higher slopes of the flood-plain. From this modest beginning stemmed an extensive and sophisticated system of irrigation whose growth is summarized in Figure 4.

The first canals were probably excavated with simple digging-sticks; their banks were unlined, and their beds consisted of alluvial silt, occasionally stone-lined to give stability. Their evolution would have been experimental, accretionary and localized. However, as the population and hence the need for some more corn and more cultivable land increased, so the necessity arose for a more coordinated and carefully planned system. This began to emerge during the period of the cult of Chavin (*circa* 500 BC), and as a result of the sort of cooperative effort at which the pre-Inca people excelled, something like 20 square miles of irrigated fields were brought under cultivation along the north bank of the Moche, and a smaller area along the south bank. Archaeological evidence suggests that over the next few centuries canal irrigation continued in a planned fashion, with more and more land being gradually brought into use. All this involved work on a comparatively small scale; but there came a time when the canal engineers were obliged to think big. For they ran out of water.

The Moche is not a large river – it is doubtful if its discharge was ever greater than 16 cubic yards per second – and as the number of irrigation channels multiplied it began to run dry. The Peruvian engineers then embarked on an ambitious project. They diverted water from the valley of the Chicama to the valley of the Moche, a traverse as the crow flies of more than 50 miles across difficult undulating desert. The resulting inter-valley canal was by any standards a magnificent feat of engineering. It was 46 miles in length. In several places it flowed through deep artificial gorges cut out of solid rock; in other places it crossed constantly shifting sand-dunes prone to flash-flood. It contained three sections of aqueduct, the section in the Chicama Valley being a mile long, 50 feet high and consisting of over a million cubic yards of earth. Perhaps most remarkable of all, it contained no sluice-gates and only a single storage reservoir which was seldom used; for so precisely were its intake, size and slope designed that throughout the year it delivered the right amount of water to the right fields at the right time. In his article, 'Water Resources and Irrigation Agriculture in pre-Hispanic Peru', Chris Park writes:

The canals were built, operated and maintained by prehistoric engineers with remarkably sound empirical knowledge of the principles of open flow hydraulics and water distribution. These engineers were highly successful in the design, construction and maintenance of stable irrigation canals which covered considerable distances, flowed without extensive lining, and operated over long periods without net scour or fill . . . They have left a lasting epitaph to their skills in the now largely abandoned irrigation systems of the Moche Valley.

We cannot be certain when this great canal was built, although the diagrams in Figure 4 may provide a clue; for the huge increase in cultivated land which occurred about AD 1,000 can only be explained by the introduction of a huge new source of water – the Chicama Valley canal. To strengthen this supposition all authorities agree that the years immediately prior to AD 1,000 were 'a very formative period . . . handicraft reached its apogee, as did engineering and architecture'. (Mason). It therefore seems highly probable that it was the Mochica who built what must be regarded as one of the most useful structures of the ancient world.

Later civilizations – in particular the Chimu and the Inca – extended the Moche Valley irrigation system almost as far west as the coast and as far north as the Chicama, so that by the time of the Spanish invasion the whole valley and its environs were, according to the Spanish chronicler Cieza de León, 'a veritable garden ... Only land that could be irrigated was under cultivation, but this ground was watered and manured like a garden. Corn was the principal crop, reaped twice a year and yielding abundantly. Also grown were yuccas, many kinds of potato, beans, pepinos, guavas, avocado, star-apple and cotton.' Ducks and llamas were bred in large numbers, although they were of minor importance compared to the cornucopia of crops.

It would be wrong to suggest that irrigation in other parts of the Andes followed an equally intensive pattern; but without doubt what happened in the Moche Valley was repeated on a smaller scale in hundreds if not thousands of other valleys throughout the range. It has been estimated that at the time of the Spanish invasion there were in the Inca empire a minimum of 20,000 miles of first-class roads and 200,000 miles of irrigation channels. Most people today have heard of the Great Royal Road of the Incas which ran almost dead straight for 3,000 miles from present-day Colombia to present-day Chile. What is not so well known is that 'beside this road, for almost the whole of its length, ran a rivulet of fresh water from which both travellers and draft animals could quench their thirst'. The provision of running water beside a highway which crossed steep-sided valleys, arid plateaux and lifeless deserts must have been an even greater feat than building the highway itself.

The people of the early Andean civilizations were magnificent agriculturalists. Their history is the history of their farming, and the history of their farming is the history of their irrigation.

Based on this commonly shared way of life each of the civilizations developed its particular skills; and as might be expected these skills were for the most part practical ones – the building of well laid-out cities, the weaving of strong, colourful fabrics, and the creation in gold of some of the world's most beautiful *objets d'art*.

The first civilization to emerge was the Chavin.

It is best not to be too dogmatic about either the origin or nature of the Chavin culture, for almost everything about it is subject to constroversy. However, it is generally agreed that round about 850 BC there began to emerge in the northern highlands of the Andes what archaelogists call 'a horizon', a recognizable architectural style. This horizon was dominated by a feline deity – a curvilinear puma with massive head, locked and curved fangs, claw feet, prominent nostrils and eccentric eyes – which was reproduced in stone carvings over a wide area. Perhaps the most persuasive theory about the Chavin horizon is that it was not so much a homogeneous culture as a widely diffused religious cult: a cult that was centred around what are now the ruins of Chavin de Huantar in the valley of the River Huallaya.

Chavin de Huantar is an interesting site, both architecturally and geographically. It is interesting architecturally because although its buildings are among the oldest in South

Opposite The Urubamba, Peru: the royal valley of the Incas, described by Hiram Bingham (the discoverer of Machu Picchu) as 'the most beautiful valley in the world'.

The Nazca lines in the *pampa* south of Lima: an archaeological enigma.

Above Mud arabesques from the Chimu city of Chanchan.

Right Burial mantle from the tombs of Paracas.

Below Gold mask of the Incas' Sun God.

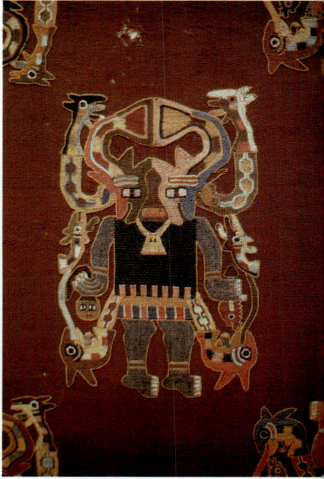

America they are highly sophisticated both in design and construction, and could only have been built by a people who had behind them many centuries of architectural expertise . . . The site consists of a number of terraces, plazas and grain-stores laid out around a sunken courtyard and dominated by a massive edifice which the Spaniards called the *castillo* but which was in fact a temple. It is a huge, impressive building, three stories high and measuring at its base 245×235 feet; it is precisely orientated to the cardinal points of the solstice; it is built of 'some of the most beautiful plain stone masonry in the world' (Mason); yet it has no outside windows, and so was clearly not designed to be lived in. The interior consists of a dark labyrinthine layout of passages and galleries – connected by both ramps and stairs and air-conditioned by a sophisticated network of shafts – all leading towards the building's focal point: a huge granite monolith, decorated with the head of the ubiquitous feline deity and known as the *Lanzon* (or spearhead). The *Lanzon* looks – and is obviously meant to look – like a shaft driven deep into the ground to mark some sacred spot; and it is this which makes the site so geographically interesting. Why did the people of the Chavin cult build what was obviously their holiest of holies in this particular Andean valley?

The valley of the Huallaya is not especially fertile, and it seems unlikely that the area around Chavin de Huantar ever supported a large population. On the other hand it *was* a crossroads, being at the intersection of the north-south route along the spine of the Andes and the east-west route across the range to settlements on the Peruvian coast; it was a centre for travellers. The South American Indians had always marked the centre of their particular world in a tangible fashion; the early settlements all had their *huacas* – piles of stones set up in the middle of the village and used as a focal point for meetings and ceremonies – so it was perhaps only to be expected that a religious cult should build its headquarters at what was reckoned to be the geographical centre of its world. Only natural too that this headquarters, and in particular the monolith at the heart of it, should come in time to be thought of as 'the navel of the world': a place identified with both its gods and demons, and with those who worshipped them. This concept of a god and his élite tied to a geographical location at the centre of the cosmos is fundamental to Inca and pre-Inca beliefs. Guidoni and Magni write in their book *The Andes*:

The *Lanzon*, situated at the centre of the *castillo*, which itself is situated at a crossroads in the Andes, anticipates the development of Inca cosmology. Centuries later the elements symbolized in this monolith were to provide the basis for the state organization and administrative systems of the Inca empire centred at Cuzco.

It was perhaps the most significant achievement of the Chavin culture that it nurtured this concept of spatial mysticism, a concept which did much to bring about the rise of the Incas and even more to bring about their fall.

Another concept which the Chavin cult nurtured was that of the *fiesta*. It has been suggested that the *castillo* in Chavin de Huantar eventually became a shrine which was visited by countless generations of pilgrims from all over the Andes. If this is so, it is easy to see how the pilgrimages could have become *fiestas*. Initially, those coming to the *castillo* probably brought with them nothing but offerings for the gods. However, as the pilgrimages became annual events attended on set occasions by more and more people, it

Opposite Inca terraces at the approaches to Machu Picchu.

would have been surprising if those taking part had not begun to bring with them not only gifts for the gods but gifts for their friends and items for display and for sale. Thus to the sanctity of the temple would have been added the bustle, gaiety and socializing of the marketplace. William Weber Johnson in *The Andean Republics* describes a present-day *fiesta*:

Religious celebrations, especially annual holidays, provide the Andean peoples with a refuge from their hard lives and harsh environments. Some of the festivals commemorate Inca times; others celebrate holy days of the Christian religion; all have a pungent flavour imparted to them by the Indians, who celebrate by wearing their gaudiest clothes, performing dances and drinking heroic amounts of native beer. The festivals commonly last for two or three days, the solemn religious observances quickly giving way to carnival. Afterwards the exhausted revellers return to their long hours of work and poor living conditions with little to look forward to but the next fiesta.

A description which probably fits a festival of 500 BC almost as well as one of today.

In other fields the people of the Chavin horizon were competent if uninspired potters, most of their work being heavy and undecorated. They were also competent gold- and silver-smiths, although a lot of their jewellery was marred, according to present-day criteria, by being daubed with coloured pigments. They have been described as 'master artisans' in media such as semiprecious stones, bone, shell and wood; but it is for their stone carvings that they are best known. All over the northern highlands and the coastal valleys of Peru archaeologists have found buildings that contain carvings of cats (mostly the puma) and birds (mostly eagles and hawks) depicted in a particular stylized and deified form. Mason descibes these carvings as 'massive, strong and sometimes even dreadful': flared nostrils, curved fangs, staring eyes and hair alive with snakes; deities as awesome as the terrain in which they were conceived.

For 500 years, from roughly 950 to 450 BC, the cult of Chavin seems to have prospered, its people leading agriculturally-orientated and basically peaceful lives. This is the period in human evolution which Rousseau described as 'the true youth of the world': a period of alleged innocence when the evils of personal aggrandizement, property-owning and war were unknown. In this Arcady – and who can say for certain whether it was mythical or real – the people of the Chavin horizon lived in scattered single-room, primitive homes, yet they managed to build huge and surprisingly sophisticated temples. These temples were dedicated to a god who may have looked ferocious yet who demanded no sacrifices and was propitiated solely by pilgrimage-cum-*fiesta*. Such a civilization could hardly be called advanced, but it was undemanding, and the indications are that its people had at least some of the attributes of the French philosopher's Noble Savage. Its end is as shrouded in uncertainty as its beginning, but it seems to have broken up slowly and painlessly as its various communities became increasingly anxious for autonomy.

This desire for autonomy spawned, over the next millennium, a large number of what might be termed local Andean cultures, which flowered briefly then either merged with or were assimilated by their neighbours or successors. The coastal valleys of Peru saw the rise and fall of the Gallinazo, Mochica, Paracas, Nazca and Chimu civilizations; the mountains and the altiplano saw the rise and fall of the Huaraz, Chanapata, Chiripa and Tiahuanaco. Of these the most interesting are the Mochica, Nazca, Tiahuanaco and Chimu.

The Mochica civilization was based originally in the Moche and Chicama valleys, but over the centuries it expanded both north and south by conquest, until it dominated the Peruvian coast from roughly the 6th to the 10th parallels. It reached its apogee towards the end of the first millennium AD.

The Mochica, like all the early Andeans, had no written language, although they may have used a primitive form of *quipu*. The resulting lack of records makes it difficult for us to reconstruct their lives in detail. We can, however, learn a fair amount about them from their remarkably fine pottery. Archaelogists have recently unearthed large numbers of bowls, vessels and sculptures – much of it funerary ware – on which Mochica artisans depicted plants, animals, birds, buildings and, above all, people in accurate detail. Experts have pointed out that in fact what the potters did was to stress some salient feature, such as the head and head-dress of a figure, and represent this with such fidelity that it was hardly noticed that the rest of the figure was stereotyped. Be that as it may, the net result is that we have an authentic contemporary record of what sort of houses the Mochica lived in, what sort of clothes they wore, what they grew, ate and drank, and what pastimes they indulged in; there is even a magnificent selection of erotic pottery depicting their sex life.

From the evidence of these ceramics we can deduce that the Mochica lived in houses which usually consisted of three or four rectangular rooms, were often built on terraces or patios, and were solidly constructed of timber, adobe-brick and thatch. The houses were not laid out according to any overall plan, but were dotted haphazardly in small villages. The way the Mochica dressed suggests that their society was rigidly stratified. Important people are shown wearing ornate brocaded shirts and ponchos, being carried in litters, and eating at raised tables; such persons are often depicted symbolically as jaguars or condors. Unimportant people, on the other hand, are shown wearing nothing but a breechcloth, and are depicted as centipedes or lizards. It was evidently a man's world; in all the ceramics that have been unearthed women are never shown doing anything except domestic chores. It seems also to have been an authoritarian world, for scenes depicting punishment – usually mutilation or stoning – are commonplace. Further evidence of the authoritarian nature of Mochica society can be found in their huge state-run building projects; in the ruins of their magnificent aqueducts and their huge temples, like the Huaca de la Luna and the Huaca del Sol, which could only have been built by an enormous corporate effort. (Huaca del Sol, sited near the town of Trujillo, is one of the most impressive structures of the ancient world. Measuring 750 × 450 feet, it is composed of over 130,000,000 adobe bricks and dwarfs all but the largest of the Egyptian pyramids.)

As well as learning about the Mochica from their ceramics, we can learn about them from their artefacts. Objects unearthed from their graves and middens indicate that they excelled in practical skills such as metalwork, weaving, agriculture and war. Their jewellery was bold, their copperware solid and practical, and they were proficient at soldering, annealing and gilding. Their textiles were strong and well-designed, although due to saltpetre in the soil few have survived intact. Their agricultural instruments were well designed and functional; it is true that they lacked both the wheel and the plough, but they seem to have done very well without them. Their weapons included maces, battle-axes, spears and shields. They played a wide variety of musical instruments:

drums, tambourines, cymbals, trumpets, panpipes and flutes. Medically, they practised circumcision, and were *au fait* with techniques of bone-setting and simple surgery. Spiritually, they were a theocracy, their religious life being inextricably intertwined with their social, political and military life, and under the control of the same élite.

The overall picture is of a dynamic, confident and expansionist people, well advanced along the road to civilization. To modern eyes their society was unduly stratified, but a more cogent criticism would probably be that it was unduly warlike. Nobody can say for certain what happened to the Mochica, but it seems probable they were submerged during the era which Mason describes as 'a period of conquest, disruption and decadence' – the counterpart of Europe's Dark Ages – which preceded the empire of the Incas.

If the Mochica are an enigma, the people who flourished a few hundred miles further south and a few hundred years later are a complete mystery.

Nazca civilization was surely the most idiosyncratic the world has ever known. They were a peaceful, democratic people who built graves rather than cities, designed what are arguably the world's most beautiful textiles, were obsessed with ancestor-worship, and sculpted inexplicable dead-straight lines and emblematic figures on the surface of the *pampa*.

The Nazca River enters the Pacific a couple of hundred miles to the south of Lima. It was not here, however, that the Nazca civilization was conceived, for this part of the Peruvian coast is desert; rain is virtually unknown and rivers disappear into the sand. Only in the oases, about 60 miles inland is human life possible. It was here, during the first millennium AD that a civilization evolved which was as isolated from its neighbours as if it had sprung up on a Pacific atoll. A hundred years ago few people knew that the Nazca had ever existed. It was through aerial photography that their fantastic graveyards and linear excavations became known to the world.

Their principal graveyards, the Cavernas and the Necropolis, are sited at the approaches to the Atacama Desert, a wilderness of red-brown sand devoid of vegetation or life. Nothing moves in the Atacama except the wind; it is the epitome of desolation.

The site known as Cavernas is described by Alden Mason:

Paracas Cavernas was so named because the bodies were found in communal bottle-shaped chambers excavated in the rock at the foot of vertical shafts, at a depth of approximately 20 feet [6 or 7 metres]. Many of the tombs also have a stone-lined upper chamber at the surface. As many as fifty-five bodies were found in one of these sepulchres, of both sexes and all ages. The bodies were wrapped in coarse cotton cloths and accompanied by mortuary offerings.

Both the carbon dating and the design of these offerings indicate that the site is an old one – the motif on some of the funerary bowls is almost identical to the cat-god of Chavin de Huantar.

The site known as Necropolis is larger; it contains more bodies and more funerary ware, but is not so old. The cemetery is surrounded by a stone wall, and although the graves are comparatively shallow, so great is the aridity that even after a thousand years the bodies in them are perfectly preserved. About 500 bodies have been exhumed, and from the artefacts buried with them we are able to piece together a picture of Nazca life.

From the fact that there is no great difference in the size of the graves or in the value of their contents, we can deduce that the Nazca – unlike the socially-stratified Mochica – were an egalitarian society. Women were interred with as much care and lavishness as men, which suggests that there was a degree of sexual equality. Since few weapons have been found, it would seem the Nazca were not warlike. What *was* found in the graves was a cornucopia of ceramics and textiles. Many of these, particularly the textiles, are of great beauty; they all appear to have been individually crafted yet never used, the inference being that they were designed specifically as funerary ware. To modern eyes it seems something of a waste that these peaceful and artistic people should have spent so much of their time creating objects of unbelievable beauty only to bury them unused beneath the desert sand; but at least this has led to examples of their art surviving.

Nazca pottery is attractive in shape, intricate in design and delicate in colouring. The most commonly found artefacts are bowls, effigy-jars, beakers and single- and double-spout water-carriers. The designs consist of either stylized animals, birds, fish and plants, or, more commonly, mythological creatures incorporated into a geometric pattern. The basic colouring is usually a white background with four or five pigments applied after firing, the most common being red, brown, yellow, violet and grey. These ceramics are pleasing rather than outstanding. The textiles are another story. Many experts consider them the most beautiful in the world. Beside almost every body in the Necropolis a variety of garments had been carefully laid out: ponchos, mantles, shirts, loin-cloths, underclothes and turbans. These had been made by just about every known technique: warp-and-weft weaving, tapestry, brocading, embroidery, knitting and three-dimensional knitting. They were patterned with intricate designs: stylized flora and fauna and a whole hierarchy of mythological gods and demons – the spotted cat the bringer of life, the demon cat the bringer of death, the bird-demon, the centipede-god and the multiple-headed god. However, their particular splendour is their colour. Even after a thousand years they pulsate with the brilliance of a rainbow. Experts have distinguished as many as 140 different tints in a single garment, all derived from natural dyes and the oil of the untreated cotton or wool. Even more amazing than the variety of the colours is their beauty. They glow as though woven with sunlight. Some of the most exotic of these garments can be seen today in the National Museum in Lima, and it is impossible to look at them without feeling wonder and admiration at the artistry of their creators.

The picture that has so far emerged of the Nazca is of a talented, individualistic but somewhat morbid people; morbid because so much of their lives appears to have been preoccupied with ancestor-worship and death. It is possible that this preoccupation may explain one of the great mysteries of our planet, the lines on the Nazca plateau.

The Nazca plateau or *pampa* lies roughly between the coast and the main cordillera of the Andes. It consists of a bedrock of compacted sand overlaid by myriads of tiny iron-impregnated stones. It is a lonely and desolate place. Rain seldom falls; clouds seldom soften the sky; perpetual sunlight by day alternates with perpetual starlight by night; silence is absolute, and time meaningless. Over an area of roughly 40 × 10 miles this *pampa* is criss-crossed by a network of lines, most of them dead-straight, but some depicting with startling if stylized accuracy birds, monkeys and spiders. The scale, clarity and complexity of these patterns has to be seen to be believed. In his book *Pathways to the Gods* Tony Morrison gives an excellent description of them:

The desert below the wing tip of our plane was a network of lines and crazy patterns stretching for miles to the horizon. One line slid into the viewfinder of my camera, perfectly straight as if it had been made by some dextrous giant, some supergod. It led into more lines which formed a narrow triangle, like a strange runway. More true lines were followed by others depicting figures, a beautifully expressive bird, a monkey fleeing; then another triangle, a huge rectangle and a double spiral. Some lines led straight as arrows over dry riverbeds and hills. Others converged on hummocks like cartwheel spokes on a hub. Beside the large rectangle a switchback-like pattern of thin parallel lines lay as neatly as tracks in a railway shunting yard. I kept shooting pictures as we circled again over the desert to look at South America's most amazing archaeological mystery.

For the last fifty years people have been asking how the lines got there and what they mean. The first question is easier to answer than the second. The lines are definitely not a natural phenomenon, a quirk of nature brought about by faults in the rock or the juxtaposition of different strata. They were brought about by human hands deliberately removing surface stones from certain areas of the *pampa* and piling the stones up along the edges of these areas so that the light-coloured sand beneath was revealed. The lines could have only come into being as a result of a lot of accurate and painstaking work by a lot of people.

For what purpose? One theory is that the lines were devised as landing strips to facilitate the arrival, long ago, of alien spacecraft; and it has to be said that this is exactly what they look like. Eric von Daniken is the chief exponent of this theory. 'What is wrong with the idea,' he asks, 'that the lines were laid out to say to the gods: "Land here! Everything has been prepared as you ordered"?' To my mind two things are wrong. First, if there had indeed been an alien landing on the *pampa* then surely the South American Indians would have had so vivid a recollection of it, it would have been encapsulated in their mythology. Second, if aliens had indeed had the technology not only to build and fly a spaceship to earth, but to get the 'locals' to prepare a landing-strip for them, why should they have created such a hotchpotch of 'runways', about 90 per cent of which were useless? And, moreover, why the symbolic bird, the fleeing monkey and the spiders and flowers?

A more plausible theory was advanced by Maria Reiche, a gifted and dedicated German mathematician who has spent more than 40 years in the *pampa* examining the lines; she reckons that they have an astronomical connotation. 'It has been found,' she says, 'that a great number of the lines and triangles coincide with the rising of an important star in the east and its setting in the west. They [the ancients] believed this had some mysterious significance.' A computer was brought in to analyze the lines and discover to what extent they were orientated towards individual stars: great things were expected of this new technique; but the computer, alas, failed to find any overall pattern. Something was missing from its programming. It would therefore seem that although astronomy is part of the answer, it is not the whole answer.

I suggest what was missing from the computer-programming was the human factor: that we won't solve the mystery of the Nazca lines until we solve the mystery of the Nazca people.

We know it must have been the Nazca who built the lines, for the *pampa* is close to their heartland, fragments of their pottery have been found beside the lines, the design of the creatures carved into the *pampa* is identical with the design of the creatures engraved on their ceramics, and carbon dating places the excavations at *circa* AD 500 which is in the early Nazca period. It seems that the lines were intended to be seen from the air, because there is nowhere on earth from which their designs can be properly appreciated; this implies that they were built, at least in part, for the edification of gods and spirits. We know they were constructed with great precision, skill and hard work – some of them run perfectly straight and parallel for up to 5 miles, and it has been estimated that to clear the largest of the rectilinear 'runways' more than a billion stones must have had to be moved. Although we know all this, we still can only guess at the fundamental purpose of the lines. Were they wrapped up with the Nazca preoccupation with ancestor-worship? Were they pathways which the living used to reach ceremonial sites on the *pampa*, and which the spirits of the dead were supposed to see from the air and use for the same purpose? Were they mini-pilgrimage routes, which the Nazca reckoned it was both safe and holy to follow? (What gives credence to this last suggestion is that even today South American Indians like to approach a shrine – be it Christian or pagan – by a route that is traditional, straight and clearly marked.) The avenues of conjecture are limitless but it could be that a possible solution is emerging.

We talk of the Nazca 'lines' because this is how we see them from the air, but in fact they are pathways, slightly sunken, with the stones piled up along either side.

Such pathways are known to the Indians are *ceques*, a word that is difficult to translate, although as long ago as 1609 the Jesuit Father Cobo made a valiant attempt. '*Ceques*,' he wrote, 'are straight lines along which holy stopping places, venerated by all, are placed at intervals.' The phrase 'holy stopping places' may conjure up a vision of shrines built by humans for the worship of the gods; this, however, is a European not a South American concept. To the South American Indians a holy place is a manifestation not of the work of humans but of the work of the gods themselves. They saw a tree struck by lightning, rocks split by frost, a boulder displaced by flash-flood, and the places where these things had happened became their holy places, places to be venerated. They also venerated places where some important incident had taken place: where a tribal elder had died, or a child had thrust his hand into a scorpion's nest and lived. Their world was dominated by gods, demons and spirits and the sites associated with them. Even as late as 1617 – when the Nazca civilization had long been superseded by the Tiahuanaco, and the Tiahuanaco by the Inca and the Inca by the Spanish – spirit and ancestor worship was still widely practised throughout the Andes. Spanish records bear witness to this. According to the *Archivo General de Indias*, in one year alone (1617) in one small province (the south coast of Peru) more than 6,000 people were arrested for idolatry, 679 people were convicted of sorcery, and the authorities confiscated 617 mummies, and found and destroyed 603 major holy places (*wak'as*) and 3,418 minor holy places (*conopas*). These *wak'as* and *conopas* can be found today scattered all over the Andes, but they are most abundant in the desert surrounding the present city of Nazca. An abundance of holy sites, a multiplicity of pathways connecting these sites, an obsession with the dead. . . It all seems to point to the fact that the *pampa* was a site for ceremonial ancestor-worship, in Tony Morrison's apt terminology 'a two-dimensional temple': that the Nazca lines were designed to bring the living and the dead together on a plane both physical and metaphysical. We don't yet know the exact form this ancestor-worship took – perhaps mummies were paraded along the *ceques* in a ceremonial transition from this world to the next? Nor do we know the exact purpose of the lines – perhaps each was made, kept in good order and used for its rituals by a particular clan? However, our knowledge is increasing. Only a few years ago archaeologists were searching the *pampa* for some secret temple or burial ground which would give the lines meaning. Today it is realized that the whole Nazca desert *is* a temple, the *ceques* its walls, and the *wak'as* and *conopas* its altars: a unique record of the life and death of a unique and mysterious people.

The Nazca were superseded by a race who are easier to understand but whose origins once again are shrouded in mystery: the Tiahuanaco.

The ruins of Tiahuanaco lie close to the south shore of Lake Titicaca in the heart of the altiplano. This is bleak, chill and virtually treeless territory, more than 12,500 feet above sea level: an unexpected place in which to find a conglomeration of huge pyramids, monolithic statues, courtyards and terraces. Garcilaso de la Vega describes the site:

We must now say something of the large and almost incredible buildings of Tiahuanaco. There is an artifical hill, of great height, built on stone foundations so that the earth will not slide. There are gigantic figures carved in stone, with head-dresses and long robes reaching down to the ground; these are much worn, which shows their great antiquity. There are walls, the stones of which are so enormous it is difficult to imagine what human force could have put them in place. And there are the remains of strange buildings, the most remarkable being stone portals, hewn out of solid rock; these stand on bases anything up to 30 feet long, 15 feet wide and 6 feet thick, base and portal being all of one piece, and it can not be imagined how such enormous stones could have been brought here . . . The natives say these monuments are dedicated to the Creator of the Universe, and that the Incas subsequently built their fortress of Cuzco in imitation of them.

How old are these mysterious structures? Who built them and for what purpose?

It used to be thought that Tiahuanaco must be the centre of some forgotten prehistoric empire, the fountain-head from which all subsequent American civilizations sprang. This idea would seem to be substantiated by Inca mythology and by the appearance of the monoliths. According to Inca legend, Viracocha (the Supreme Being) made two attempts at creation. First, he created the sky and the earth (but no sun) and peopled the earth with a race of giants. However, the giants soon displeased him, so he turned them into stone – the monolithic statues of Tiahuanaco – and covered the earth with a great flood. It was only on his second attempt that he created the moon, the sun and human beings of the size they are today. The inference here is that the Tiahuanaco ruins are of great antiquity, and this is certainly the impression the monoliths give; they have the appearance of being timeless, old as the hills that encircle them. Scholars now reckon, however, that Tiahuanaco is of comparatively recent origin. What dates the buildings is partly the style of the clothes, weapons and symbols carved on the stone, and partly the buildings themselves. Not only are the great 100-ton blocks beautifully dressed and perfectly fitted, they are held together by notching and copper-cramping, techniques which were unknown to the early civilizations. Exact dating is still a matter of controversy, but it is now generally reckoned that Tiahuanaco was built between 1,000 and 1,500 years ago.

The obvious people to have done the building are the Aymara Indians. Scattered families of the Aymara are still living today on the shores of Lake Titicaca, grazing their llamas and alpacas on the pale grass and harvesting their potatoes from the arid soil, very much as their ancestors did a thousand years ago. Mason describes them as 'a stolid, taciturn people, with no high degree of culture'. Even if we accept that the population of the altiplano was greater then than it is now, and that the Aymaras' past was more prestigious than their present, it is still difficult to see how such huge monuments could have been fashioned by purely local labour. It has been suggested that Tiahuanaco, like Chavin de Huantar a millennium earlier, was a shrine: that as such it would have been visited at *fiesta*-time by large numbers of pilgrims, and that these pilgrims could, under supervision, have provided the necessary labour-force. This is a convincing theory – provided that the ruins are indeed those of a shrine and not a city.

The Tiahuanaco horizon can boast several urban centres (Huari, Pucara and Pikillata, to mention only a few) through which its culture was disseminated; but the site from which it takes its name is too small to be classed as a city – it occupies less than a sixth of a square mile – and none of its buildings can be identified as homes, whereas several can be identified as temples or parts of a temple. Among the latter is arguably the most famous monument in South America: the Gateway of the Sun. The Gateway of the Sun is made from a single block of andesite, cut into the shape of a portal 10 feet high, 12½ feet wide, and 1½ feet thick, and weighing over 10 tons. The top of the portal consists of a frieze almost entirely covered with figures, arranged in a series of symmetrically laid-out panels. These figures are dominated by a centrally placed deity with weeping eyes, its head-dress and clothes adorned with discs and trophy-heads, and its hands grasping a spear-thrower and a quiver. Arranged on either side are forty-eight far smaller warrior-attendants, apparently hurrying towards the deity as if to pay homage. The Gateway is interesting architectually because it is monolithic, and because the figures depicted on it are replicas of those worked in other media, such as wood or gold. It is even more interesting historically because of the insight it gives us into pre-Inca beliefs. Guidoni and Magni sum up what researchers have to say about the significance of the Gateway:

The mass of literature – not all of it accurate in its descriptions or its conclusions – on the Gateway of the Sun is now so great that it is not easy to find one's way through the labyrinth of fascinating but often contradictory explanations of the frieze. However, one student of Andean culture has summed up the more reliable interpretations as follows: there is the religious approach which takes the central figure to be a divinity (most probably Viracocha) to whom acolytes are paying homage; the political approach, according to which three different social classes are appearing before the majestic figure of the sovereign; and the ritual approach which interprets the 48 figures as participants, disguised with masks, wings and tails, in a dance.

These interpretations ignore the fact that Aymara artisans would never have created a work which was solely religious or solely political or solely ritual, since the people of the Andes regarded all three as being inextricably intertwined. So how *should* the freize be interpreted and what does it tell us of its creators?

Perhaps its most interesting feature is so obvious that it is seldom mentioned: it is remarkably formal and mathematical. Not only are its figures arranged in perfect symmetry, they are arranged in multiples of eight, which is the perfect number to form the basis of a stylized pattern since it quarters, halves and three-quarters into exact digits. Furthermore, the figures are not merely similar, they are identical, exact mirror-images, to create which the sculptors must have used reversible stencils. Bearing in mind that this sort of precise and stylized symmetry was also a feature of Mochica ceramics, Nazca textiles and a great many other forms of South American art, it seems obvious that the early South Americans were a people who set great store by a regimented way of life.

This regimentation led them always to have a *huaca*, a tangible holy of holies, at the centre of their lives. The people of the Chavin horizon had Chavin de Huantar as their navel of the world, and the people of the Tiahuanaco horizon had the Titicaca site as their navel; and the differences between these sites highlight the differences between the way of life of the people who built them. In the Chavin site the central feature, the *lanzon*, is dominated by a symbolic feline godhead; there is little sign of human involvement. In the Tiahuanaco site the central feature, the Gateway of the Sun, is dominated by human beings. All the minor figures, although they are decked out with condors' masks and monkeys' tails, are recognizably human. The central figure is human too; not only does it have human features, it has human characteristics, for quite clearly it is weeping. So, over a span of some 1,500 years, a religion dedicated to an abstract, feline and uncaring god gave way to a religion dedicated to a god who was corporeal, semihuman and caring. As Guidoni and Magni put it, 'It seems probable that at Tiahuanaco we are already witnessing a king identified with the sun, in the double function of high priest and supreme being.'

From these roots stemmed the faith of the Incas.

Only one thing was needed to engender the conditions which gave rise to the Inca empire: there had to be a greater alignment between the centre of spiritual power and the centre of temporal power. Up to now the holy places of the pre-Inca civilizations had tended to be shrines, centres of pilgrimage rather than centres of population. What altered this was the emergence of cities. The great city-builders were the last of the pre-Inca civilizations, the Chimu.

The kingdom of Chimu was large in extent but of comparatively brief duration. It seems to have been not so much a centralized state as a loose confederation of cities scattered throughout the coastal plains of northern Peru and southern Ecuador between the 4th and 11th parallels; it flourished from about AD 1150 to AD 1450. Most of what we know about the people of Chimu has been gleaned from a study of their magnificent capital, Chanchan.

Chanchan was the largest pre-Hispanic city in South America, covering 8 square miles, and was laid out with a simple precision which is the envy of present-day town-planners. It consists of ten separate complexes. These used to be known as 'palaces'; the word, however, is misleading, because although each complex contains palacelike buildings, it also contains large numbers of smaller dwellings, as well as streets, reservoirs, irrigation channels, storehouses, cemeteries and temples. The city is probably the most symmetrical in the world, for not only are its complexes arranged parallel to one another astride the meridial axis between mountains and sea, each is laid out on similar lines, with rectangular buildings set precisely at right angles to one another. Today Chanchan is deserted; its great walls of adobe brick are crumbling, its water-runnels have silted up and there isn't a tree in sight. However, it is easy to picture the scene as it must have been some 600 years ago, when the 'palaces' were home to more than 100,000 people, and the city and its environs – like the rest of the Moche Valley – were 'a veritable garden'.

What do the ruins of this once great city tell us about the people who lived in it? The fact that it was designed and built to an ambitious overall plan implies an authority which was in firm control, was forward thinking and – at least to some extent – paternal, since the city appears to have been designed to benefit not only an élite but the whole population. The fact that the scale was so vast and the workmanship so uniformly excellent implies a labour-force which was both skilled and willing – Egyptian pyramids were the work of slaves, but it seems likely that Chimu artisans (like their successors the Inca artisans) gave their labour willingly and indeed proudly, glad to help in the completion of worthwhile projects of value to the community. The great difference in the size of the dwellings – some are near-palaces, others single-room apartments – leads us to suppose that Chimu society was stratified into the haves and the have-nots; and this is substantiated by evidence from the cemeteries, for whereas some graves are simple and the gifts in them few in number and poor in quality, others consist of huge vaults crammed with exotic if undistinguished pottery, textiles and furniture. Finally, we can learn about the people of Chanchan from the architecture. While it is difficult to fault the workmanship, the designs are stereotyped and uninspired: an endless reproduction of rectangular buildings decorated with simple geometric motifs and crude animals. Their pottery and textiles are similarly uninspired, so much so that Chimu art is sometimes known as 'decadent Mochica' or 'decadent Nazca', since it is clearly derivative of these earlier art forms and combines the worst features of both. The people of Chimu seem to have been more efficient than artistic. In this they resembled their conquerors, the Incas.

It is perhaps surprising that so efficient and well-organized a people should have been conquered with such apparent ease. One explanation is that since their kingdom was a loose federation of city-states, these were defeated one by one. If this is so, the implication is that the Chimu empire lacked a heart, and that their capital Chanchan was to some extent a façade. Certainly, the impersonal symmetry of the Chanchan ruins suggests a city, like present-day Brasilia, which didn't evolve naturally, but was created artificially. Such cities inspire awe rather than affection – it is doubtful if a Brasilian would fight for Brasilia with the same fervour as a Frenchman would fight for Paris, or an Inca for Cuzco.

The Inca capital, Cuzco, had, on the face of it, much in common with Chanchan, for it too was artificially created, being largely the inspiration of the Inca Pachacuti. Yet there seems to have been a fundamental difference between the two capitals. Chanchan never appears to have been accepted as the navel of the world, the sort of touched-by-magic centre to which the Indians could sublimate their penchant for allegiance. Cuzco, on the other hand, appears to have become, in a remarkably short space of time, a spiritual and temporal centre accepted not only by the Incas but by those who came under their suzerainty.

What, one wonders, were the qualities of these Incas that, from their remote and isolated capital, they succeeded in doing what nobody had done before and nobody has done since: to unite under one banner the multifarious people of the Andes?

CHAPTER 4

Children of the Sun God

June: digging the potatoes.

Those who delve into the history of the Incas tend to come up with more questions than answers.

No one has summarized the character and achievements of these once-mighty people better than John Hemming:

The Incas were an austere mountain tribe, one of many Andean peoples who flourished briefly during the millennia before the European conquest of the Americas . . . [They] were the Romans of the Andean world – efficient administrators, excellent soldiers, fine engineers, but with little of the artistic brilliance of the more flamboyant civilizations that preceded them.

Yet even such an incontrovertible summary raises questions. Why was it this particular mountain tribe – and not their neighbours the Aymara, Chanca, Colla or Tampa – who managed to impose their rule over an empire which in its heyday stretched for 3,500 miles from Quito in the northern Andes to Concepcion in the southern? And what sort of empire can it have been that it was defended by hundreds of thousands of 'excellent soldiers' yet was conquered by a rabble of 120 adventurers?

These questions are difficult to answer because our knowledge of the Incas is so limited. It is limited partly by the fact that since they lacked a written language no contemporary sources record the birth and growth of their empire, and their early history has come down to us only at second hand through the eyes of their conquerors. Also, comparatively little archaeological research has been done in the Andes. Inca artefacts are for the most part derivative and standardized, and of little interest to the archaeologist. Only their stonework is outstanding, and the isolation of many of the great Inca buildings and the devastation they suffered at the hands of the Spaniards have limited research. (Machu Picchu, for example, wasn't even discovered until 1911, and some of its satellite shrines still haven't been comprehensively studied; while Sacsahuaman – the citadel of Cuzco – was deliberately dismantled by the *encomenderos* to provide stone for their houses.) This last fact pinpoints the third and greatest stumbling block to our knowledge of the Incas: much of their civilization was deliberately destroyed by the Spaniards. It is of course standard practice for conquerors to rub the noses of those they have worsted in the dirt; but seldom have a people been forced to endure such utter subjugation as the Incas. The classic condemnation of the rape of their civilization was written by Prescott in his *History of the Conquest of Peru*, and even after 140 years and through a pall of unfashionable rhetoric, his message comes to us loud and clear:

Pizarro found a country well advanced in the arts of civilization; institutions under which the people lived in tranquillity and personal safety; the mountains and the uplands whitened with flocks; the valleys teeming with the fruits of a scientific husbandry; the granaries and warehouses filled to overflowing; the whole land rejoicing in its abundance; and the character of the nation, softened under the influence of the mildest and most innocent form of superstition, well prepared for the reception of Christian civilization. But far from introducing this, Pizarro delivered up the conquered races to his brutal soldiery; the sacred shrines were abandoned to their lust; the towns and villages were given up to pillage; the wretched natives were parcelled out like slaves, to toil for their conquerors in the mines; the flocks were scattered and wantonly destroyed; the beautiful contrivances for the culture of the soil [the irrigation works] were suffered to fall into decay; paradise was converted to desert. Instead of profiting by the ancient forms of civilization, Pizarro preferred to efface every vestige of them, and on their ruins to erect the institutions of his own country. Yet these institutions did little for the Indian, held in iron bondage. He became an alien in the land of his fathers.

Contemporary sources confirm this almost total destruction of a civilization in its prime. In the words of the Spaniards, 'Whatever can be burned, is burned; the rest is broken.' In the words of the Incas, 'Night fell at noon'.

With such a background it is hardly surprising that early Inca history is a quagmire of conjecture. There is, however, one source which provides us with something approaching first-hand material; this is the work of Garcilaso de la Vega, el Inca.

Garcilaso was born in Cuzco in 1540, only a few years after the conquest, the son of an Inca princess who was a member of the *acllahuasi* (house of the chosen women) and a Spanish conquistador who acted briefly as governor of the capital. He was among the first of the mestizos, bound by ties of blood and affection to two totally different worlds; he was also a man of formidable scholarship who, for a wager, translated abstruse Christian treatises with a felicity that won the admiration of those élite of the intelligentsia, the Jesuits. No one would appear better qualified to chronicle the rise and fall of the Inca empire. Yet historians have pointed out that Garcilaso's facts are sometimes suspect, because at the age of twenty-one he left South America and settled in a remote Andalusian valley where he spent the rest of his life: his writings therefore include much second-hand material. However, blemishes should not obscure the value of Garcilaso's unique *Royal Commentaries of the Incas* and his recently discovered *Sum and Narration of the Incas*. From these two great works we have probably learned more about the people of the Andes than from all other sources combined.

Perhaps the basic point to emerge from Garcilaso's writings is that the Incas had a powerful sense of vocation. They believed their kings were direct descendants of the Sun God, and as a corollary to this they believed it to be their duty to persuade less fortunate races to worship their God and so qualify for the fruits of his benediction. It is easy to dismiss this as a convenient excuse for them to subjugate their neighbours. However, there is evidence that the Incas really did regard their campaigns as crusades rather than conquests, that their despotism was paternal, and that they did indeed confer very real material benefits on the races they brought under the aegis of the Sun God.

Garcilaso describes how this myth of Inca divinity originated. He tells us that when he was between sixteen and seventeen years old he often visited his mother's relatives in Cuzco and listened to the older members of her family reminiscing about 'the happy times before our rule was turned to bondage'. One day he asked the most senior of his relatives what, in the absence of written records, he knew of his people's history. His uncle was delighted at this question, and replied at length:

You should know that in the old days the whole of this region was covered in scrub and heath, and the people lived like wild beasts, with no religion or government, no towns or houses, without sowing the soil and without clothing. They lived in twos and threes, as chance brought them together, in caves and crannies in the rock. Like wild beasts they ate the herbs of the field, the roots of trees and fruits growing wild, also human flesh. In short they lived like animals, and even in their intercourse with women they behaved like animals, for they knew nothing of having separate wives.

Our Father the Sun, seeing men in this state, took pity on them, and sent from heaven a Son and a Daughter to teach them about Himself and persuade them to adopt Him as their God and worship Him . . . and learn to till the soil and grow plants and crops and breed flocks and use the fruits of the earth like rational beings and not like beasts. With these instructions our Father the Sun set His two children down beside Lake Titicaca, and bade them go forth, and wherever they stopped to sleep to try and thrust into the ground a golden rod which He had given them; and at the place where this rod sank into the ground He told them to set up their court. Finally He said: 'When you have reduced these people to my service, you are to care for them with reason, justice and mercy, treating them as a father treats his children. Do this in imitation of me, remembering that I always work for the good of the world, bringing it light, brightness and warmth, and circling it once a day to observe its needs . . . So that you, my children, may follow my example I nominate you lords and kings over all people.'

As soon as our Father the Sun had made known His wishes to his children and had bidden them farewell, they set off from Lake Titicaca and headed north. Whenever they stopped to rest they tried to push the golden rod into the earth, but it never sank in. Eventually they reached Pacárec (the resthouse of the dawn), and from this place they came next morning to the valley of Cuzco, which was then a wilderness.

Close to the hill now known as Huanacauri they thrust the rod into the soil, and it sank in completely and disappeared. So the Inca said to his sister: 'Our Father wishes us to remain in this valley and make it our home. It is therefore right, queen and sister, that each of us should go forth and call people together and instruct and benefit them as our Father ordered . . .' So the prince went north, and the princess south, and spoke to the savage men and women they found in the wilderness and told them that their Father the Sun had sent them from the sky to be teachers and benefactors and to bring everyone together to dwell in towns in the valleys . . . And the savages, seeing the Inca and his sister adorned with ornaments which have been given them by their Father the Sun, with their ears pierced and opened, and in clothing very different from their own, were attracted by the promises held out, and many said that they would follow our king and queen wherever they led . . .

So some were set to work to supply meals, and others were set to work to build houses according to plans drawn up by the Inca. Thus our imperial city came to be built: it was divided into two halves called Hanan Cuzco (Upper Cuzco) and Hurin Cuzco (Lower Cuzco), the former being populated by those brought in by the king, and the latter by those brought in by the queen . . . And while the city was being built, our Inca showed the male Indians which tasks were proper for men: teaching them how to break and till the soil, sow it with seeds and vegetables, and irrigate it with channels brought down from the streams. While the queen trained the female Indians in all feminine occupations, such as spinning and weaving. In short, there was nothing relating to human life that they failed to teach their vassals, the Inca king acting as master of the men and the Coya queen as mistress of the women . . .

These were the beginnings of our great and famous empire which your father and his friends deprived us of. I cannot tell you exactly how long ago these events took place, but we believe it to have been a little over 400 years.

Reduced to its basics this is a description of a military conquest followed by an agricultural revolution; and it has been suggested the Garcilaso, writing years later, invested these mundane events with the sanctity of myth in order to justify Inca aggression. There may be truth in this; however, it wasn't long before the Incas themselves came to believe the myth of their divine origin, for as their empire expanded and prospered it seemed to them increasingly self-evident that they were indeed a chosen people whose destiny was to bring under their aegis all the diverse tribes of the Andes.

Exactly how and when these tribes came under Inca suzerainty is a matter of conjecture. Garcilaso would have us believe that the Inca empire came into being as soon as his people migrated north from Titicaca to Cuzco – about AD 1200 – and that from this moment onward it expanded slowly but surely under a succession of benevolent emperors, the first of whom was Manco Capac (c. 1200-1225). *Royal Commentaries* is full of entries like:

Manco Capac settled his vassals in villages and taught them how to till the soil and to make irrigation channels and do all that was necessary to lead a civilized life. And the Indians, conscious of the favours the Inca had showered on them, praised him and blessed him . . . The second Inca king, Sinchi Roca, said it was his father's wish that all people should be taught to worship the Sun, and that he intended to set forth and deliver the neighbouring tribes from their bestial way of life. The Indians of the Puchina and Carchi tribes, being simple and ready to believe any new thing, agreed to accept the Incas' rule; in this way, without the use of arms, the empire was extended a further twenty leagues.

The words 'a further twenty leagues' provide a clue to these early events in Inca history. Everything was on a small scale. Indeed it seems likely that for more than a century after the Incas arrived in Cuzco, the whole of their 'empire' lay within sight of the hills overlooking their capital, and the Cuzco itself consisted of little more than a temple and a simple complex of timber and fieldstone huts.

According to Garcilaso, expansion accelerated during the reign of the third emperor, Lloque Yupanqui, who 'ordered six or seven thousand warriors to be mobilized, so that he could advance with greater authority than his predecessors; for he wished to rely not only on petitions but also, when faced with those who were stubborn, on arms.' By the reign of the fifth emperor, Inca armies were said to be campaigning beyond the altiplano – 'having crossed the hot land where neither grass nor anything useful will grow they came at last to the sea' – probably a little north of the Atacama. However, such far-flung excursions must have been rare, and seem to have been punitive raids rather than attempts at permanent occupation. Indeed, no attempt was made to garrison captured territory until the reign of the eighth emperor, Viracocha Inca – and then, surprisingly, we learn that the land garrisoned was less than 100 miles from Cuzco. It would therefore seem that up to this point in time Inca activity was essentially small-scale and local.

Yet by the end of another generation the Incas were in control of territory not 100 miles from Cuzco but 1,000; and their empire stretched from the shores of the Pacific to the headwaters of the Amazon, and from the cordillera of Colombia to the valleys of central Chile: that is, they controlled an area of almost ½ million square miles, with a probable population of at least 10 million – an empire to rival that of the Romans.

Modern scholars are inclining to the view that Garcilaso is wrong in suggesting that this great empire was built up steadily throughout the centuries: that it was, in fact, carved out suddenly and dramatically in the middle of the fifteen century by the genius of one man, the emperor Pachacuti (1438-71).

According to this interpretation, the Inca empire prior to Pachacuti was small, unstable and highly vulnerable. Indeed, during the reign of his father, Viracocha, it was very nearly obliterated by an invading army of Chancas. The Chancas, whose territory lay beyond the River Apurimac to the north-west of Cuzco, were old enemies of the Incas, and so powerful was the attack they launched that Viracocha and his eldest son decided that resistance would be useless and fled. However, the emperor's younger son, Pachacuti, had other ideas. On the heights above Cuzco he rallied the Inca army and, against all the odds, in one of the decisive battles of South American history, the Chancas were routed and driven back over the Apurimac. So total and unexpected was the Incas' victory that according to legend it was divinely inspired, the rocks on the hills overlooking Cuzco being metamorphosed to Inca warriors who helped turn the tide of battle – these rocks were subsequently venerated as *wak'as*. With a victorious army to back him, Pachacuti quickly had himself enthroned in Cuzco – according to most sources, without the approval of his father and behind the back of his brother. His seizure of the throne marks the end of what is usually known as the legendary Inca empire whose events were largely conjectural, and the beginning of the historical empire whose events are proven fact.

Pachacuti has been described by John Hemming as 'one of those protean figures, like Alexander or Napoleon, who combine a mania for conquest with the ability to impose his will on every facet of government'. His name gives us a clue to his achievements, for in the Incas' language (Quechua) *pacha* = land or time, and *cuti* = to turn around; so a fair translation of his cognomen would be 'reformer of the world'. It seems to have been through the achievements of this outstanding ruler that the Incas were transformed from a small and warlike tribe which exercised loose control over the terrain round its capital, to a huge and stable civilization which exercised tight control over a third of a continent.

There were three phases to this transformation.

First, in a series of spectacular campaigns, Pachacuti and his son not only increased the extent of Inca territory by some 1,000 per cent, but also created a network of roads, fortresses and warehouses which enabled their army to keep the newly conquered territory under effective control.

Second, by promulgating and enforcing a comprehensive code of laws, Pachacuti ensured that Inca ideology and Inca methods of agriculture were accepted without question throughout the empire. These laws were inflexible and restrictive rather than harsh; they regulated almost every aspect of every person's life; conformity was by *force majeure*.

Third, he rebuilt Cuzco on a monumental scale, turning it into one of the world's great fortresses and, more importantly, making it the centre from which he, as Sun God, exercised absolute temporal and spiritual authority.

The military exploits of Pachacuti and his son Topa deserve to be ranked with those of Alexander, Hannibal and Napoleon. As soon as the area within some 100 miles of Cuzco had been pacified, Pachacuti led his armies north into the Cordillera Vilcabamba. This was a world of steep-sided valleys and fast-flowing rivers, with slopes of bare scree alternating with swathes of luxuriant forest; difficult country to fight in. Yet the very difficulty of the terrain made the Incas' task easier. Most tribes of the cordillera were isolated valley-dwellers, cut off from their neighbours by barriers both physical and cultural. The Incas, with their large and well-organized army, conquered them one by one. As they advanced they built roads and, at strategic points, what are arguably the world's most magnificent temple-fortresses – Ollantaytambo overlooking the valley of the Yucay, and Machu Picchu overlooking the valley of the Urubamba. These temple-fortresses, like the eighteen cities that bear the name of Alexander the Great, served for many years as centres for the preservation and dissemination of an alien culture.

As the Inca armies worked their way north, the valleys became more fertile, more populous and more prosperous. Soon enormous quantities of booty, the exotic produce of the headwaters of the Amazon, were flowing back to Cuzco, much of it accumulated by an Inca army led by Pachacuti's brother, Capac. It seems that Capac was rash enough to boast his conquests were more glorious than those of his brother. Pachacuti, on the pretext that he was planning a rebellion, had him executed.

Having extended his empire some 500 miles to the north, Pachacuti turned his attention to the south where old rivals of the Incas, the Colla and Lupaca, were staging a rebellion in the neighbourhood of Lake Titicaca. The rebellion was short-lived. Inca armies proved as invincible in the highlands of the altiplano as in the valleys of the cordillera; the Colla and Lupaca were swiftly crushed, many of them being transported *en masse* to other parts of the empire. Pachacuti then pushed farther south, beyond the shores of Lake Titicaca and into the desert of Tapac-Ri. This was unpromising terrain. According to Garcilaso, one of the troops reported: 'There is not one foot of good land here, nothing but cliffs, rocks and stony wastes. The only things that grow are cactuses, with thorns as long as a man's finger. There are many hot springs emitting great clouds of steam and the stench of sulphur.' Probably feeling that such a bleak new world was hardly worth the conquering, Pachacuti returned to his capital.

By now he had been in the field for almost ten years and had had his fill of campaigning. He decided to name his favourite son, Topa Yupanqui, as his successor, and to devote the rest of his life to promulgating a new and comprehensive code of laws for governing his expanding empire and to rebuilding Cuzco. It was therefore Topa and not Pachacuti who in 1485 led the Inca army once again to the north in one of the great campaigns of military history.

We cannot say for certain how many troops Topa took with him. Garcilaso says 40,000, modern historians say 200,000; perhaps a realistic estimate would be 15,000 Inca troops plus levies of 50,000 or 60,000 from the conquered tribes. Passing through the cordillera, which had been pacified a decade earlier by his father, Topa came to the Maranon River flowing north into the unknown. This again was difficult terrain to pass through, let alone to fight in: vertiginous valleys trembling to the roar of fast-flowing rivers, sunlit foothills crowned with the fortified villages of the pre-Inca Yarivilcas, and among and often above the clouds the great snow-capped peaks of the Cordillera Blanca. The Incas advanced on tribe after tribe, demanding allegiance. Those who agreed to accept the ideology of the sun God were absorbed peacefully into the empire; those who refused were crushed and colonized and thus absorbed by force. What happened to the people of Chachapoya was typical. Garcilaso writes:

With the coming of summer reinforcements were brought up, and the Inca ordered his army to advance against the land of the Chachapoya. According to the usual custom a messenger was sent in advance to offer peace or war. To this messenger the Chachapoya replied that they were ready to die in defence of their freedom; let the Inca do his worst, they would never become his subjects.

On receipt of this reply there began a cruel and bloody war, with many dead and wounded on both sides. The Incas were determined not to retreat; the people of Chachapoya were determined to die rather than yield. They had prepared prepared formidable defences, building forts and blocking the ravines which were in places so steep and rugged that the only way to advance was by climbing ropes. Owing to these difficulties the Incas suffered great loss of life in forcing their way through the passes and occupying the strong points ... At last they captured a fort on the hill known as Pias, which is one of the chief places in this province. They found the fort unoccupied, except for some old men and women and young children who were too weak to take to the mountains. Topa ordered all these people to be treated with mercy and care.

From Pias he sent forward a force of 300 picked men to reconnoiter the mountain passes; but they were caught in a great snowfall, which buried them and froze them to death; not one was able to escape ... When the fury of the snow had abated, Topa continued his conquest, reducing the villages, and building as he advanced the royal highway, a laborious task in so difficult a country. In the village of Cuntur Marca, the Chachapoya made a last stand. They fought valiantly for many days, but such was the might of the Incas that they were overcome by the mass of men bearing down on them, and were forced at last to submit. Topa received them with his usual clemency, and bestowed on them gifts and favours, both to pacify them and induce others to surrender ... He appointed teachers to show them how to settle in villages, till the soil and make clothes of wool and cotton. Many large channels were dug for the watering of the fields, and the province was soon cultivated so thoroughly that it became one of the best in the empire.

After subjugating the Chachapoya, the Inca army continued its progress north. On the shores of the Gulf of Guayaquil, the Canari bowed to the inevitable:

These people were won over by flattery and kindness rather than force of arms. They promised that instead of worshipping the Moon they would henceforth worship the Sun: and in return the Incas built storehouses for them, dug irrigation channels, and extended their cultivated fields. The Canari were delighted and became excellent subjects, many of them joining the Inca army.

Astride the equator, the Quitenos were not so amenable. A powerful people in a fertile land, they resisted the Incas for the better part of five years; but in the end their kingdom, 'rich in trees, deer and gold', was forced to submit. The Incas set great store by this new addition to their empire, and Quito became a favourite resort of their royal family, who found its lush beauty a welcome change from the barren hills around Cuzco. Still further to the north, the Incas met resistance from the forest-dwellers of the Cordillera Central:

a primitive, verminous people who bored a hole through the membrane between their nostrils and inserted an ornament of copper, silver or gold which hung down over their lips like an earring; they worshipped great serpents, and offered human hearts in sacrifice.

There was little incentive for further advance, and here, some 1,500 miles from Cuzco, among the volcanic peaks of the South Colombian rain forest, the northward surge of the Incas finally petered out – largely because there seemed to be nothing more in this direction that was worth the conquering.

After some twenty years of campaigning the Incas controlled both the altiplano and the central cordillera of the Andes. The ancient civilizations of the coastal plain now lay at their mercy.

What followed was not so much a campaign as a procession. As Topa led his army south down the coasts of present-day Ecuador and Peru, the once-powerful civilizations collapsed like ninepins. It has been suggested that the speed of their downfall was due to the fact that they had become decadent, but a more likely explanation is that they were attacked one by one in their isolated valleys and oases and submerged by weight of numbers. For the Inca army, over the last decade, had been progressively augmented by levies from every tribe that was conquered; by now it probably numbered at least 200,000. In the face of such overwhelming odds it is hardly surprising that the people of the coastal civilizations opted for discretion rather than valour.

Having 'pacified' the Pacific seaboard, Topa next turned his attention to the opposite side of his father's empire. Crossing the Andes, he led his army into the headwaters of the Amazon. This was difficult terrain for the Incas: difficult for their phalanxes of troops to fight in, difficult for their engineers to build roads through, and difficult to occupy with any degree of permanence. Indeed the rain forest of the Amazon was to the Incas what the mountains of Afghanistan were to the British and the Russians: a no-go area which was dangerous to penetrate and impossible to control. Chroniclers tell of Inca flotillas descending the Madre de Dios and Tambalata rivers, but any victories they achieved would have been pyrrhic, and it was probably a blessing in disguise that before the campaign got properly under way Inca troops were called to their heartland to deal with yet another uprising on the shores of Lake Titicaca.

The events of the next few years demonstrate the mobility and versatility of the Inca army. Topa swiftly transferred his troops from the rain forests of the Amazon to the plains of the altiplano. He crushed the rebels, then headed into the unknown world of the Southern Andes in a new and dramatic burst of empire building.

His initial problem as he led his army south was the terrain. The only route by which he could reach his objective – the fertile valleys of Chile – was by crossing first the Bolivian highlands, then the main cordillera of the Andes, and finally the Atacama Desert. The Bolivian highlands are a desiccated mosaic of saline flats, lava-coated plateaux and glaciated massifs. The climate is harsh, uncomfortably hot by day, numbingly cold by night, with little but violent rain. This can have been no easy march for an army of some 50,000 troops and their entourage. The corderilla were an even more formidable barrier: a chain of huge volcanic peaks, many over 20,000 feet, with the few passes through them all rising to over 14,000 feet. Those with first-hand knowledge of this frozen and lunar world agree that Topa's crossing of the Southern Andes was a greater achievement than Hannibal's crossing of the Alps. Moreover, he was still faced with the greatest obstacle of all, the Atacama. Garcilaso tells us:

Scouts and spies were sent into this desert to find a route into Chile. These men suffered terrible privations, but managed to cross the Atacama, leaving markers every two leagues to show those who followed them the way. They came and went like ants, reporting on whatever they found, and laying secret caches of supplies, until at last the Inca army was able to advance in two columns, each of 10,000 men and each laden with supplies on beasts of burden [llamas] which were also to serve as rations.

By the time he had crossed the Atacama Topa was operating more than 1,500 miles from his base, and the logistics of keeping his army equipped and fed must have been formidable. Yet the chroniclers tell us:

During the whole of the campaign that followed the Inca took particular care to keep his men supplied with reinforcements, arms, provisions, clothing and footwear. He thus came to have a force of 50,000 warriors in Chile, as well supplied with everything they needed as if they had been in Cuzco.

At first the Inca armies swept all before them; but about 300 miles south of the Atacama they found themselves facing fierce resistance from a proud and warlike race, the Araucanians. There followed one of the bloodiest battles of the medieval world.

Topa found the Araucanians and their allies drawn up along the line of the River Maule. He offered them the usual inducements to surrender, but was told that the people of Chile would 'fight till they conquered or died'. 'So the next day,' writes Garcilaso,

both armies left their camp and attacked one another, fighting with great spirit, courage and obstinacy. The battle lasted all day, without either side gaining advantage but with huge numbers of killed and wounded. As night fell, both armies retired to their camps. On the second and third day they fought with the same determination, the one for their honour the other for their freedom, until more than half the warriors in each army had been killed and almost every single man had been wounded. On the fourth day both armies again prepared for battle, but were content to stay in their camps, making themselves strong in case their adversaries should launch an attack. [This stalemate continued for several days] until on the seventh day both armies withdrew, each fearing that the other had brought up reinforcements.

Garcilaso's account of what happened next is highly dubious.

The Incas considered it more in keeping with the policy of their rulers to give rein to the bestial fury of the enemy rather than destroy him by bringing up reinforcements, which could easily have been done. It was therefore decided to return to territory already pacified . . . So the Incas brought their conquest of Chile to an end, setting up boundary marks, and fixing the River Maule as the southernmost limit of their empire.

One wishes Garcilaso had admitted that the Incas, for once, had met their match: that the Araucanians had inflicted on them their first major defeat in some forty years of campaigning.

With the stabilizing of its southern frontier, the delineation of Tawantinsuyu (the empire of the four corners of the earth) was complete.

The creation of so vast an empire in so short a time was a remarkable achievement, and one wonders what were the special qualities of the Inca armies that they achieved such spectacular success? The troops themselves were no supermen, but were tough and resilient. Most of them, coming from the altiplano or the cordillera, were accustomed to heat by day, cold by night and a harsh environment, and were able to march long distances and campaign in a wide variety of terrain. Temperamentally they were amenable to discipline, and well suited to a regimented and physically demanding life. They were excellent soldiers: loyal, brave and highly disciplined.

Their weapons were mainly designed for hand-to-hand combat. Most warrior-races throughout history have had their own particular weapon, the Zulus their assegais, the conquistadors their swords and the Incas their clubs. These clubs were usually about 2½ feet long, made of wood and weighted with stone, copper or bronze. Inca troops also used heavy, wooden, double-edged swords, and axes of stone or bronze. For defence they relied on small, usually rectangular shields; these had wickerwork frames and a covering of hide. They protected their heads with plaited-cane helmets, and their bodies with quilted-cotton 'armour', which was effective against native weapons but not against the tempered steel of Spanish swords. Although bows and arrows were used for both hunting and warfare by the people of the rain forest, the Incas never incorporated these weapons into their arsenal; for long-range combat they relied on slings and bolas. Horses were unknown in the Andes, and for draught animals the Inca army used llamas. These 'little camels' could carry only comparatively light loads; but they were agile climbers, and – like the dogs who saw Amundsen to the pole – when no longer needed for transport they provided excellent meat.

It may have been Napoleon who coined the catch-phrase that an army marches on its stomach, but this fact was well understood, centuries earlier, by the Incas. Indeed the success of Inca armies was due in large part to the excellence of their commissariat. The Incas were a highly numerate people who excelled at logistics; and wherever their troops were operating - in rain forest, altiplano or desert – they were invariably kept 'as well supplied with everything they needed as if they had been in Cuzco'. Supplies were moved from place to place either by backpack or by trains of llamas, and were stockpiled in buildings known as *qollas*. Archaeologists and historians have often marvelled at the number and sophistication of these storehouses and the cornucopia that was kept in them. At Vilcashuaman (midway between Cuzco and the coast) in one site alone there are 700 *qollas*, laid out as symmetrically as troops on a parade-ground; while at Cotapachi (in Bolivia) another site contains 2,400 qollas, each exactly 3 metres in diameter and positioned at exactly the same distance from its neighbour; all were completely weatherproof, and many had underfloor ducts for ventilation. As for their contents: 'Here,' writes Guaman Poma, 'are stored *chuno* frozen, dried potatoes, *moraya* cooked, *caya* cooked, and frozen *oca* [sorrel], dried meat, wool for weaving . . . also maize, sweet potatoes, chili peppers, cotton, coca and *cumo* which consists of various foods especially treated for conservation and which could be eaten without cooking.' 'In Cuzco,' writes another chronicler, 'the storehouses are full of cloaks, wool, weapons, metal, cloth, shields, leather bucklers, beams for roofing houses, knives and other tools, sandals, breastplates, and deposits of iridescent feathers.' These storehouses mushroomed up all over the Andes, some in isolated villages, others spaced out at intervals along the roads; and the distance from one to another was never more than the distance that could be covered by a day's march. In time of war the *qollas* facilitated the fast and trouble-free movement of troops. In time of peace they provided the local people with a built-in insurance against the possible failure of crops or flocks.

If the key to the Incas' commissariat was their *qollas*, the key to their *qollas* was their network of roads.

Inca roads were one of the wonders of the world. They were almost as extensive as the Roman roads and are regarded by experts as far greater feats of engineering, since they traversed more difficult terrain and were better built; also they were more artistically landscaped. In the words of that exact and scholarly scientist Alexander von Humboldt, 'they are the most stupendous and useful works ever executed by man'. If this sounds an exaggerated claim, there are facts to prove it. The principal Inca highway, known as

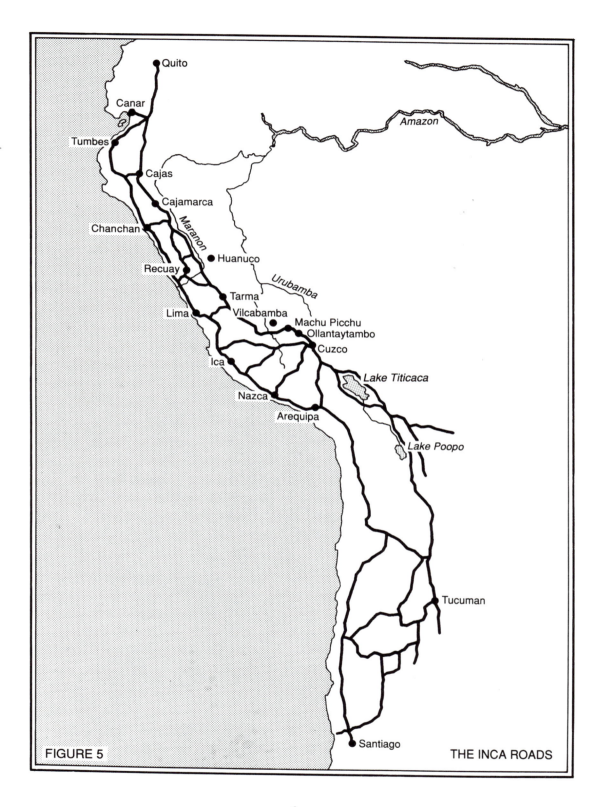

FIGURE 5

THE INCA ROADS

64

Capac-nan (the beautiful road) runs from Cuzco to Quito, a distance of over 1,500 miles. For most of the way it is perfectly straight, a uniform 25 feet in width, and built of beautifully dovetailed blocks of stone. 'The Indians who worked these stones,' wrote the missionary José de Acosta, 'used no mortar; they had no steel for cutting and working the stones, and no machines for transporting them; yet so skilled was their work that the joints between the stones were barely noticeable.' Capac-nan spanned huge ravines by means of suspension bridges; it passed through swamps, rain forest, glaciated plateaux and arid deserts, and in several places, as it crossed the cordillera, it rose to over 15,000 feet. 'In one spot,' writes Victor von Hagen, 'Inca engineers, anticipating the future path of a glacier, raised a huge retaining wall to divert the snow and cascading rocks.' Another writer to sing the praises of the Capac-nan is the poet Jorge Carrera Andrade:

On either side of it the Incas built walls of stone; they packed earth on top of these and at regular intervals planted agave cactuses. This was in addition to the rows of trees which lined the road and provided shade for travellers. [The Incas attached great importance to these trees; there were stringent laws for their preservation. The penalty for felling one was death.] At intervals of every twelve miles the Incas built *tampus*, where travellers could rest or spend the night . . . Beside most of the road ran a rivulet of fresh water [an artificial canal] to quench the thirst of wayfarers and draft animals . . . At a time when the roads of Europe were little more than muddy pot-holed tracks, the Incas had the finest highways in the world.

The Capac-nan was no isolated *tour de force*; it was part of a complex network which ranged the length and breadth of Tawantinsuyu. Another magnificent highway ran for almost 3,000 miles through the ancient cities of the coast, across the Atacama and deep into Chile, while at least ten subsidiary roads over the Andes linked these two major highways. Figure 5 shows the probable extent of the network, 'probable' because it is one of the tragedies of history that the Spaniards allowed these magnificent highways to disintegrate under the iron-shod hooves of their horses and the heavy metal wheels of their ox-carts, while whole sections were deliberately dismantled by Spanish settlers to provide stone for their homesteads. Today's visitors to the Andes can catch only occasional glimpses of the remnants of these roads which in their heyday were the arteries of empire, bringing mobility to the Inca army in war and prosperity to the Inca people in peace.

An adjunct of the roads were the bridges – a frequent necessity in terrain characterized by steep-sided valleys. The Incas perfected three types of bridge: pontoon, cantilever and suspension. The first they used for crossing wide and slow-flowing rivers like the Desaguadero, which flows into Lake Titicaca. The second they used for crossing small streams up to about 30 feet in width; in the case of wider streams cantilever construction was impossible, for although the Incas were arguably the world's greatest-ever workers in stone, they never perfected the arch. This meant that wide rivers with high banks had to be crossed by suspension bridge. Von Hagen has estimated that the Inca road-system incorporated about 100 of these suspension bridges, the most famous being that over the Apurimac, which he describes as 'undoubtedly the most outstanding example of native engineering in the Americas'. Basically the bridge was constructed not of wood- which was in short supply in the bleak headwaters of the Apurimac – but of plaited and twisted *cabuya* which was woven into cables 'thick as a man's body'. Five of these great cables spanned the river, and were extended some 40 feet beyond either bank where they were anchored into the ground by massive stone pillars. Wood and bamboo planks were then laid across the cables to form the 'floor' of the bridge, the whole being bound together, in an apparently haphazard fashion, by interwoven lianas. Two further cables served as handrails, running the length of the bridge some four feet above the 'floor', to which they were attached by a succession of vertical stays. A good description of the bridge and its approaches is given by that most precise and perspicacious of travellers, the American George Squier:

As we descended, the gorge narrowed until it was shut in by precipices of stratified rock strangely contorted, while huge masses of stone, rent and splintered as from some terrible convulsion of nature, rose sheer before us. There was foothold for neither tree nor shrub as our mules picked their way warily, with head and ears pointed downwards, among the broken and angular masses ... Now we could hear the voice of 'the Great Speaker' *Apu* in Quechua = great; *rimac* = speaker], and could see, swinging high in a graceful curve between the precipices on either side, looking wonderfully frail and gossamer-like, the famed bridge of the Apurimac... We had timed our journey so as to reach the bridge in the morning, for in the latter part of the day a strong wind sweeps up the canyon with great force, and then the bridge sways like a gigantic hammock, and crossing it is next to impossible ... We carefully measured its length and altitude, and found it to be 148 feet long, and at its lowest point 118 feet above the river.

The diaries of the conquistadors are full of horrified descriptions of these suspension bridges and the perils of crossing them; but in fact they were safer than they looked. In this they resembled those classic deep-water vessels, Arab dhows and Polynesian outriggers, which in appearance are frail and ramshackle but in fact are remarkably resilient. Where more solid structures would have disintegrated under the hammer-blows of the elements, the *cabuya*-bridges swayed with wind and earthquake and survived. There were of course accidents on them, but the catastrophe for which they are best known is fictitious: the bridge over the Apurimac was the inspiration for Thornton Wilder's classic disaster-novel *the Bridge of San Luis Rey*.

As evidence of how much importance the Incas attached to their roads and bridges, the penalty for tampering with or neglecting them was death.

Competent troops, adequate weapons, a first-class commissariat and a high degree of mobility deriving from their magnificent network of roads ... these were bonuses for the Inca armies, but the basic reason for their success is so obvious it is often overlooked. They nearly always outnumbered their adversaries – and this, in battles involving hand-to-hand fighting between troops with similar weapons, was usually the deciding factor.

The first Inca forces to venture beyond the immediate vicinity of Cuzco were probably no more than skirmishing parties of a couple of thousand men. However, following Pachacuti's defeat of the Chancas, the army appears to have developed into a large, permanent and efficient fighting force; and when, *circa* 1475, the Sun King moved north into the Cordillera Vilcabamba he probably had with him well over 12,000 men. This number would have been augmented by levies from each successive tribe as it was conquered. For the Inca army, like the Roman, was composed mainly of 'foreign' troops, the Incas themselves providing no more than the bodyguard of their emperor, a small

66

core of 'regulars', and most of the high-ranking officers. It has been estimated, perhaps surprisingly, that only about 15 per cent of the conquering armies were pure Incas. Another surprising fact is that most of the troops were volunteers. It is true that every able-bodied male Inca was a potential warrior, was given a modicum of military training as a young man, and was conscripted in emergency; but there seems to have been no obligation on either the Incas themselves or the conquered races to provide troops on a permanent basis. The truth would appear to be that army life was popular; it provided the people of the Andes with a chance to break free from the restrictive routine of their *ayllus*; it gave them a rare opportunity to widen their horizon and improve their lot, and as a further incentive the army was efficient, respected and, above all, successful.

In short, the well-being of Tawantinsuyu depended very largely on the well-being of its army. When the army was successfully campaigning – as under Pachacuti and Topa – the empire prospered; when the army was idle – as under Topa's successors – the empire was susceptible to dissension and civil war, a susceptibility of which the European invaders were to take full advantage.

Inca armies may have been the instrument by which Tawantinsuyu was carved out, but Pachacuti had the good sense to realize that the retention of his empire would depend not so much on military expertise as on sound administration; thus his retirement to Cuzco in 1484.

The code of laws which Pachacuti devoted the rest of his life to promulgating were summarized in the seventeenth century by Father Bernabé Cobo, a perceptive Jesuit priest:

Pachacuti gave the state a new and comprehensive code of laws and statutes . . . He set everything in order, abolishing some rites and ceremonies and adding others. He expanded the official religion, inaugurating special services and ceremonies by which the gods were to be worshipped. He enriched the holy places with magnificent buildings . . . In short, he overlooked nothing and organized everything with great efficiency.

The inference from this entry in Cobo's *Historia del Nuevo Mundo* is that Pachacuti imposed on his subjects a regime which demanded both spiritual and secular conformity. However, it is hard to say exactly how he did this, since his reforms were never recorded and there was never a written legal code. Here the Incas were the antithesis of the Romans. The Roman Empire was controlled by a large number of inflexible written statutes; the Inca Empire, on the other hand, appears to have been controlled by a far smaller number of flexible and traditional lores, with the Incas (like the Polynesians) knowing by tradition what was taboo and what were the penalties for breaking a taboo. It was among Pachacuti's greatest achievements that he managed so to improve, simplify and standardize Inca lore, that it became accepted throughout his empire.

The instruments by which he enforced this rule of law were his government officials. The Inca Empire has been likened to an efficiently run welfare state, analogous in some ways to present-day Singapore, with its prosperity imposed on it willy-nilly by a benevolent despotism. Inca beliefs, laws and customs controlled almost every aspect of every person's life from cradle to grave. Local customs may have been permitted (and were indeed encouraged) in non-essentials, but when it came to the basics everyone was expected to toe the line: to acknowledge the divinity of the Sun God, to conform to His beliefs, to obey His commands and to work hard to ensure His prosperity – laziness was considered almost as serious a 'crime' as heresy. This authoritarian regime was administered by a huge pyramid of officials. At the bottom of the pyramid were the agricultural labourers, the work-horses on whose efforts the prosperity of the empire depended. Every ten labourers were controlled by a field-leader, every ten field-leaders were controlled by a foreman, every ten foremen were controlled by a headman; and so the pyramiding continued from the village unit to the tribal, from the tribal to the provincial, from the provincial to the regional (one of the four quarters of Tawantinsuyu) and finally from the regional to the Inca Himself. Such a bureaucratic system may have been cumbersome – it has been estimated that out of every 10,000 Andeans more than 1,300 were officials – but it worked. Spanish chroniclers were, without exception, full of praise for the efficiency and thoroughness of Inca administration, their careful censuses, their precise tabulation of crops grown and taxes collected. 'In the capital of each province,' wrote Cieza de León,

there were accountants who used *quipus* (knotted and coloured strings) by which they kept a record of the tribute paid by the people of that district in silver, gold, clothing and flocks, right down to the most insignificant things like bundles of wood; and by means of these *quipus* at the end of each year they submitted their report to an official whose duty it was to check all records so thoroughly that not even a pair of sandals was unaccounted for.

The administrators' task was made more difficult by the way the land was divided up and by the multiplicity of crops it produced. Throughout Tawantinsuyu arable land was divided into three parts: the produce of one part going to the government, one part to the church and one part to the people. These proportions varied not only from district to district but also from season to season, with priority always being given to the needs of the people – a fact which illuminates a basic truth about Inca administration: it may have been cumbersome and despotic, but it was also flexible and paternal. It was as though the administrators realized that life for everyone in the Andes centred around the need to wring a livelihood out of the difficult terrain, and that the prosperity of the empire depended on the prosperity of its individual peasant-farmers. John Hemming describes the life of these farmers, and how a paternal administration was able to improve their standard of living:

What Pizarro's men saw as the marched into the Inca empire was a well-ordered agricultural society. The ordinary Peruvians lived simple peasant lives. They farmed and lived collectively, with no private property, strongly bound to their families and clans, villages and fields. Because of Peru's isolation, its plants, animals and diseases were unique, all unknown to the European invaders. The Peruvians had no draught animals to help with their farming. They ploughed with foot-ploughs, long poles hardened at the point and equipped with foot-rests and handles. The men stood in lines to plough, prising up the earth with their pole; their wives crouched opposite, breaking the sod, hoeing and planting . . . They lived in simple thatched huts, smoky and smelly, fully of guinea-pigs, dogs and fleas. Apart from the guinea-pig, and occasional dried llama meat or fish, their diet was vegetarian – mostly maize, potatoes or rice-like quinoa. For Peru is a hard country: most of its level ground is desolate puna, too high for normal cultivation, or the strip of coastal plain where miles of desert separate the river valleys. All that is left for normal cultivation and habitation are the river valleys - tight, crumbling canyons in the mountains or shallow beds of vegetation on the Pacific side. Almost nowhere in Peru are there stretches of rich farming land as found in Europe or North America. To these topographical difficulties are added the relative meanness of natural endowment. Peru had few domestic animals, few crops, and few trees outside the Amazon forests.

The Incas applied their extraordinary organizational genius to overcome these natural deficiencies. Their agricultural collectives were organized to build and maintain elaborate terraces, shoring up the hillsides in great flights of fieldstone terracing. The water resources of the dry coastal plain were husbanded, and the heavy rains of the sierra were tamed by fine irrigation canals and ditches. The imperial administration kept storehouses full of food and herds of llamas and alpacas, primarily for the use of its own administrators and armies but also as insurance against bad harvests. It moved the rural population to equalize the standard of living throughout the empire, and also to plant colonies of loyalists amid potentially restive tribes.

As a result of this administrative efficiency, and a steady regime of disciplined agricultural labour, the population of the Inca empire flourished.

Never before or since have the people of the Andes enjoyed so much prosperity as under the paternal despotism of Pachacuti and his son.

The instruments by which this despotism was enforced may have been the Sun King's multitudinous and efficient bureaucrats, but there is no doubt where the real power lay: with the Inca Himself. It was the last and in some ways the most remarkable of Pachacuti's achievements that he managed to elevate his personal status from that of tribal chief to monarch-cum-god.

The last few Inca emperors were arguably the most absolute rulers the world has ever known. Like the emperors of ancient Egypt and medieval Japan they claimed not only to be descended from the Sun God, but to *be* the sun God – a delusion subsequently reiterated by Louis XIV. Alden Mason sums up the Inca emperor's position:

He was an absolute despot but not a tyrant. To his subjects he was an omnipotent god, merciless to his enemies but firm and just to his subjects, whose comfort and peace were his constant concern . . . As a lineal descendant of the Sun he ruled by divine right, and was worshipped and implicitly obeyed as being himself divine.

The steps by which Pachacuti invested himself with these extraordinary powers were cumulative.

First, he rebuilt Cuzco on a monumental scale, turning it into not only a magnificent administrative centre for his expanding empire but, more importantly, into a magnificent earthly residence for the Sun God.

The people of the Andes were accustomed to have a *huaca* at the geographical centre of their world, and in his remodelled Cuzco Pachacuti gave them a *huaca par excellence*. He razed the old city centre, drained the marshes to the south, channelled the streams which had formerly flowed through the city into stone-lined conduits, and redesigned the centre of Cuzco around one of the world's most exotic temples, the Coricancha; while guarding and overlooking his refurbished capital he built one of the world's most formidable fortresses, Sacsahuaman.

Coricancha (the Temple of the Sun) was probably one of the most beautiful buildings the world has ever known – 'probably' rather than 'definitely' because so little of it now remains that even its layout is a matter of conjecture. Part of it was deliberately destroyed by the Spaniards, another part was incorporated into the structure of a Dominican church and the remaining parts are today little more than ruins. However, to judge from the reports of Spanish chroniclers who saw the building intact, the original design had a classic simplicity – six rectangular chapels opening on to a central courtyard – it also had walls of the most beautifully-dovetailed stone overlaid with gold. The indefatigable Squier visited the site a little over a hundred years ago:

The temple of the Sun, was [once] the most imposing edifice not only in Cuzco but in all Peru, if not in all America . . . The structure was about 400 paces in circuit, with walls of finely-cut stone enclosing a court[yard] on which opened a number of chapels . . . The buildings stood about eighty feet above the Huatenay River, towards which the ground fell away in a series of terraces, faced with stone, which formed the famous Gardens of the Sun. The temple proper occupied the whole of one side of the court[yard]. The cornice of the walls, outside and in, was of gold, and the inner walls were lined with gold. At the eastern end [of this chapel] was a great plate of solid gold, representing the sun; and ranged beneath it, in royal robes and seated on golden chairs, the embalmed bodies of the Inca rulers. Surrounding the other sides of the court[yard] were structures dedicated to the Moon, Venus, the Pleiades, Thunder and Lightning and the Rainbow. All these are described as having been richly decorated with gold or silver.

If descriptions of walls that were lined with solid gold sounds a tall story, here is what Pizarro's matter-of-fact secretary, Pedro Sancho, tells us. He records that when the Inca Atahualpa promised to hand over to Pizarro a room full of gold, he ordered Coricancha to be stripped, and its treasures to be brought to where he was held captive. This treasure, Sancho tells us, arrived in over 200 consignments, 'and in one consignment alone were 700 plates taken from the wall of this temple and looking for all the world like boards from a chest'. Each plate, when melted down, yielded not less that 4½ pounds of pure gold (i.e., in terms of present-day currency this single consignment alone was worth about 22 million US dollars.)

As well as enriching Cuzco with the greatest of Inca shrines, Pachacuti guarded it with the greatest of Inca fortresses, Sacsahuaman.

Sacsahuaman was built not so much onto as into a steep-sided hill of sedimentary rock which overlooks Cuzco. Its south face consisted of sheer natural cliff – unclimbable – its other faces were guarded by three gargantuan terraced walls. These Squier describes as 'cyclopean', adding that the Spaniards regarded them with awe and dubbed them the ninth wonder of the world. As well as being a fortress, Sacsahuaman seems also to have been a temple and the major arsenal of the Inca army; incorporated into its layout were *qollas*, the Inca's throne, a huge parade-ground, palaces, vaults and reservoirs. Everything about it was on a majestic scale. 'This fortress,' wrote Sancho, 'has too many rooms and towers for a person to examine them all. Many who have visited it, and who have travelled in Lombardy and other foreign countries, say they have never seen a building to compare with it . . . Nothing built by the Romans is as impressive as this.'

How, one wonders, did the Incas – without the aid of cutting tools or mechanical devices – manage to construct such a magnificent fortress?

Of all the legacies left by the Incas none has proved more durable than their masonry-work. 'Their buildings,' writes John Hemming, 'were simple in plan and design, but their stonework was technically and aesthetically astounding.' The best examples of this stonework are found in their great temple-fortresses: Ollantaytambo and Saihuite, Tarahuasi and Vilcashuaman, Machu Picchu and Sacsahuaman. Machu Picchu epitomizes one aspect of the Incas' love affair with stone: the way they integrated their buildings with the landscape, the contours of their ramparts and the position of their altars mirroring the nature of the surrounding terrain. Sacsahuaman epitomizes another aspect: their skill in creating structures of staggering size, strength and technical virtuosity.

As with Coricancha, it is difficult today to visualize how magnificent Sacsahuaman must have been, for so much of it was wantonly destroyed. However, its main feature, its three massive, terraced walls, remain, albeit in ruins. These walls rise one behind the other, roughly parallel, to form the fortress's northern defences. Each is a little over 400 yards in length and 60 feet in height, and is sawtoothed (so that attackers have to approach it diagonally rather than head-on) and consists of the most enormous blocks of perfectly interlocking stone – and how enormous the stones are! One monolith measures $16 \times 15\frac{1}{2} \times 8\frac{1}{2}$ feet, while many (indeed probably the majority) weigh well over 100 tons. How, one wonders, did the Incas manage to quarry such enormous stones, drag them – often for many miles – to the site, shape them with such precision, and finally raise them into position? Garcilaso writes: 'These walls were the most ambitious structures that the Inca ordered to be built. To those who have not seen them their dimensions sound incredible. To those who have seen them, it appears they could only have been raised by magic – by wizards rather than by men.' Sancho echoed this sentiment: 'These ramparts are the most amazing in the land. They are built of stones so large that anyone seeing them would say they could not possibly have been raised into position by human hands.'

So how *did* the Incas build Sacsahuaman? They had the benefit of no clever technical devices or magic formulas. They built the fortresses by millions of work-hours of patient human endeavour, laboriously quarrying the stones by hand, dragging them to the site with robes of *cabuya*, shaping them with stone axes, obsidian pebbles and abrasive sand, and finally raising great earthen ramps up which each stone could be laboriously rolled and levered into position. Chroniclers have left a description of each of these stages.

Some stones – the limestone and green diorite – were quarried only a few hundred yards from site; but others – the great blocks of andesite – were quarried around Huacoto and Rumicolca, far to the south-east. It must have cost the Incas blood, sweat and tears to drag these huge 100-ton stones for more than 12 miles over rough terrain, much of it uphill. Garcilaso describes the moving of one such block, known as the Weary or Blood Stone:

More than 20,000 Indians brought this stone up, dragging it with great cables. Their progress was very slow, for the road up which they came is rough and has many steep slopes to climb and descend. Half the labourers pulled at the ropes from in front, while the rest kept the rock steady with other cables attached to it, lest it should roll back downhill. On one of these slopes, as a result of carelessness on the part of those who failed to pull evenly, the weight of the rock proved too much for the strength of those controlling it, and it rolled back down the slope, killing more than three thousand Indians. Despite this disaster, the rock was again dragged up and deposited on site

. . . Near the top of this stone are two holes which look like eyes; and after rain red liquid (doubtless produced by the red earth) seeps out of these 'eyes', so that the Indians say the stone is weeping blood, hence they call it the Blood Stone.

Other chroniclers describe the fitting-together of the stones. As in most of the great temple-fortresses, the walls of Sacsahuaman are polygonal: that is to say the stones interlock like the pieces of a jigsaw puzzle. Some stones have as many as 12 corners on their outer face alone, and if viewed in three dimensions have up to 30 corners, all interlocking with mathematical precision. Father Cobo expresses his wonder:

Even though [the stones] are so large they are cut with amazing skill. They are elegant, and so finely positioned one against another, without mortar, that the joints are scarcely visible . . . Some are large, others are small and all are irregular in shape, yet they are positioned with joints as precise and delicate as those of coursed ashlars . . . Such work must have been immensely laborious! To interlock the stones so perfectly, it must have been necessary to remove and replace them repeatedly to test them. When one realizes that 100 men working for a month would have been altogether inadequate to cut a single stone, it is obvious how much labour must have been involved.

Cobo goes on to describe how the cut stones were raised into place:

Having no cranes, wheels or lifting devices, the Indians made a sloping ramp up against the wall and lifted the stones by rolling them up this. As the wall rose, so they raised the ramp proportionately. I saw this system being used in the building of Cuzco cathedral. Since the labourers engaged in this work were Indians, the Spanish architects and foremen let them organize their work by traditional methods. They made ramps to raise the stone blocks, piling earth against the side of the cathedral until it was level with the top.

Between 25,000 and 30,000 men are thought to have been working almost continuously on Sacsahuaman for more than fifty years, from roughly 1480 to 1532. It has been estimated that by the time work was brought to a halt by the Spanish invasion, some 5 billion work-hours had been devoted to the fortress. If one wonders why the Incas were unable to defend so formidable a structure, the answer has already been hinted at: it was, at the time of the invasion, still unfinished. From the point of view of the Spaniards, their invasion was extremely fortunately timed. A decade earlier and Pizarro would have had to face a confident people on the crest of a wave of expansion; a decade later and he would almost certainly have had to face a people who had patched up their internal quarrels and completed their magnificent fortresses.

Coricancha and Sacsahuaman were the most spectacular but by no means the only buildings in Cuzco for which which Pachacuti was responsible. He also restored the palaces of the former emperors and built his own, the Cassana; he designed and built the Acclahuasi (the house of the 4,000 virgins of the Sun); he laid out gardens 'filled with the most charming trees, flowers and herbs'; and in the city centre he built upwards of 100 minor *huacas*, all precisely orientated both to the Temple of the Sun and to the roads which fanned out from the centre of Cuzco to the four quarters of Tawantinsuyu. Even Pizarro's secretary, who was not easily impressed, was forced to admit, 'This is the most beautiful city, even by Spanish standards. It is full of palaces wonderfully made and buildings most remarkable.'

In a surprisingly short time Pachacuti transformed Cuzco from a stronghold fit for a tribal chief into a residence fit for a god. He then proceeded to invest himself with the trappings of that god.

The lack of written records makes it difficult to assess Pachacuti's character. He was clearly ruthless, able and, to say the leaast, ambitious. However, it would, I think, be wrong to rate him solely as a great conqueror, a sort of New World Genghis Khan. He was also a great administrator – to quote that knowledgeable South Americanist Sir Clements Markham, 'the greatest man that the aboriginal race of America has produced' – and he used his administrative skill to bring stability and prosperity to his people. It therefore seems probable that his self-aggrandizement and his claim to divinity were no more than the means to an end.

The people of the Andes have always worshiped gods that are visible and tangible, and they have always enjoyed pomp and pageantry; Pachacuti, in his own person, offered them both. His first step on the road to divinity was to curtail the power of the priest-nobles, the *orejons* (literally the long-eared ones, so called because they wore heavy gold earrings which elongated the lobes of their ears). By the middle of the sixteenth century the *orejones* were becoming cult figures with the status of demigods, many of them having their own personal shrines and, more importantly, their own personal followers. 'These priests,' write Guidoni and Magni, 'were threatening the power of the emperor. It was therefore necessary for Pachacuti to advance the theory that there was a single all-powerful god who in the last analysis controlled everything . . . there was a prolonged theological debate which in the end was decided in favour of the emperor.' Having established that there was indeed one such god, Pachacuti proceeded to identify with him. Almost every decree he issued was presented in a way that emphasized both its paternal nature and its divine origin; while many of his reforms, either directly or indirectly, had the effect of increasing his status. When, for example, he standardized the calendar, he did away with festivals which were non-Inca in origin and inaugurated others which involved the ritual worship of the Sun God. No record *per se* exists of these reforms, but the historian Father Blas Valera enumerates some of them.

He regulated the ceremonies and sacrifices made in the temples. He enriched the schools and extended their curriculum, appointing teachers of great learning and giving special encouragement to pupils with an aptitude in science . . . He bid his people eat with frugality, although they were allowed more licence in drinking . . . He confirmed the law by which children were expected to obey their parents until they were 25 and not marry without paternal consent. He established tribunals to stamp out idleness, and ordered that everyone should occupy themselves with their trade, and work for the good of the state. Even boys and girls of five, six and seven were expected to occupy themselves with tasks suitable for their years. The blind, the lame and the dumb were also given various jobs. The old were expected to scare birds off the newly-planted fields . . . and all drew ample supplies of food and clothing from the public storehouses. Lest the people be wearied by too much toil, Pachacuti decreed that there should be three holidays each (lunar) month, also three festivals which fell on feast-days and were the occasion of much ceremonial splendour.

One gets the impression of a caring and above all a practical welfare state concerned with the everyday needs of its people. To give just one example of this concern, there were secret drop-off points in Cuzco where mothers could leave unwanted newborn babies, knowing they would be cared for in one of the state-run orphanages – a facility much used, according to the recently discovered *Sum and Narration*, by the 4,000 virgins of the Sun! Such facts reinforce the claim that the Incas' system of government was more humane and in many ways more advanced than that of any contemporaneous nation in Eurasia.

Yet there is a contradiction here between the Incas' modern laws and the archaic adulation they lavished on their emperor. For no prophet or potentate was ever accorded more reverential treatment than the Sun King. Each day he wore new and specially made clothes (the old ones being ceremonially burned); he was carried everywhere in a golden litter; he ate and drank from golden tableware, and those to whom he granted an audience were required to have burdens strapped to their backs to emphasize their subservience. Deification extended to both his personal habits and important affairs of state. If he wished to spit, he didn't do it on the ground, but a woman held out her hand and he spat into it; if hair fell on his clothing, a woman removed it and ate it. When he married, the only person considered to be a fit consort was someone who was his equal and the only person considered his equal was a genetic replica, that is to say his sister; so he married her – a concept which had its parallel in the incestuous marriages of the Pharaohs.

This glorification of the Inca was an important buttress to his absolute rule, and it might be argued that so long as this rule was benevolent the glorification was excusable. However, there were two circumstances in which their emperor's absolute despotism was likely to prove disastrous for the Incas. The first was if the emperor wielding absolute power proved unworthy of it - in which case the empire would almost certainly be torn by dissatisfaction and dissent. The second was if some disaster should overtake the person of the emperor – in which case the empire would be left at the mercy of events it had no mechanism to control.

It would be an exaggeration to say that the Incas who succeeded Topa were unworthy of power, but they were not rulers of the same calibre as their predecessors. Topa's son, Huayna Capac, was profligate, and his grandson, Atahualpa, cruel. The chroniclers tell us that Huayna had at his disposal 700 concubines, living in specially guarded houses in Cuzco; he is said to have had a bodyguard of over 100 relatives of royal blood, and to have fathered more than 200 illegitimate children. Atahualpa, at the end of a bitter civil war, is said to have murdered all 200 his brothers, the sons of Huayna,

some being hung, some being weighted with stone and thrown into rivers or lakes, and others being hurled to their death from high cliffs . . . also all his brothers' wives, sisters, aunts, nieces and cousins were hung, some from trees, some from gallows, some by the hair, some by one arm and others in ways which decency forbids me to relate; and they were handed their babies whom they held on to for as long as they could, until at last they fell and were killed.

These accusations may be exaggerated, but without doubt contain an element of truth.

However, the most serious criticism of Pachacuti's successors is that they allowed Tawantinsuyu to be split into warring factions. The main culprit was Huayna Capac.

Huayna's problems stemmed from two of his multidinous offspring. His reign is usually regarded as the high noon of the Incas. After a successful campaign on the borders of present-day Colombia and Ecuador, the empire reached its maximum geographical extent; the building of roads, *qollas* and temple-fortresses continued, as did the contruction of the most magnificent agricultural terraces like those at Moray, Pisac and Machu Picchu. Yet cracks were beginning to appear in the fabric of empire. Given the Andean peoples' penchant for fragmenting into disparate communities, it was probably inevitable that almost as soon as Tawantinsuyu came into being there was pressure for secession. This pressure was increased when divisions began to bedevil the Inca royal family . . . Even with written records it would be no easy task to piece together Huayna's genealogy; without such records it is almost impossible. However, the basic fact seems to be that there were two contenders for his throne: Huascar, a son born to him by his young sister, the Coya Queen Araua Occlo, and Atahualpa, a son probably born to him by the daughter of the former ruler of Quito. Huascar lived in Cuzco, where he had the support of the *ancien régime* – the nobility, priests and bureaucrats. Atahualpa lived in Quito, where he had the support of the farmers, the army and the most experienced generals. The Inca succession was not necessarily a matter of primogeniture; the next ruler was usually nominated by the existing emperor. Huayna suggested a compromise: that he should leave the southern part of Tawantinsuyu, centred around Cuzco, to Huascar, and the northern part, centred around Quito, to Atahualpa. On his deathbed the omens for such a division were found to be inauspicious, but before Huayna could be persuaded to change his mind he died of a strange and terrible disease which for the first time was sweeping the Andes.

It has been estimated that before the Incas ever set eyes on a European nearly a quarter of a million of them had died from has been called 'the white man's most deadly legacy': smallpox, its virus brought to the mountains of South America via the Caribbean and the Amazon.

The death of Huayna Capac sparked off a bitter civil war between his sons, neither of whom was satisfied with half an empire. According to Spanish chroniclers, the war was punctuated by the most appalling atrocities. These began with Huascar killing and mutilating the envoys sent to him with an offer of peace from his brother, and ended with a blood-bath in which Atahualpa tortured and put to death more than 300 of Huascar's family. Such stories may have been blown up out of all proportion by the Spaniards who would have been anxious to depict Atahualpa in a bad light so as to justify the way they treated him; but whatever the truth may be about the atrocities, there is no doubt that the war left Tawantinsuyu weakened and fatally divided.

And at the exact moment the Incas were most vulnerable, Pizarro and his 168 adventurers came marching into the sierra. It was the disaster that soothsayers had predicted.

Only a few weeks earlier, at the feast of the Sun, an eagle – symbol of the Sun God – had come plummeting out of the sky, pecked to death by buzzards. Garcilaso describes what happened next:

There followed earthquakes of such violence that great rocks were shattered and whole mountainsides collapsed. The sea became furious, overflowing its boundaries and invading the land. Comets flashed across the sky . . . On one unusually bright night the moon was haloed by three huge rings, the first the colour of blood, the second greenish-black, and the third apparently consisting of smoke.

The blood-red ring, according to soothsayers, predicted war: the greenish-black ring predicted the end of the Incas' faith and laws; and the third ring gave rise to the most terrible prediction of all: 'that all that you have done and all that your ancestors have done will vanish as though it had never been, as though in smoke.'

It is one of the tragedies of history that the soothsayers were right.

'Night Fell at Noon'

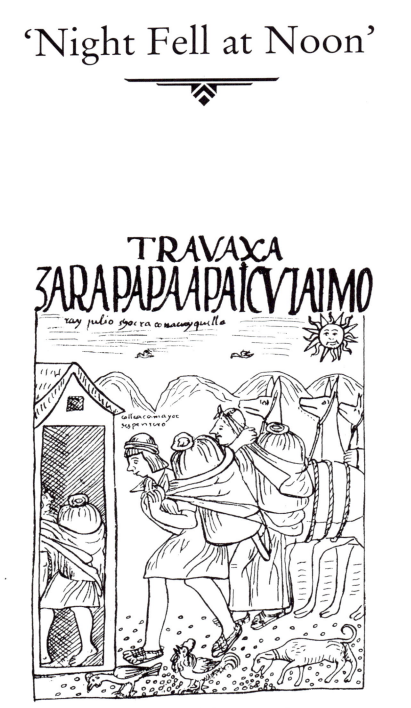

July: storing the grain in state granaries.

He stood defiant on the beach of a little island – subsequently known as Isla del Gallo – which lies off the coast of Ecuador. He was so thin that his ribs stood out like the bars of a cage; his skin was blotched with sun cancer and running sores, and his clothes were in rags. The members of his near-mutinous crew who surrounded him were in no better shape; they were clamouring to be taken back to Panama. The man drew his sword, and with it traced a line in the sand.

'To the north of this line,' he cried, 'lies Panama and poverty – and safety. To the south lies Peru and riches – and toil, hunger, thirst, weariness, sickness and maybe death. Now choose, each one of you, which way you will go. For my part, I go south.' He stepped over the line.

Out of his crew of over 100 only fifteen crossed the line to join him; but for Francisco Pizarro fifteen loyal companions were enough. So long as there was breath in his body, a sword in his hand, and a fellow-countryman to follow his lead, there would be no turning back.

What sort of men were Pizarro and his companions, that they dared first to reconnoitre and then to try and conquer an empire a third the size of Europe and guarded by a ¼ million first-class troops? To understand the conquistadors we need to understand early sixteenth-century Spain.

For nearly 800 years (from 711 to 1492) the people of Spain had been engaged in a bitter and protracted crusade against the Islamic invaders who were occupying a large part of the Iberian peninsula. During this time, virtually every male Spaniard regarded himself as a fighting machine, 'born,' as Hammond Innes writes, 'to the saddle and the sword, burning with a wild religious fervour, and utterly devoted to the task of freeing his homeland from the Infidel.' For generation after generation Spaniards had been led into battle by their priests; their prowess in war had been romanticized by minstrels and poets; the qualities they admired and aspired to were courage, pride, honour and chivalry. Fighting was what they were good at, but in 1492 the last Moorish stronghold in the peninsula, Granada, fell to the besieging Christians, the last Moorish troops were evacuated to North Africa, and there was suddenly no one left for the Spaniards to fight. However, at the very moment one challenge subsided in Europe, another arose in the New World. The year Granada fell was also the year Columbus discovered America. 'So,' writes Innes, 'the men who had fought their last battle against the Moors turned soldiers of fortune; they followed the sailors across the sea to seek out new infidels, and blaze a trail of murder and heroism halfway around the world.' This background explains – but doesn't excuse – the fact that a Spanish arquebusier could kill a native nursing mother simply to prove his prowess as a good shot, and should then justify her murder by saying, 'What matter if the heathen are consigned to hell today, since they will go there in any case tomorrow.' They regarded non-Christians as less than human.

If the conquistadores' prowess was fuelled partly by their religious fanaticism, it was fuelled even more fiercely by their lust for gold.

It is difficult for us today to realize how completely post-Renaissance Europe was dependent on gold. If a nation didn't have gold in the vaults of its treasury it could neither trade nor pay its armies, and was liable to be left starving and defenceless. What was true of nations was true also of individuals: a person's wealth more often than not consisted of gold coins hidden in straw beneath the bed. In the fourteenth and fifteenth centuries about 90 per cent of Europe's gold came from mines on the west coast of Africa – hence the names the Guinea Coast and the Gold Coast. European sailing ships were unable to make the round voyage to these mines because of adverse winds and currents. The gold had therefore to be brought by camel-caravan across the Sahara, a long and costly journey every step of which was controlled by the Islamic peoples of Mali, Songhai and the Hausa. For centuries Europeans had dreamed of an alternative source of gold which was under their own control, and they were understandably delighted when reports came back from the New World of 'rivers of gold nuggets of such quality it was a marvel'. It was soon realized that an adventurer could pick up in Central and South America the sort of rewards that couldn't be earned by a lifetime of labour in Europe. With the ending of the crusade against the Moors, Spain was full of out-of-work adventurers, and the toughest and most enterprising of them set out for the New World, their attitude summed up in the wry admission of the ablest of their leaders, Hernan Cortes: 'We have a sickness of the heart for which there is only one cure: gold.'

With such a background to sustain them, and such an incentive to spur them on, the conquistadors were to prove able if brutal despoilers.

So Pizarro and his fifteen supporters remained on Gallo, while his ships and the rest of his disenchanted crew headed back for Panama. Their navigator, Bartholomew Ruiz, had promised to return to pick them up, but as they watched their ships disappear into the tropical haze they must have wondered if they would ever see them again. Ruiz, however, was as good as his word. He came back. By the end of 1527 Pizarro and his men were again standing south on their reconnaissance. Crossing the equator, they found themselves in waters no European before had ventured into. They were now on the threshold of great discoveries, about to catch their first glimpse of both the Andes and the Incas.

Those who sail south down the coast of Colombia are unlikely to see a great deal of the Andes – the coastal plain is too broad, and the distant mountains are veiled in near-perpetual cloud. However, in Ecuador, only a little inland from the Gulf of Guayaquil, a jumble of great volcanic peaks lies within a few miles of the sea; and one morning, as the mist cleared, the conquistadors saw to their amazement the snow-capped bulk of Chimborazo 'rising above our masthead higher even than the clouds'. A couple of days later they sighted their first Inca city, Tumbes, its towers and temples etched sharply against the bright-green fields of its delta.

This was the first meaningful contact between Incas and Spaniards, and it was friendly. As Pizarro's ship edged into Tumbes harbour, it was surrounded by balsawood sailing rafts – very similar, from all accounts, to Thor Heyerdahl's *Kon-Tiki* and the ocean-going *Uro*. The Spaniards asked for provisions, and the hospitable people of Tumbes brought them fish, fresh vegetables (including sweet potatoes) game, and even llamas. Two chiefs were invited aboard, and they were followed later in the day by an Inca official who was wined and dined and presented with a steel-headed axe. Next morning the Spaniards were invited ashore, and two of the crew were taken on a tour of the city. They were particularly impressed by the magnificent temple-fortress, its outer walls great unmortared blocks of stone, its inner walls 'literally tapestried with plates of silver and gold'. Pizarro, however, affected to have no interest in silver or gold, for in military parlance he was keeping his powder dry.

The Spaniards spent several days in Tumbes. What the Incas thought of them we will probably never know; but the Spaniards were certainly impressed with the Incas, marvelling at their magnificent roads, great temples and complex works of irrigation – and of course their gold. When Pizarro left, his ship was loaded with fresh vegetables, and many of the people of Tumbes were loaded with Spanish gifts.

During the next few weeks, as the conquistadors worked their way south, they found more evidence that they were on the periphery of a great and hitherto unknown civilization. There are few harbours on this part of the coast, but wherever Pizarro was able to land – at Paita, Trujillo and the River Santa – he was greeted by a people who were living in prosperous, well-organized communities. Moreover, these communities, he was told by his interpreters, were no more than the outposts of a mighty empire whose heart lay in the distant mist-and-cloud-encompassed mountains which for mile after hundred mile lined the eastern horizon. As Pizarro stared at the great snow-capped peaks of the cordillera, compared to which the Pyrenees and the European Alps were little more than foothills, and listened to stories of the Sun-king-god who lived in these mountains in a city of silver and gold that was guarded by tens of thousands of well-armed troops, it must have been obvious that here was a world in which there would be no easy pickings. Yet he seems to have had neither doubts nor fears about his next step. Having discovered this vast and rich new empire, he would conquer it and loot it.

'So Pizarro,' wrote Innes, 'shed the cloak of the discoverer and put on the armour of the conqueror.' He returned to Panama and set about raising a force – a couple of hundred men, he reckoned, would be enough – to subjugate this great new civilization he had discovered. He seems to have expected the governor of Panama to authorize his plans on the spot, and the people of Panama to flock instantly to his standard: but in this he was disillusioned. He was referred to Spain, and it was to take him the better part of three years to get his expedition under way.

What happened in Spain was to influence what happened subsequently in Peru. After much to-ing and fro-ing between the Spanish court and the Council of the Indies, Pizarro's expedition was at last given official sanction. He was appointed *Adelantado* and *Alquaril Mayor* (Governor and Chief Constable) of whatever territory he conquered. His associates – his brother Hernando, and Almagro – were given grandiose titles but little authority. The conquered territory was to be known as New Castile and to be administered from Spain, the Spanish crown receiving its customary one-fifth of whatever booty was acquired during the conquest. The expedition itself was to consist of three ships and 250 men (150 to be conscripted in Spain and 100 in Panama). All expenses, except for a small token sum donated by the crown, were to be met by Pizarro and his associates. The last of these clauses was the telling one. In the long term, Spain was to have all the advantages of conquest without having risked either money or men; in the short term, Pizarro was to have the advantage of retaining four-fifths of whatever treasure he accumulated. Pizarro and his conquistadors resembled not so much a state-financed army of invasion, as a privately-financed band of mercenaries. Their concern was not conquest but loot.

It was largely because the expedition was self-financing and those who joined it had no guarantee of regular wages that Pizarro found difficulty raising men. He visited Estremadura, the province where he was born, but about the only people who joined him were his kinsfolk – 'all poor,' observed a contemporary chronicler, 'and all as proud as they were poor'. In the end his ships were obliged to sail with little more than half their stipulated complement, hoping to make up their numbers in the Indies. However, this too proved difficult. When at last, in January 1531, the expedition left Panama, it consisted of only 180 men and 27 horses, an inadequate force, one might have thought, to embarrass so omniscient a monarch as the Sun God. Yet within less than a year Atahualpa was a prisoner, and his empire plunged from brightest noon to darkest night.

How did Pizarro do it?

His campaign got off to a bad start. Ruiz had planned to take the conquistadors direct to Tumbes by a track far out to sea. However, the ships encountered tropical storms and headwinds. After a fortnight of being soaked with both seawater and rainwater, the men were in poor shape, and Pizarro decided to put them ashore some 350 miles to the north of Tumbes and let them continue the journey on foot. This turned out to be an unfortunate decision, for the terrain was difficult, a mixture of mangrove swamp and rain forest; astride the equator the heat was appalling, especially for men in heavy armour; the humidity was debilitating; the conquistadors, bitten by insects and lacerated by jungle foliage, broke out in terrible suppurating ulcers; many fainted as they marched; several died. It was about the most depressing start to a campaign that could be imagined. Worse was to come. At the approaches to the Gulf of Guayaquil Pizarro came to a small, undefended town. He attacked it and burned it, massacring the inhabitants and looting their silver, gold and emeralds to the value of 20,000 pesos. For the sake of this small immediate gain, he sacrificed the goodwill of the local people and all hope of surprise. From now on the villages that the Spaniards marched through were deserted. Tumbes, when at last they came to it, was on the alert.

It was now that Pizarro first became aware that the people of the Andes were in the aftermath of a bitter civil war. Province had been divided against province, and on the periphery of the empire the recently subjugated tribes had taken the opportunity to revolt. This was the sort of situation that a would-be conqueror dreams of: a situation where the invading army, by offering its help, can find ready-made allies. Pizarro was not a particularly intelligent man, but he had a basic cunning; he made use of what was later to become the classic colonial strategem 'divide and rule'.

However, his first attempt to put this strategy into effect backfired. He established a camp on the island of Puna, whose people, he knew, were hostile to those of Tumbes; but as a result of his efforts to play one tribe against another several of the Puna chiefs were killed. The people of the island, in fury, attacked his camp and, although they were driven off, the Spaniards suffered casualties they could ill afford – among them Hernando with a javelin wound in the leg. Pizarro was forced to evacuate Puna and camp on the mainland. About this time his numbers were augmented by a small force of cavalry under de Soto, and he now felt strong enough to enter Tumbes. Three years ago the city had been prosperous, now it was an empty shell, not a building remained standing except the great temple-fortress and a handful of stone-built warehouses, and these had been stripped of their treasures. In the recently ended war the people of Tumbes had backed the wrong brother. To say the conquistadors were disappointed would be an understatement. Throughout their miserable voyage and more miserable march, they had been buoyed up by dreams of easy pickings in Tumbes. Now, it seemed, they would have to penetrate more deeply into the Inca Empire to win the rewards they had set their heart on.

Pizarro led them south. He spent several months in the arid and uninviting region of the Chira and Piura Rivers, welding his men into an efficient fighting unit, and attempting to win over the local population. Chiefs who accepted him were encouraged to join him with troops; chiefs who opposed him were first put in chains then burned to death. He established a base camp at what can claim to be the first colonial township in South America – Tangarara on the River Chira: a church, an arsenal, a law court and a couple of dozen wooden houses encircled by a pallisade. Here he melted down the small amount of silver and gold he had been able to lay his hands on and, as soon as a ship was available, sent the ingots back to Panama to settle his expedition's debts.

He must have been wondering what to do next, when his Indian allies brought him the news that was to topple an empire. Atahualpa had left Cuzco and was making a triumphal tour of his newly consolidated domain; he had already reached the northern sierra, and was camped beside the hot springs of Cajamarca. This was almost too good to be true. Over the last few months it had been becoming increasingly obvious to Pizarro that he and his men stood little chance of forcing their way through the Andes to confront Atahualpa at Cuzco, for the Inca capital was 1,300 miles away and could be reached only by passing through some of the most daunting and easily defended terrain on earth. Cajamarca, on the other hand, was little more than 300 miles away, and the route to it comparatively easy.

Luck had brought the Sun God to within striking distance of Pizarro's diminutive force. On 24 September 1532 he led his conquistadors into the sierra.

There were only 168 of them – 106 foot-soldiers and 62 horsemen – and this number was soon reduced by defections, for their route took them parallel to the Sechura Desert, one of the most arid in Peru, and, not surprisingly, the desolation of the landscape and the uncertainty of their future began to prey on the men's minds. Where, some of them wanted to know, was Pizarro leading them, and where were their easy pickings of gold? Pizarro called a halt and gave the faint-hearted the option of returning to Tangarara. It seems that only nine men (five horsemen and four foot-soliders) took advantage of the offer; then the rest were heading into the foothills via one of the minor Inca highways which runs from Saran to Cajas.

The higher they climbed, the more evidence the Spaniards found that they were now entering the heartland of a powerful and well-organized empire. There was the road itself, wider, more even and more solid than any in Europe; there were the well-built and well-stocked *qollas* beside it; there were the strategically placed observation-posts from which, they realized, the Incas were monitoring their advance; and soon there were the Incas themselves. One Spanish soldier told Garcilaso that not far from Cajas an Inca nobleman, an emissary from Atahualpa, 'entered our camp as casually as if he had been brought up all his life among Spaniards . . . The local chief was so afraid of this man that he dared not remain seated in his presence.' Gifts were exchanged, the Inca bringing from

Atahualpa two ceramic drinking vessels cast in the mould of castles, and two stuffed ducks – the suspicious Spaniards were afraid that the castellated drinking vessels might represent the many fortresses ahead, and the stuffed ducks the fate that awaited them as intruders! In return Pizarro gave the Inca a cap, a shirt and two goblets of Venetian glass. 'This man then enjoyed himself for two or three days among us . . . counting our numbers and examining our horses, swords and armour.' Before the emissary left he invited Pizarro to visit his master the Sun God in his camp beside the springs of Cajamarca – an invitation which the conquistador was quick to accept.

The Spaniards didn't advance directly on Cajamarca. They chose instead a circuitous route via the gorges of the Zana and Nancho rivers. This involved a difficult climb over passes of more than 12,000 feet. Although it was midsummer and not far from the equator, the ground was covered in snow. The horses suffered from frostbite and the men from altitude sickness. The road degenerated into a spiral stairway. If the passes had been defended, the Spaniards would have had little hope of forcing their way through; as Pizarro himself admitted, 'They could easily have taken us here. For on the road we could not use our horses, no matter how great our skill; and off the road we could take neither horses nor foot-soldiers.' Yet the fortresses guarding the route were manned by no more than skeleton garrisons. Atahualpa had decided to watch but not impede the Spaniards' advance. When they reached the top, he sent them a present of ten llamas.

A couple of days later Pizarro led his men into the valley of Cajamarca, one of the richest and most beautiful in the Andes. It was not, however, the magnificence of the valley that took away the Spaniards' breath, it was the magnificence of Atahualpa's army quartered around the hot springs. Ruiz de Arce, one of Pizarro's veterans, described it:

The Indian camp looked like the most beautiful city. There were so many tents that we were filled with apprehension. We never thought that Indians could maintain such a proud estate in such good order. Nothing like it had ever been seen before in the Indies, and it filled us Spaniards with fear and confusion. However, it would have been fatal to show fear, or to turn back. For had they sensed weakness in us, even the few Indians who were accompanying us would have killed us. So with a show of good spirits, having taken a careful look at both town and camp, we descended into the valley and entered Cajamarca.

There can be no doubt as to how Pizarro felt as he led his men that morning into the near-deserted town. He climbed to the top of Cajamarca's temple-fortress, looked out on the well-ordered ranks of the Inca army – conservatively estimated at 80,000 men – and was appalled. It seemed obvious that he had bitten off a great deal more than he could chew. Soon, to add to his troubles, high winds came sweeping down the valley and it started to hail.

He decided to send a deputation to Atahualpa: fifteen horsemen under de Soto, followed by another twenty under his brother Hernando. The Spaniards found the Inca, surrounded by his bodyguard and entourage, 'sitting with all the majesty in the world on a low stool at the entrance to his quarters'. It was unheard of for the Sun God to give an audience in person and in public, and this is probably why Atahualpa feigned not to notice de Soto as the Spaniard rode up to him, even though de Soto approached so close that 'breath from his horse's nostrils stirred the fringe on the Inca's headpiece'. De Soto offered the motionless Inca his ring as a token of friendship, and delivered a prepared speech inviting him to visit his 'Governor' Pizarro. Atahualpa made no reply, and one of his dignitaries explained that the Sun God was engaged in a ceremonial fast. Hernando Pizarro then made a similar speech and, as soon as Atahualpa understood that the man now addressing him was the 'Governor's' brother, he looked up and asked quietly why the Spaniards had been treating his people with such cruelty, putting his chiefs in chains and burning them to death? This was hardly an auspicious opening, and Hernando – who, like many of the conquistadors, had more courage than sense – made matters worse by hotly denying the accusation, and going on to boast that ten Christian horsemen would be enough to conquer Atahualpa's enemies, or indeed Atahualpa himself. 'At this the Inca smiled, in the manner of someone who did not think much of us.'

Luckily for the Spaniards de Soto now came to the rescue. Noticing that Atahualpa seemed interested in the horses, he asked the Inca if he would like to see one put through its paces. Atahualpa assented, and de Soto proceeded to give an exhibition of equestrian skill which excited both wonder and fear, his horse 'wheeling and leaping with great dexterity and much foaming at the mouth'. According to one chronicler, a section of the royal bodyguard shrank back as the horse reared up in front of them. Their frailty was to cost them their lives, 'for that night Atahualpa ordered them to be killed because they had shown fear'. The deputation ended on a more harmonious note than it had begun, with the Spaniards being offered and accepting chica-wine, and Atahualpa promising that he would visit Pizarro the following day.

This last assurance was what the Spaniards had hoped for, and that evening back in Cajamarca they laid plans for a coup which for cold-blooded audacity has no equal in history. They planned to capture the Sun God.

The fact was that they had got themselves in a near impossible situation. That night one of them wrote:

We discussed what should be done, and there were many different views. All of us were full of fear, for we were so few in number, and so deep in this [alien] land where we could not be reinforced . . . Few of us slept that night. We kept watch from the square, and could see all around us the camp fires of the Indian army. It was a fearful sight. They were camped on a hillside, and so close to one another that it looked like a brilliantly star-studded sky.

Of the options open to them, that of kidnapping Atahualpa was the most dangerous, but held promise of the most lasting success – indeed, it was to prove even more sucessful than the Spaniards anticipated, because the Inca Empire without its Sun God was to prove like a chicken without its head: blind, paralytic and doomed. In the end it was agreed that Pizarro should decide at the last moment which of their several plans to put into operation. If Atahualpa could be persuaded to make some gesture of political or spiritual submission, they would prolong their façade of friendship. If not, they would rely on their cannon, their cavalry, their steel swords, and the element of surprise.

Atahualpa was in no hurry next morning to visit the extraordinary strangers who had descended so unexpectedly on his kingdom. He had decided to turn his audience with them into a ceremonial parade – partly perhaps to impress them, but more as a thanksgiving for his recent military successes over his brother. There was therefore much preparation that morning in the Inca camp but no advance, and as the hours passed the Spaniards became increasingly apprehensive. At last, however, an envoy arrived to say that Atahualpa was on his way, and that he was coming – as the Spaniards the previous evening had come to him – armed. To this Pizarro replied, 'Tell your lord to come in whatever way he pleases. I will receive him as a friend and a brother.'

By early afternoon a spectacular procession, the Sun God and his retinue resplendent in their ceremonial regalia, was advancing on Cajamarca. First came 'a squadron of Indians wearing a livery of chequered colours, like a chessboard, and as they advanced they removed all straws and dirt from the roadway and swept it clean'. Next came the Inca himself, carried in a wooden and silver-inlaid litter, and surrounded by his most trusted kinsfolk and advisers, 'all with crowns of gold or silver on their heads . . . and dressed in blue ceremonial robes'. Flanking the litter, in battle order, were some 7,000 well-drilled troops, while watching motionless from the encircling hills were the remainder of the Inca army. There is no doubt about how the watching conquistadors felt. 'I saw many Spaniards urinate without noticing it,' writes Pedro Pizarro, 'out of pure terror.'

The Incas came to a halt in a meadow about half a mile from the town, and there was yet another exchange of messages, Atahualpa saying that he intended to pitch his tents and remain where he was for the night. This was the last thing Pizarro wanted, for he was particularly afraid that the Indias would attack him under cover of darkness. He therefore sent back a message to 'ask the Inca to come at once to dine with me . . . I give him my promise that no harm or insult will befall him. He can come without fear.'

Was it, one wonders, this last jibe, with its imputation of cowardice, that now goaded Atahualpa into making an extraordinary decision? He decided to enter Cajamarca unarmed. (It is claimed by some historians that the Incas in fact had 'weapons concealed beneath their tunics', but the facts of the coming massacre refute this; much more likely the concealed weapons were a figment of Spanish chroniclers' imaginations, anxious to give the impression that Pizarro and his men were under threat.)

The sun was nearing the rim of the altiplano as the Incas entered Cajamarca. Soon something like 7,000 of them were crowded into the narrow streets and open square. Atahualpa was surprised to see no Spaniards – it seems never to have occurred to him that they might be planning an ambush, and he is said to have admitted afterwards that he thought they must be overawed by the pomp and circumstance of his entry and were hiding in fear. 'Where are they?' he called out. At this, the Dominican Friar Vicente de Valverde, a cross in one hand and a Bible in the other, pushed his way through the mass of troops to where Atahualpa was seated. There are several versions of what happened next, but the gist of all of them is that the friar handed Atahualpa the Bible and started to proclaim from a document known as the Requirement. This epitome of casuistry demanded that any non-Christians to whom it was read should instantly acknowledge fealty to the King of Spain and the Pope; if they refused, they laid themselves open to attack, the enslavement of their families and the confiscation of their property, 'and [they were told] any deaths or losses that may result from this will be your own fault'. Even many Spaniards admitted that they didn't know whether 'to laugh at the Requirement's impracticality or weep at its injustice', and Atahualpa's reaction when the friar's demands were translated to him was predictable. He had just taken under his aegis an empire a third the size of Europe; he had at his beck and call 10 million people and ¼ million troops; and, most significant of all, he was god, the earthly embodiment of an all-caring sun whose diurnal traverse brought light, warmth and life itself to the people of earth. And this handful of tatterdemalion strangers was demanding his fealty! His face flushed with anger, he threw the Bible to the ground.

To Pizarro, as he watched from a doorway in the temple-fortress, it seemed that only the most hazardous of his options remained. He dropped his handkerchief – the prearranged signal. His artilleryman Pedro de Candia touched off his two cannon. Grapeshot scythed into the close-packed ranks of the Incas.

A moment of shocked silence. Then, with cries of 'Santiago', the Spanish cavalry and foot-soldiers who had been hidden in the surrounding buildings came pouring into the square, their swords flashing first white in the evening sun then red with blood, as they slashed and hacked at the mass of defenceless human bodies. Eyewitnesses describe the carnage:

The Indians were thrown into confusion and panicked as we fell upon them and began to kill . . . They were so filled with terror that they climbed on top of each other, forming great mounds and suffocating one another . . . our horsemen rode over the top of them, wounding and killing, and since they were unarmed they were routed without danger to any Christian.

A group of foot-soldiers, led by Pizarro, hacked their way through to Atahualpa's litter. The litter was carried and surrounded by the flower of the Inca hierarchy, relatives of the Sun God, high-ranking soldiers and trusted councillors. All were unarmed; all were butchered – literally to the last man:

Many Indians had their hands and arms cut off, yet they still tried to support their ruler's litter on their shoulders. Not one of those escorting the Inca abandoned him; all died around him.

The litter was overturned, and Atahualpa was captured and dragged into the temple-fortress. Meanwhile the slaughter in the square continued. All exits were blocked by troops, and the weaponless Incas had only one chance of escape; several thousand of them flung themselves at a section of wall, 6 feet thick, broke through it and fled into the open plain. Even here the blood-crazed Spaniards pursued them.

Our horsemen jumped the rubble, and with cries of 'After them! Spear them! Let none escape', continued to hunt down and lance [the Incas] long after it was dark. Very many were killed, before they sounded a trumpet for us to reassemble.

In the meantime, those remaining in the square had been methodically massacred:

In the space of two hours – all that remained of daylight – virtually everyone who had entered Cajamarca was killed, and during all this time no Indian raised a weapon against a Spaniard.

It has been estimated that more than 6,000 Incas were killed that evening – Atahualpa is said to have put the figure at over 7,000. Of the Spaniards only one man, Pizarro himself, was wounded – and this a superficial cut from one of his own men's swords during the struggle to drag Atahualpa from his litter.

That evening the Sun God was forced to dine with his captors, who treated him with a combination of solicitude and condescension. He was given clean clothes, fine food and whatever women he wished for, and was told, he had no reason to be sorrowful, because wherever we Christians go we make friends of the country's former rulers and turn them into our vassals . . . He [Atahualpa] asked the Spaniards if they were going to kill him. They told him no, because although Christians may kill in the heat of the moment they did not kill afterwards in cold blood.

One wonders if the Inca remembered this assurance a few months later as the garrotte bit into his throat.

Two things about the Cajamarca massacre are not altogether clear. Why did Atahualpa enter the city unarmed, and why didn't his army drawn up on the nearby hillside make an effort to save him?

There seems little doubt that the Incas *were* unarmed. Several eyewitness reports specifically state this. More tellingly, if the Incas (as was later claimed) had indeed 'carried battle-axes beneath their tunics', they would surely have used them, and it seems inconceivable that some 7,000 troops who were armed would not have inflicted a single wound on the 160-odd men who attacked them. Common sense indicates that they carried no weapons. As to why, the simple answer is that Atahualpa, puffed up with pride after his victories over his brother, misjudged and underestimated the Spaniards. It must have seemed to him that summer, as he monitored their advance from the coast to Cajamarca, that at any moment he could crush them, as easily and as casually as a farm labourer crushes a beetle; an impression strengthened by the reports of the envoy whom he had sent to make contact with Pizarro; for this man had told him that 'the Christians do not seem to be great warriors, and if he [the envoy] were given 200 troops he could overpower and tie up the lot of them'. It must have seemed inconceivable to Atahualpa that while he was closely guarded by his huge and victorious army, such a tiny handful of men would dare even to think of trying to capture him. In the sombre and weighty words of Prescott, 'he did not know the character of the Spaniards'.

The fact that there was no attempt at rescue underlines the basic weakness of the Inca regime. Too much depended on the Emperor himself; no action could be taken without his authorization, and when Atahualpa needed help quickly there was no one with the necessary authority to act on the spur of the moment. Two other factors told against the likelihood of rescue. Atahualpa's most trusted generals and most experienced troops were not with him at Cajamarca; they were still campaigning some 1,000 miles to the south, and had just completed mopping up the remnants of Huascar's supporters in the hills around Cuzco. The troops with him at the hot springs consisted of a small core of Incas, who were unquestioningly loyal, who accompanied him into Cajamarca and who were killed almost literally to the last man, together with a large number of levies from other tribes – troops who might be described as fair-weather allies, who owed no personal or racial allegiance to the Inca, and who were unlikely to leap spontaneously to his rescue. Having failed to make a spontaneous rescue, the army was expressly forbidden to make a planned one. For Pizarro made it clear to Atahualpa that any attempt to free him would cost him his life. The Inca therefore ordered his troops to offer no resistance to the Spaniards, but to greet them with the sign of the cross as a gesture of surrender and subservience.

Atahualpa is an enigmatic figure. It is difficult to know whether or not one can believe what is said about him, for our only two sources of information are Spanish chroniclers, who naturally went out of their way to show him in a bad light, and Garcilaso de la Vega, el Inca, who might have been expected to champion him but who in fact was a supporter of his brother Huascar. So Atahualpa, like King John of England, got a bad press. He was obviously a highly intelligent man but, it would seem, unheroic. Rightly or wrongly the verdict of posterity has been that he rated his personal safety more highly than the survival of his empire, and that he kowtowed to the Spaniards in an effort to save his life.

In the aftermath of the massacre Pizarro and his conquistadors could hardly believe their good fortune. They had acted in terror and desperation, and within a couple of hours had acquired an empire.

That night the Spaniards steeled themselves to face an attack from the 70,000-odd troops still encamped round the hot springs, but it never came. Next morning the stunned Indians offered no resistance but made the sign of the cross (as Atahualpa had ordered) to indicate their surrender.

Now at last the conquistadors were able to get their hands on what they had come for: women and loot.

In the royal baths they found 5,000 women, of whom they did not fail to take advantage; they also took possession of many fine tents, all kinds of provisions, linen, valuable tableware and vases of solid gold. Atahualpa's tableware alone, which was entirely of gold and silver, was worth one-hundred-thousand ducats. There were also many large emeralds.

This was no more than the beginning, for when Atahualpa saw how highly the Spaniards valued silver and gold, he decided to offer them more of these metals in exchange for his freedom. He showed Pizarro a room (probably adjoining the one in which he was held prisoner) 22 feet long and 17 feet wide, and undertook to fill it with gold and silver ornaments to a height of more than 8 feet, provided the Spaniards would allow him to return as emperor to Quito. Pizarro was delighted, and his secretary drew up a document formally recording the bargain.

There was now no immediate need for the conquistadors to advance more deeply into Inca territory. Knowing that the loot which was their desideratum would be brought to them, they were able to settle down in Cajamarca – each with his retinue of women, servants and booty acquired in the aftermath of the massacre – to await the reinforcements which Pizarro had called for and the ransom which had been promised.

This breathing space was more advantageous to the conquistadors than to the Incas. For during their stay in Cajamarca the Spanish leaders succeeded beyond their wildest dreams in setting Inca against Inca, and the Spanish rank and file succeeded, again beyond their wildest dreams, in amassing a personal fortune.

While Pizarro was waiting for Atahualpa's ransom to accumulate, he managed to get in touch with the Inca's brother Huascar, who had been taken prisoner by the armies of the pro-Atahualpan north and was being brought captive to Cajamarca. What price, Pizarro asked Huascar, would he be willing to pay if the Spaniards procured him *his* freedom? Huascar replied that he would give the Spanish three times as much gold as his brother was giving them – 'It will not be up to any line drawn on the wall, but up to the ceiling that I shall fill the room.' This was exactly what Pizarro had hoped for, and he was relishing the prospect of having the two claimants to the Inca Empire captive under the same roof

Above Sacsahuaman, the Inca temple-fortress overlooking Cuzco. The walls, made of 100-ton perfectly fitting blocks of stone, were described by the conquistadors as 'the ninth wonder of the world'.

Right Machu Picchu, the Incas' magnificent 'monument in stone', which blends into and mirrors the landscape in which it is set.

Overleaf In the rain shadow of the Andes are some of the most arid deserts on earth. In parts of the Atacama rain has never been recorded.

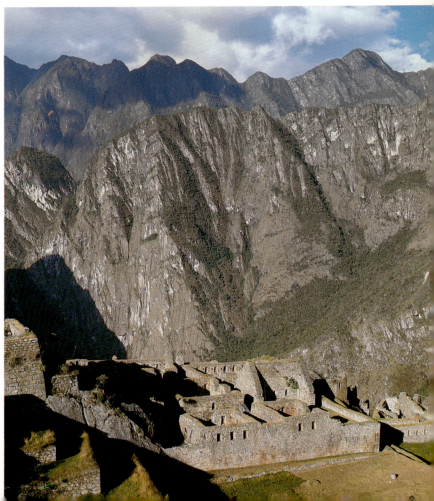

Above Francisco Pizarro (*c*.1472-1541), leader of the conquistadors and *left* Manco Inca (*c*.1516-44) who led his peoples' resistance to the conquistadors.

Below The massacre at Cajamarca: 'Our horsemen rode over the top of them, wounding and killing': a seventeenth-century painting from the Cuzco School.

and being able to play them off against the other, when Atahualpa forestalled him. Fearing – with every justification – that his brother was conspiring against him with the Spaniards, he arranged to have Huascar murdered by his guards before he ever got to Cajamarca; an act which may have prolonged his life, but which fuelled the flames of the Incas' dynastic feuding.

The treasure, meanwhile, was accumulating steadily, brought in by 'caravans' of llamas:

On some days twenty-thousand and on other days sixty-thousand *pesos de oro* would be brought it . . . There were goblets, ewers, salvers, vases of every shape and size, ornaments from the temples and royal palaces and tiles from public buildings, all in solid gold.

Many of these artefacts were of great value. Atahualpa's throne, for example, was of solid gold and weighed 183 pounds; the wall-plates from Coricancha were also solid gold, they weighed 4½ pounds apiece and the Spaniards in one consignment alone got some 700 of them. Many artefacts were of great artistic merit, the masterpieces of skilled craftsmen, and what happened next was an act of tragic vandalism. Pizarro ordered the *objets d'art* to be melted down and converted into ingots. It has been estimated that 24 tons of silver artefacts and 11 tons of gold artefacts were fed to the furnaces and forges; and at the end of a month of smelting and pressing the artistic treasures of the Incas had been reduced to 26,000 bars of silver and 13,000 bars of gold. When these were distributed, each of Pizarro's foot-soldiers found himself with a fortune worth, in today's currency, well over £100,000; the horsemen got twice as much, Pizarro himself ten times as much.

This near-embarrassment of riches fuelled the El Dorado legend . . . The Incas soon realized that what mattered most to the Spaniards was gold. So to please them, pacify them, get rid of them or simply to co-exist with them, they offered them gold on every possible occasion. This was like a drug to the Spaniards; the more they were given, the more they wanted; to get that which mattered most to them they were willing to climb any mountain or sink to any depths. At first there was gold enough to keep them happy, but the Incas' treasures were not inexhaustible. When their temples had been desecrated, their palaces had been looted, their public buildings had been stripped bare and they had been robbed of their personal bric-à-brac and jewellery, there was nothing left, and no matter how cruelly the Spaniards tortured them, burned, mutilated and killed them, they were unable to reveal the whereabouts of more. It was then that the legend of El Dorado came into being – the legend that in some secret place where the rainbow ended lay a fabulous crock of gold – and in pursuit of this crock of gold the conquistadors combed ice cap, desert and rain forest, leaving in their wake a trail of suffering and destruction. The Spanish conquest of the Incas was not so much a military campaign as a succession of forays in search of plunder.

Pizarro planned the first and arguably the greatest of these forays in the winter of 1533. However, before he led his men south into the heart of the Andes, he had a problem: what to do with Atahualpa?

Now that his ransom had been paid, Atahualpa had outlived his usefulness. Some of his captors may have grown frond of him, and some may have felt that since the Inca had kept his side of the bargain they ought to keep theirs; but by now Pizarro had been joined by a posse of reinforcements under Diego de Almagro, and the attitude of these newcomers to Atahualpa was unclouded by sentiment. He was, they pointed out, a liability, a potential rallying point – 'so long as he lives our lives will be in constant danger . . . it is expedient he is killed'. At a hasty trial, its indictment (in the Spaniards' own words) 'a badly contrived document devised by a factious and unprincipled priest, an amoral and incompetent notary and others of like stamp,' Atahualpa was found guilty of 'treason, incestuous polygamy and worshipping false gods'. He was condemned to be burned to death. On the evening of 26 July 1533 the chroniclers tell us:

The Inca was brought out of his prison and led to the middle of the square to the sound of trumpets proclaiming his treason, and was tied to a stake. The friar [Valverde] consoled him and, through an interpreter, instructed him in our Christian faith . . . The Inca was much moved by the friar's arguments, and requested baptism. This was at once administered to him. He was christened Francisco after the Governor. His conversion did the Inca much good. For although he had been sentenced to be burned alive, he was in fact garrotted by a rope that was tied round his neck . . . So with the Spaniards who surrounded him saying a credo for his soul, he was strangled. May God in his holy glory preserve him, for he died repenting his sins, in the true faith of a Christian. After the sentence had been carried out, fire was thrown on him to burn his clothes and his flesh, and his body was left in the square overnight. Next day the Governor ordered all the Spaniards to attend his funeral. He was carried to the church with a cross and the rest of the usual religious ornaments, and was buried with as much pomp as if he had been the most important Spaniard in our camp. All the lords and chiefs in his service were very pleased with this; they appreciated the great honour that had been done to him.

The truth is another story. The Incas were stunned and horrified by Atahualpa's death. For days the streets of Cajamarca were full of men and women prostrating themselves and rolling about, as though drunk, in a frenzy of despair; while night after night 'his wives and sisters searched for him softly through the rooms where he had been held captive', buoyed up, it seems, by the doctrine of the resurrection; when the Spaniards 'disabused them and told them that dead men do not return, they made long and terrible lamentations . . . One might have thought [the chronicler adds] that the world was coming to an end.' As indeed for the Incas it was.

As soon as they had freed themselves from the incubus of Atahualpa, the Spaniards, with amazing audacity, set out for Cuzco. With a force of under 200 men and without hope of reinforcements, Pizarro, Almagro and de Soto were planning to push 1,000 miles into the heart of an unknown and hostile empire in an effort to capture its capital which they knew to be guarded by well over 100,000 hostile troops.

Their route to start with lay through pleasant and well-wooded country, where progress was uneventful and the going easy. The Spaniards, however, were taking no chances – 'always maintaining a vanguard and a rearguard, they advanced with great diligence'. They had with them a puppet Inca, the young Tupac Huallpa, who was known to be popular in the south; also Atahualpa's greatest general, Chalcuchima, who was known to be extremely unpopular and was kept for much of the journey in chains. Thus the Spaniards were able to pose as champions of the pro-Huascar south come to liberate the people of the cordillera from the tyranny of the pro-Atahualpa north. The effectiveness of this pose is shown by what happened in the Mantaro Valley. As the foothills of Cajamarca gave way to the snow-capped peaks and steep-sided gorges of the Cordillera Blanca, the Spaniards began to run into difficulties. They suffered from cold and altitude sickness; the road became too steep for their horses; and their scouts reported that in the passes ahead Quitan troops were massing to block their advance. 'Our men,' writes Pedro Sancho, 'had to remain constantly on the alert, their horses saddled. For days they had nothing to eat, for they lacked both firewood and water. Having no tents and no shelter, they felt themselves close to dying of cold. It rained and snowed without respite so that their armour and clothes became sodden.' Soon, to add to their discomfort, they came across the bodies of more than 4,000 local Andeans, killed in the recent civil war – evidence of the fighting prowess of the Quitans. Next morning they found themselves face to face with these formidable warriors, a small number (about 600) who had been left to set fire to the town of Jauja as part of a scorched earth policy, and a far larger number (about 10,000) who were drawn up for battle on the far bank of the Mantaro. What happened next underlines the Incas' suicidal disunity. For as the Spaniards advanced on Jauja, 'the natives all came out on to the road to look at the Christians and to celebrate their arrival, for they thought this would mark the end of their subjugation under the Quitans'.

The battle that followed was the first meaningful trial of strength between Spaniards and Incas. As the vanguard of Spanish horsemen rode into Jauja they surprised Quitan troops setting fire to the storehouses. Without hesitation the Spaniards charged, driving the Quitans back through the narrow streets, cutting down those who resisted, and forcing those who fled into the river. Even the waters of the Mantaro were no obstacle to the Spaniards. They urged their horses into the river and up the opposite bank. The Incas were in two minds whether to fight or to flee. Those who decided to fight were scythed down by the rampant horsemen and, to quote John Hemming, 'the battle ended in a field of maize at the river's edge, with the slaughter of the frightened warriors who tried to take refuge there'. Of the 600 who had been setting fire to the *qollas* in Jauja less than 50 survived. From the point of view of the Incas worse was to come. Demoralized by the ferocity of the Spanish attack, they decided to fall back on Cuzco. The consquistadors, however, were too quick for them. Pizarro sent 80 horsemen in pursuit of the retreating army. Eighty against 9,000 may not sound very favourable odds, but the cavalry caught up with their quarry in a broad and open valley and attacked without hesitation. The Inca rearguard put up a spirited resistance; but as soon as they were overrun the rest of the troops and their entourage fled for cover in the rock-strewn upper slopes of the valley. Many were too slow, and were ridden down without mercy. 'The pursuit continued for four leagues,' the chroniclers tell us, 'and many Indians were speared . . . We won a good haul of both gold and silver, also many beautiful women, among them two daughters of Huayna-Capac.'

How, one wonders, did the conquistadors achieve such overwhelming victories in the face of such adverse odds?

They owed almost everything to their horses. In battle, a man on horseback has an overwhelming advantage over a man on foot, a fact underlined by the exploits of the armour-clad knights who dominated the battlefields of Europe for a thousand years, the efficaciousness of their charge being blunted only by long-range weapons such as the longbow and musket. The Incas had virtually no long-range weapons; they relied on close hand-to-hand combat, and this made them particularly vulnerable to Spanish horsemen wielding either the lance or the double-edged sword. As well as being potent weapons in battle, horses gave the conquistadors a speed and mobility on the march which repeatedly threw their opponents into confusion; for Spanish cavalry could ride faster than Indian messengers could run, and time and again the conquistadors were able to launch effective surprise attacks, as they did after crossing the Mantaro. Contemporary chroniclers all stress the Incas' terror of horses. Lopez de Gomara, for example, writes, 'The Indians thought more of killing one of these animals than of killing ten men, and they always placed the head of a slain horse where the Spaniards could see it, garlanded with flowers as a symbol of victory.'

Another advantage enjoyed by the Spaniards was the quality of their weapons. The wooden clubs and stone-and-bronze-headed axes of the Incas were no match for the magnificent Toledo-steel swords and steel-tipped lances of the conquistadors; nor was their quilted fabric as effective a protection as the conquistadors' steel armour and chain-mail. Spanish troops in the early sixteenth century were the élite of Europe, their weapons, tactics and morale honed to razor-sharpness by half a millennium of campaigning against the Moors. Even if the Incas had been united they would have been hard pressed to stand up to them. The fact that the Incas were *not* united played into the Spaniards' hands.

In the early days of the conquest the conquistadors enjoyed the advantage of surprise; the explosion of their arquebuses and the speed and ferocity of their cavalry-charges were phenomena completely new to the Incas, who in the early battles thought horse and man were one and that they were being attacked by a mutant species. By the latter stages of the conquest this element of surprise had worn off and the Incas had discovered that both the Spaniards and their horses were mortal. By this time, however, the conquistadors had succeeded in setting the people of the Andes faction against faction and tribe against tribe, so that in every march they made and every battle they fought they had allies. Spanish chroniclers, anxious to stress the heroic nature of the conquest, play down the role of these Indian allies; Garcilaso de la Vega, el Inca, anxious to conceal the disunity of his mother's people, has little to say about them. Yet without the help of tribes such as the Canari, Chanca, Colla and Lupaca, and without the cooperation of their puppet-Incas, the conquistadors would have had little prospect of success.

The first of these puppet Incas, Tupac Huallpa, hardly lasted long enough to be useful to his masters, for while Pizarro was setting up a forward base of Jauja, the Inca died in mysterious circumstances. It is quite possible that he was poisoned at the instigation of the captive general, Chalcuchima, who had good reason to hate the puppet, both as a member of the southern pro-Huascar dynasty and as a collaborator. It was the Spaniards' good fortune that no sooner had they lost one puppet than they gained another; for only a few weeks after Tupac Huallpa's death, his brother Manco came riding into the Spanish camp.

Manco was described by contemporary chroniclers as 'the greatest and most important lord in the land . . . and the man whom all influential people wanted as emperor'. For the past year he had been a fugitive from the armies of the north, and he was delighted to see the Spaniards, whom he regarded as deliverers from the yoke of Atahualpa and the instruments by which he could regain his throne in Cuzco. In the long term Manco was to be disillusioned by Spanish brutality and greed, and was to lead the most heroic and successful of the Inca resistance movements; but in the short term he threw in his lot with Pizarro. One of his first acts was to denounce the old northern general Chalcuchima, who was promptly tied to a stake and burned alive. The consquistadors were then able to resume their advance on Cuzco in the guise of friendly strangers helping to restore the legitimate Inca to his throne.

By this time Pizarro's numbers had been reduced by sickness, injury and his decision to leave a garrison at Jauja. So, in the final stage of his march, his force consisted of no more than 30 foot-soldiers and 100 horsemen. Between them and the Inca capital lay at least 75,000 hostile troops and 500 miles of daunting terrain.

The central section of the Andes through which Pizarro was now about to march has been described as 'wild, magnificent country: a vertical land of mountains deeply cut by fierce rivers plunging towards the Amazon'. The Spaniards had to follow the line of and cross both the Cordillera Occidental and the Cordillera Vilcabamba. Dominating both these ranges are a succession of great snow-capped peaks, many over 17,000 feet. Beneath the peaks lies the puna: a bleak, treeless landscape where the Spaniards and their horses suffered from heat by day, cold by night, and the breathlessness that stems from lack of oxygen. Below the puna one finds a mosaic of isolated valleys, full of maize and flowers; and lower still the beds of the canyons, airless and arid, little more than ribands of cactus and sand. It would have been almost impossible country to traverse if it hadn't been for the Incas' roads and bridges, although the usefulness of these was diminished by the fact that the roads were ill-suited to horses, and the bridges had usually been burned by the retreating Incas. Pedro Sancho describes a typically terrifying stretch of road:

Now we had to climb another stupendous mountain. Looking up at it from below, it seemed impossible for birds to scale it by flying through the air, let alone men on horseback by climbing by land. But the road was made less exhausting by ascending in zigzags rather than in a straight line. Most of it consisted of large stone steps that greatly wearied the horses, and wore down and hurt their hooves, even though they were being led by their bridles.

As for the bridges, the one over the Mantaro had been destroyed, but the bridge-keepers, who were well disposed to Manco, had managed to hide their stocks of repair material, and the Spaniards were able to build a makeshift bridge and cross it so swiftly that they surprised the Quitan army and captured most of their entourage before the Indians realized that their adversaries had even crossed the river. A few weeks later, finding that the bridge over the Apurimac had also been destroyed, the Spaniards swam their horses across the fast-flowing river – a feat never attempted before and seldom since – and inflicted another surprise defeat on the Quitans.

South American Indians were far from incompetent fighters; they were well disciplined, and for the most part brave and determined. Yet time and again they were outmanoeuvred and outfought by the conquistadors – witness the four pitched battles that took place during the advance on Cuzco.

The first of these, the encounter at Jauja, had been not so much a battle as a massacre.

This was the first time that the Incas had faced either arquebuses or horses. They had been terrified and disorganized. The few who tried to stand and fight had been snuffed out like candles, and the rest had fled. It has been estimated that in the streets of Jauja, in the waters of the Mantaro River and later in the open reaches of the Mantaro Valley, upwards of 1,000 Indians were killed and at least as many wounded. Spanish casualties are thought to have been three wounded horsemen, whose injuries were superficial.

The next encounter was at Vilcashuaman, about 250 miles southeast of Jauja. Here again the speed of the Spaniards' advance took the Indians by surprise, and de Soto and his horsemen managed to capture the Quitans' base-camp, 'together [according to Pedro Sancho] with all their tents, women and possessions with hardly a blow . . . for their warriors were away hunting.' This time, however, as soon as the Quitans realized what had happened, they launched a counter-attack, and Diego de Trujillo tells us:

Because of the roughness of the terrain, they gained on us rather than we on them . . . They killed a white horse belonging to Alonso Tabuyo. We were forced to retire to the square in the town centre, and spent the night under arms. Next day the Indians attacked with great spirit, carrying banners made from the mane and tail of the horse that they had killed. We were forced to release the booty we had captured – the women and the men in charge of their flocks. They then withdrew.

It has been estimated that this battle cost the Indians at least 600 dead. Spanish losses are believed to have been one horse killed and two injured, also five soldiers wounded, one of them seriously. The Quitans discovered at Vilcashuaman that the conquistadors could be made to retreat and that their dreaded horses were mortal: but for this knowledge they paid a high price.

The third battle took place about ten days later, among the steep-sided hills to the south of the Apurimac. The Spanish vanguard, forty horsemen under de Soto, disobeyed orders and pushed on unaccompanied towards the Inca capital. 'Since we had endured the hardships,' the conquistador wrote, 'we thought we should also enjoy the entry into Cuzco without waiting for reinforcements.' Their rashness cost them dear. It was late afternoon, and de Soto and his men were climbing towards the head of a steep-sided valley, leading their horses by the halter; both men and animals were exhausted by the heat and suffering from altitude sickness. Suddenly the skyline was dark with figures, an ambush of 4,000 Indians. Behind a barrage of stones and javelins they came pouring over the rim of the valley. The Spaniards had only one hope. Scrambling on to their horses, they tried desperately to force their way through their attackers and gain the comparative safety of high ground. 'But,' Sancho tells us, 'the horses were so exhausted that they had insufficient breath to charge the enemy with élan. The Indians never stopped harassing and worrying the animals with javelins, stones and arrows; they so exhausted them that they could hardly raise a trot, and seeing the state they were in, they attacked with redoubled fury.' Five Spaniards were cut off from their companions. They were dragged off their horses and bludgeoned to death – the first occasion on which the Incas had managed to engage the conquistadors in the sort of hand-to-hand fighting at which they excelled – all the Spanish dead had their heads split open by blows from battle-axe or club. The survivors, with great difficulty, gained the comparative safety of a small hillock at the head of the valley. Here they spent the night 'with little victory and plenty of fear', surrounded by a great throng of Indians, who showered them with abuse and the occasional volley of arrows. The Spaniards were in trouble. Five men and five horses had been killed, and eleven men and fourteen horses had been wounded, many of them seriously. The Indians were reinforced during the night by 1,000 warriors from Cuzco, and they were almost certainly planning a dawn attack in which de Soto and his cold and exhausted survivors were likely to have been overwhelmed by sheer weight of numbers. However, in the small hours of the morning the Spaniards' hopes of survival enjoyed an unexpected boost. Faint at first, but growing louder with every passing hour, came the peal of a European trumpet – Almagro and some forty horsemen had heard of the battle, and were riding through the night to the rescue. At dawn the Indians found that their battered adversaries had been miraculously doubled in number and were advancing on them through the early morning mist. Disappointed, they melted away . . . The battle of Vilcaconga was described by the Spaniards who took part in it as 'a fierce fight . . . a highly dangerous affair'. If the Incas had managed to destroy de Soto's vanguard, they might well have gone on to destroy Almagro's and Pizarro's contingents as well, for, as John Hemming points out, Indian troops annihilated far larger Spanish forces in the later stages of the conquest. However, more by luck than judgement, the conquistadors survived, and their combined forces were able to continue the advance on Cuzco.

The final encounter took place in the hills overlooking the capital. The Quitan commander had drawn up his army to defend a pass only a few miles north of the city. Ruiz de Arce describes the battle that followed:

We found all their warriors waiting for us at a place where the road cut through the hills. They attacked us in great numbers, with much shouting and determination. At first they drove us back, killing three of our horses – including my own which had cost me 1,600 castellanos – and wounding many Christians . . . The Indians had never seen us retreat before, and thought this was a trick to lure them into the open plain; they therefore remained in the security of the hills, until our Governor came up with reinforcements.

The Spaniards spent an anxious night, surrounded on all sides by the camp-fires of the Indian army; but the arrival of Pizarro with reinforcements had disheartened the Quitans. They left their camp-fires burning, and slipped away in the darkness. Next morning the road to Cuzco lay open.

On 15 November 1533 Pizarro and Manco rode side by side into the Inca capital.

Pizarro now had the opportunity to establish a regime in which Spanish suzerainty might well have been accepted almost gratefully by the Indians, who would have been thankful to submit to any authority that was reasonably paternal and left them free to work the land. Pizarro, however, had little interest in creating a well-administered Spanish colony. His interest was in accumulating loot, and the story of the next two decades is a story of torture, rape, murder and spoliation as a succession of pillaging expeditions stripped the Inca empire of its silver and gold.

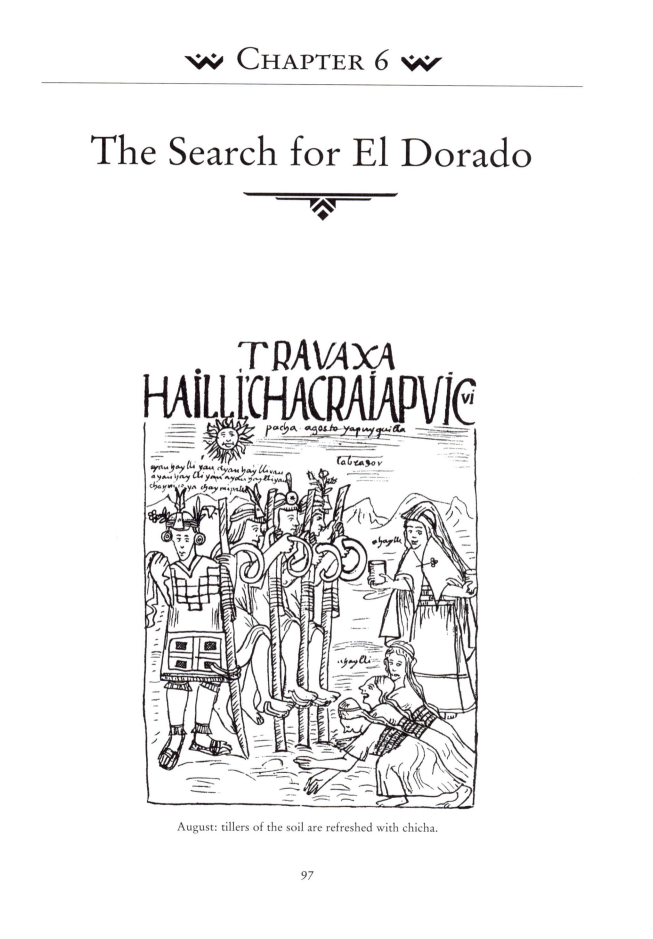

CHAPTER 6

The Search for El Dorado

August: tillers of the soil are refreshed with chicha.

Within a couple of weeks of the conquistadors' arrival in Cuzco their leaders had installed themselves in the most luxurious palaces, Manco had been crowned with much pageantry as Inca, and the serious business of looting the capital was under way.

Pedro Pizarro writes: 'Some began immediately to dismantle the walls of the temple, which were of gold and silver; others to disinter the jewels and gold ornaments that were with the dead . . . They sacked the houses, also the fortress, which still contained much of the treasure of Huayna-Capac. In short they acquired an even greater quantity of gold and silver from looting Cuzco than they had obtained from Atahualpa's ransom.' As at Cajamarca objects of great artistic beauty were thrown into the furnaces and melted down to make ingots. It has been estimated that the resulting bars of gold were worth 588,266 pesos, and the bars of silver 228,310 marks. This looting was carried out in an orderly fashion, much emphasis being placed on its alleged legality and its careful documentation. There was little protest from the Incas; and when the spoils were divided out, Pizarro's veterans were more than happy with their share. Not so happy were the swarms of adventurers who now began to descend on the Inca Empire in Pizarro's wake, like vultures on to a dying animal, for these late-comers found no easy pickings; before they even set foot in the Andes the treasure of the Sun God had been converted to ingots and shipped to Spain.

The first Inca gold to reach Europe was unloaded at Seville in December 1533. Here was indisputable evidence that the riches of Peru were not legend but fact. Official interest in South America quickened, and soon a whole spate of expeditions was setting out for the New World. Over the next decade the Andes were crossed and recrossed by literally dozens of bands of adventurers, whose ostensible objective may have been pacification but whose real desideratum was gold, that mythical El Dorado which the conqistadors were ever hoping lay beyond the next fiercely flowing river or mist-encompassed hill. Three of these expeditions – those of Diego de Almagro, Jimenez de Quesada and Gonzalo Pizarro – epitomize this phase of the conquest.

Diego de Almagro, we are told by a contemporary chronicler, was 'a foundling of humble birth . . . a man of short stature and ugly features, who had great courage and powers of endurance'. His relationship with the Pizarro brothers was to outward appearances cordial but was basically flawed, Almagro feeling (with some justification) that because of his humble birth he had never been given the recognition which, as co-leader of the original expedition, he deserved. However, soon after the occupation of the Inca capital he was granted a licence 'to discover, conquer and settle those lands which lie along the coast of the South Sea, from Cuzco to the Strait of Magellan'; and in July 1535 he set out with a force of 200 Spaniards and 15,000 Indians to explore his vast new domain. The 15,000 Indians were in theory troops provided by Manco to ensure the expedition's safe conduct; in practice they were used as load-carriers, and it is doubtful if the members of any expedition before or since have ever suffered such hardships. These hardships were due partly to the brutality of the Spaniards and partly to the harshness of the terrain. The priest Christobal de Molina, who accompanied the expedition, records his disgust at the way the Indians were treated:

Those who would not accompany us voluntarily were dragged along bound with ropes or chains.

By night they were kept in rough shelters, well guarded; by day they were forced to carry heavy loads with no rest and no food except for a little maize and water. [Those who fled were] hunted down and brought back in chains together with their wives and children and any attractive women whom the Spaniards could get their hands on for personal service . . . When the mares of the Spanish horsemen produced foals, these were carried in litters by the Indian women. Some Spaniards even had themselves carried in litters, leading their horses by the hand so they could become strong and fat . . . A Spaniard who could boast that he had killed many Indians acquired the reputation the being an important person. One [Spaniard] locked twelve Indians together in a chain without food until they all died, and then boasted of his achievement. In another chain, when one of the Indians died his head was cut off and he was left in place to terrify the others and avoid having to undo their shackles.

Almagro's Indian guides advised him to head south via the coastal road and the Atacama. The conquistador, however, thought he knew better, and decided to head south via the inland toad and the cordillera. It was winter.

'As they advanced,' the chronicler Alonso de Ovalle tells us,

they met nothing but vast deserts and a wind so cold it pierced them through and through. It is not possible to imagine what they endured . . . Here a man would fall into the snow and be buried alive. Here another would lean only for a second against a rock and be frozen on to it in death. If any stopped they would die almost instantly, fixed and immovable as though cast in iron; and a Negro leading his horse by the hand did but pause and turn his head to see who called him, and he and his horse became frozen solid like two statues. The Indians, being unprovided with clothes, died apace. The Spaniards, being better provided for, suffered less; nonetheless many lost toes and fingers without knowing it. The greatest suffering was in the night time; for there was no food and no wood to make fires, and the Indians ate the bodies of their companions out of hunger. It is said that there died in these mountains 70 horses and more than 10,000 natives.

The remnants of the expedition struggled through to the plains of Chile, where the tribes who might have been expected to massacre them gave them shelter and food. Almagro spent several months recuperating, then pushed south as far as the River Maule. Here, like the Incas before him, he met fierce resistance from the Araucanians 'who engaged us with great valour, so that Spanish blood which was usually shed so sparingly was here shed in abundance'. It was while fighting the Araucanians that Almagro first heard rumours of an Inca uprising in Cuzco; these rumours and the lack of easy pickings in Chile persuaded him to cut short his campaign and return.

In the course of his Chilean venture Almagro passed close to the greatest natural deposits of silver in the world (Potosi) and through some of the richest farming country (the Vales of Paradise); but because the conquistadors were seeking short-term loot rather than long-term prosperity, they described Chile as 'sterile' and their expedition as a 'disappointment'. Most of them returned to Cuzco via the Atacama Desert. Years later a handful again crossed the cordillera by their original route, this time in summer. Here they found the bodies of their companions and their horses, 'still frozen solid as though they had died but yesterday'. It has been estimated that of the 15,000 Indians who set out on this expedition no more than 1,000 returned.

Almagro, like most of the conquistadors, met a violent death. In the aftermath of the Inca uprising the Spaniards fell to fighting among themselves for control of Cuzco.

Almagro found himself leading a faction opposed by his erstwhile friends the Pizarro brothers. After a battle in which more than 150 Spaniards were killed, Almagro was defeated and captured. Within forty-eight hours he had been given a hastily-convened trial, sentenced to death and garrotted – the same fate, ironically, as he had engineered for Atahualpa.

Almagro's expedition was typical of those launched by the conquistadors from their bases in Peru; Jimenez de Quesada's was typical of those launched from Spain. It was a big, elaborate and hopelessly ambitious venture, its objectives being to establish a trade route between the Atlantic and the Pacific, and to acquire gold peaceably from the Indians. As regards the first of these objectives, what Quesada's sponsors hoped for was a swift paddle up the Magdalena, an easy portage across the spine of the Andes, and then an even swifter current-assisted paddle down one of the rivers that entered the Pacific near Quito. As regards the gold, his orders were equally unrealistic: 'You are to give good treatment to the Indians . . . Tell them how badly I [the King of Spain] need gold, and when they give it avoid vexing them so that later they will willingly give you more.' There was, however, a sting in the tail to these naive instructions: if the natives failed to hand over their gold, Quesada was 'to read the Requirement to them, and if this fails to wage war on them with fire and blood'.

He set out from Santa Marta, on the Caribbean coast, on 5 April 1536. Reports vary as to how many men he took with him, but it seems probable that his land-force consisted of about 500 men, and that he was hoping to rendezvous with a sea-borne force of a further 300 a little upriver from the mouth of the Magdalena. It was a huge expedition, financed, equipped and armed on a lavish scale. However, right from the start things went wrong. Quesada's ships were wrecked by a storm before they even arrived at the rendezvous, and most of the survivors who struggled ashore were 'cruelly killed by the cannibal Caribs and buried in their stomachs'. The land-party didn't fare much better. First they had to cross an area 'sterile in drinking water', a wasteland dotted with brackish and mosquito-breeding lagoons; here they were debilitated by malaria and yellow fever. Worse was to come. Their guides – almost certainly on purpose – took the wrong route, and in dense rain forest the Spaniards came under attack from the Chamila Caribs, whose poisoned arrows were one of the few things the conquistadors feared. 'If an arrows draws blood, the wounded man will be raving within twenty-four hours and dead within three days,' wrote the contemporary Friar Pedro de Aguado, 'for the poison flowing along the bloodstream and reaching the heart, causes trembling, convulsions and loss of reason, so that dying men say unbelievable things, and often the living are prompted to kill them rather than let them endure so terrible a death.' By the time they had hacked and fought their way through to their rendezvous (Tamalameque) on the mainstream of the Magdalena more than a hundred had died. At Tamalameque they met up with the remnants of their seaborne expedition. The sick and wounded were sent back to the coast, and after a brief recuperation Quesada led his combined but depleted force up the Magdalena. They made the mistake of trying to keep close to the river, their supplies being paddled upstream by canoe while the men and their horses squelched along the jungle-covered banks. It was purgatory. There was no trail, for the local Indians moved always by canoe, and the men had to cut a path with axes and machetes through dense stands of ivory-palm and swathes of tough nacuma grass. Each tributary they came to was a major obstacle and had to be crossed by makeshift bridge or raft. Men were killed and eaten by caymans as they waded chest-deep in the flood water; they were killed and eaten by jaguars as they hacked a path through the jungle; and they were almost literally eaten alive by swarms of mosquitoes, black-flies, ticks, leeches and worms. 'Our soldiers suffered in many ways, on water and on land,' wrote Fernandez de Oviedo, 'from fighting, from illness, from hunger and thirst, from heat, from nakedness, and from lack of clothing . . . there were dead and dying every day, and in the heavy rains no way to succour or relieve them.' By the time they reached the higher ground at La Tora another 150 had died.

Quesada's hopes suffered a major setback at La Tora. When he sent boats to reconnoitre upriver, they reported that after only a few miles the Magdalena became unnavigable: a succession of narrow gorges where 'the waters bore down with such force it was impossible to make any progress forward,' wrote Quesada. 'I was horrified to find we could ascend that river no farther'. Most of the men had by now lost heart and wanted to turn back. Quesada was not defeated so easily. He sent reconnaissance parties up the Magdalena's tributaries; and the canoes reconnoitring the Opon met Indians who indicated 'we were on the threshold of a powerful province called Meta, which was rich in gold'. The only indication that they might indeed be approaching an unknown civilization was that the Indians were dressed in skilfully woven clothes and were trading in cakes of rock salt – up to now all the river tribes through whose territory they passed had used sea salt. On the strength of this slender evidence Quesada led 60 of his fittest men on a further reconnaissance of the Opon. 'It was,' writes John Hemming, 'another terrible ordeal. The rains fell continuously. The river was flooded and "forced our men to advance like fish through the water by day and climb into trees like birds to sleep by night." The few surviving horses had to sleep with water up to their bellies. The men carried their own supplies, and the daily ration was no more than 40 grains of maize per man.' Soon they were suffering from hunger: a solitary dog that was rash enough to follow the explorers was killed and eaten, 'feet, legs, head, tripes and even the skin, with as much relish as if it had been the most tender lamb'. Eventually they struggled through to a high, rolling, fertile and apparently well-populated plateau, where a raid on one of the villages yielded well-woven cloth, a number of sophisticated agricultural instruments, emeralds and gold. Meta, it seemed, was not legend but fact, and Quesada hastened back to his camp at La Tora with the news.

By the time he got there his expedition had been incarcerated in the Colombian rain forest for more than eight months, and of the 800-odd men who had set out with such high hopes from the Caribbean no more than 250 were still alive, and of these many were too ill to move. When, on 28 December 1536, Quesada finally set out for 'the powerful kingdom of Meta' he had with him only 70 horses and 170 men; 60 of these men were so weak that they could walk only with the aid of a stick, and Quesada himself was unable to stand or ride unsupported. Yet he seems never to have doubted that his sickly, starving and half-naked rabble would be able to subjugate whatever opposition they encountered. He had a difficult time getting his horses up the steep and heavily forested mountains; often the unfortunate animals had to be hoisted up in cradles made out of creepers and lianas, and on one particularly hazardous cliff-face a horse and twenty Spaniards were killed. But at last the survivors struggled through to more open terrain, and saw ahead of them a vista of well-cultivated farmland dotted with homesteads.

The conquistadors knelt in prayer, 'thanking God that in His mercy He had given them so rich and well-ordered a kingdom to plunder'. Then they proceeded to plunder it.

Quesada spent nearly two years in what later became known as 'the land of the Muisca', one of the most prosperous farming communities in the Andes, indeed in the world. It would not be wrong to say that in these two years he stripped the Muisca of their wealth, then tortured their ruler to death in an effort to extract more. Such a statement, however, does less than justice to his achievement; for with a force of only 150 men – many of whom were initially so weak that they had to be carried on stretchers – he subjugated an empire which was stable, prosperous, civilized and had a population of over 1 million.

As the conquistadors headed south into the high valleys of the Cordillera Oriental it was literally a new world which opened up ahead of them; the landscape, the food and the people were all quite different from anything they had known in Europe. The landscape was beautiful: wide fertile valleys, sheltered by well-wooded limestone hills, and watered by the snows of the encircling cordillera; here was the site, according to South American theologians, of the New World's Garden of Eden. What made it different from anything in Europe was its height. Even the lowest of the Muisca's fields were at 8,200 feet, while the highest were at 9,400; this, close to the equator, was the ideal altitude for farming – low enough for maize and high enough for the best quality potatoes and quinoa. And, to European eyes, what a bizarre cornucopia was harvested from these fields: white, yellow and pink potatoes, non-hybrid maize, quinoa rich in protein, tomatoes, broad beans, chilli-peppers, pineapple, guavas and avocados – all at that time unknown in the Old World. Wildlife was scarce. A few deer were found in the woods, but apart from guinea-pigs and cavies the Muisca had no domestic animals. As for the people, their largely vegetarian diet seems to have suited them, for they were a strong, virile and healthy race, though not (according to the conquistadors) in the least skilled in war. What they *were* skilled in was husbandry, and all contemporary accounts agree that they enjoyed an orderly and rewarding way of life as farmers-cum-merchants. Evidence of their prosperity was the abundance of their produce and the quality of their homes – 'well built of wood, thatched, often ornate, and as fine as any we had seen in the Indies'. What heightened the impression that these New World Arcadians and the conquistadors might have come from different planets was the fact that they couldn't communicate. On most of their Andean forays the Spaniards had with them a go-between, an interpreter who had at least a smattering of the local language. The Muisca, however, cut off from the rest of the world by near-impenetrable forest, had developed a language quite unlike any other; it was only by signs that Quesada and his men were able to communicate with them.

Undeterred by the novelty of the situation, the conquistadors set about subjugating the Muisca in their usual forthright manner. They headed straight for the heart of their empire, intent on storming their most impregnable citadel and capturing their most important chief; any opposition was brushed contemptuously aside. Not that there *was* much opposition. For the Muisca thought that the Spaniards must be 'children of the Sun and the Moon', and were more intent on placating them as gods than opposing them as invaders. According to Quesada, they showered them with food and gifts: 'There was not a single day when food of all variety failed to arrive at [our] camp, on some days as many as 100 deer, on other days as many as 1,000 guinea-pigs, on yet other days young children. [We] made them understand by signs that children were not [our] type of food . . . and soon there arrived mantles beautifully woven, fine emeralds and gold. So peace was established between us, though for a short time only.' Quesada made a genuine attempt to preserve this peace. He issued orders that there must be no looting and no mistreatment of the Indians – a soldier who was caught stealing a Muisca poncho was summarily hanged. However, one of the local chiefs tried to ambush the Spaniards and, in the confused skirmishing that followed, looting proved impossible to control, especially since the conquistadors, as they pushed south, came across an increasing number of gold and silver artefacts. Eventually they reached the Muisca heartland, the present-day Valley of Bogota, to which Quesada gave the romantic name Valle de los Alcazares (Valley of the Castles) because its magnificent wooden palaces reminded him of the castellated Moorish forts of his homeland.

Many of these Muisca palaces contained artefacts of gold – some decorative, some funerary and some the regalia of local chiefs – and, presented with these easy pickings, the conquistadores' greed got the better of their good resolutions. The palaces were looted, often with casual incompetence. At Tunja Quesada's men ransacked the local ruler's quarters, 'tossing his treasure into a courtyard so that it formed a pile the height of a mounted horseman'. This, when melted down, yielded 621 kilos of fine gold and 280 emeralds. At Sugamuxi they inadvertently set fire to the most holy of the Muiscas' temples, 'which burned for five days so that we lost much treasure, although from nearby shrines we obtained gold worth 40,000 pesos'. At Bogota they inadvertently murdered the Muiscas' most powerful ruler – 'since he was fat and elderly he had difficulty fleeing, and was killed by mistake before he was recognized'. Here the Spaniards obtained little treasure, because, they convinced themselves, it had been carried away and hidden.

In the course of the next few months Quesada and his men embarked on a series of pillaging forays into the surrounding hills. Some of them were frozen to death and some were impaled with poisoned arrows; they were lured into pit-traps, and sent on a wild-goose chase to find 'a tribe of women who live on their own with no men among them and are known as Amazons'. They were surreptitiously given hallucinogenic herbs by the women they slept with. 'It was amazing how many Christians would wake up each morning crazed, and do foolish things at which everyone was horrified . . . and once the men had been driven mad the women were able to run to safety.' They met tribes so primitive that their only food was crushed ants. They found alluvial gold, reef gold and emerald mines. Every man who survived accumulated a personal fortune. Yet they always wanted more. In particular they wanted the Bogota treasure, which became an obsession to them – a sort of mini El Dorado. They convinced themselves that on the night the Zipa (or chief) of Bogota had been murdered, his followers had carried away a great cache of gold and hidden it in the hills. They were determined to find it.

They installed a puppet-chief named Sagipa, and entered into an arrangement with him whereby in return for help against his traditional enemies – the forest-dwelling Panche –

Sagipa would help them locate the treasure. The Spaniards duly campaigned against the Panche, and suffered not inconsiderable losses from their poisoned arrows; but when the fighting was over Sagipa failed to produce the eagerly anticipated cache of gold. What happened next is a good example of the tragic gulf between Spanish intention and achievement. When Quesada first entered Muisca territory he had ordered no looting and no ill-treatment of the Indians; now, six months later, after an orgy of looting, Sagipa was tortured in an effort to make him reveal the whereabouts of the treasure.

In another of those ridiculous 'trials' in which the Spaniards sought to justify actions for which no justification is possible, Sagipa was accused of 'rebellion' and of concealing the Zipa's gold. In spite of his protests that he knew nothing about any treasure, he was found guilty and sentenced to torture. After being suspended from a beam with his hands tied behind his back, he undertook to fill a hut with gold within twenty days. His friends did indeed bring in a great quantity of gold, together with many beautifully woven mantles, rare feathers and other objects valued by the Muisca; but the Spaniards were not satisfied, and there was more torture. The luckless Sagipa, in an effort to buy time, suggested that the Spaniards dug for gold in the spot where the Zipa had been killed. This they did, but found nothing. Reckoning they had been tricked, 'they gave Sagipa two or three very severe tortures, throwing him on his back and putting burning fat on his belly . . . Then they placed a shackle round each of his ankles and set fire to his feet . . . They repeatedly scoured the soles of his feet and applied large quantities of fire to them, so that they turned inwards and shrivelled. They also gave him other forms of torture, two or three times, so that a few days later he died.' The treasure was never found. In all probability it never existed.

The expedition had an improbable end. Quesada was about to return to the coast, when two other conquistadors arrived unexpectedly in Muisca territory – Benalcazar from Peru and Federmann from Venezuela. 'Jimenez de Quesada,' writes John Hemming, 'now needed all his skills as a lawyer and diplomat. His ragged veterans were heavily outnumbered by the new arrivals. Each of the other expeditions was better armed and had more horses; each had endured great hardships, and each was led by an ambitious lieutenant-governor,' who reckoned that the rich lands of the Muisca lay within his jurisdiction. Here was the tinder of conflagration; but after several weeks of tension common sense prevailed and the three leaders agreed to submit their claims to Muisca territory to royal arbitration. They travelled together to Cartegena and thence to Spain. Here Quesada met with a cool reception, largely because of his treatment of Sagipa. In an age which believed in the divine right of kings, the death of 1,000 or indeed 10,000 ordinary Indians was unlikely to cause concern, but the death of a single king (albeit a puppet-king) caused a furore. Quesada found himself facing an avalanche of accusations and indictments; it was ten years before he cleared his name and was back in favour, and ten years after that before he led his second and even greater expedition, this time in search of the legendary El Dorado.

Quesada was one of the most determined, popular and humane of the conquistadors; yet in terms of suffering and death his expeditions were a disaster. On his first, he had lost 700 men out of 800 and had been responsible for the death of several thousand Indians. On his second he fared even worse. In 1569 he set out to explore the llanos, those vast and featureless plains-cum-swamps which lie to the east of the Cordillera Oriental. He had with him large numbers of cows, pigs and llamas, 300 Spaniards, 1,100 horses and 1,500 Indians to serve a load-carriers. For two and a half years his men hacked, squelched and staggered through the llanos, plagued by swarms of mosquitoes, debilitated by fever, and dying of starvation. They achieved nothing; and no more than a handful of them, emaciated and half dying, managed to struggle back to Bogota: of Quesada's 300 Spaniards he lost 250, of his 1,100 horses he lost 1,065, of his 1,500 Indians he lost 1,470. Few expeditions before or since can have left in their wake such a trail of dead and dying.

Jimenez de Quesada was one of the few conquistadors who survived into old age and died in his bed; but his death was as steeped in horror as that of any of his contemporaries. He died at the age of 79 of leprosy.

The most important and in many ways the most typical of the conquistadors' pillaging forays was that of Gonzalo Pizarro and Francisco de Orellana.

Gonzalo Pizarro was the epitome of a conquistador. He was brave, handsome, magnificently dressed, a fine horseman and swordsman; but he was also foolish, headstrong, mean, arrogant and cruel. In February 1541 he set out from Quito with 220 Spanish adventurers, 200 horses, great numbers of pigs and llamas, 4,000 press-ganged porters, and a pack of hunting dogs. This was the expedition on which 500 Indians died while crossing the Andes east of Quito, and many others were tortured to death in an attempt to make them reveal the whereabouts of the non existant El Dorado. Too proud and too greedy to admit defeat, Pizarro, with more courage than sense, hacked his way east through unyielding rain forest.

Rain forests are difficult to move through at the best of times – even those who live in them prefer to traverse them by boat rather than on foot. Finding one's way is the first problem, for there is never an horizon on which to pick a point to aim for and, because of the dense canopy of foliage, neither the sun by day nor the stars by night can be used as aids to navigation. Wherever one looks one is faced by the same dense and apparently uniform wall of foliage. And how dense this foliage is. The botanist Richard Spruce wrote:

'Imagine two millions of square miles of forest, uninterrupted save by the streams that traverse it . . . Here the most enormous trees are crowned with thick foliage, decked with fantastic parasites and festooned with lianas which vary in thickness from slender threads to python-like coils, rounded, flattened and twisted. Here too are bamboos 60 feet or more in height, some upright and some entangled in thorny thickets which even an elephant could not penetrate. Everything is covered with tree-ferns, mosses and lichens . . . and the mud, which often comes up to one's knees, makes progress slow and painful.

Before an explorer can move he has to hack out a path. This is exhausting and dangerous work. The festoons of creepers and bryophytes often have to be pinned down and cut individually, and each blow with the machete is liable to bring down a shower of ants, ticks, jiggers (fleas which burrow under the skin to lay their eggs), scorpions or tree snakes. By day the forest swarms with blackfly; by night it swarms with mosquitoes. Much of the vegetation is serrated or thorny, and after only a few hours' cutting men's skins become a festering mosiac of bites and scratches, and their glands swollen with poison. Rain – some 450 inches of it a year – falls almost continuously, and for much of the time a canopy of mist-cum-cloud shrouds the forest in perpetual twilight. The South American Indians have adapted to this somewhat daunting environment; by accepting the forest and becoming part of it, they are able to lead contented, community-orientated and partly nomadic lives; they regard the forest not as a foe to conquer but an ally to live with. The Spaniards, in contrast, hated the forest. It rendered their horses useless, blocked their progress, rusted their swords and their armour, and was frequently a fatal source of hunger, debilitation and disease. Their attitude to it was summed up by Gonzalo Pizarro who, six months after leaving Quito, found himself hopelessly lost, on the banks of a river he couldn't cross, short of food and with every one of his 4,000 Indian load-carriers either fled or dead. 'Pizarro,' we are told by a contemporary, 'was much distressed at finding this terrible country went on and on and he could not get out of it . . . he frequently deplored having undertaken the expedition.' Having got himself lost, he decided that his best hope of survival lay in building a boat. There was no shortage of timber for planking, lianas for cordage or resin for pitch; the camp was scoured for metal that could be turned into nails, 'and in this manner, with the labour of all, a boat was built'. Local Indians had told the Spaniards that there was a country rich in gold and food only a little way downstream, and to see if this was true Pizarro ordered his second-in-command, Francisco de Orellana, to take the boat and 60 men on a reconnaissance.

There are two versions of what happened next. Orellana claims that his boat was swept so far and so fast downriver, and his men were so weak – seven died of starvation in the first couple of days of the voyage – that he was unable to fight his way back: 'Although we wanted to return to the expedition where the Governor [Pizarro] had remained behind, it was impossible to go back because the currents were too strong.' Pizarro claims that he was betrayed and deserted: 'I gave him the brig and 60 of our best men. But instead of bringing back food he continued to head downriver, thus displaying towards the expedition the greatest cruelty that a faithless man could show. He knew he had left us trapped in a vast region among great rivers . . . And he carried off with him all the expedition's arquebuses, crossbows and munitions.'

One can understand how Pizarro felt. However, the river in question was almost certainly the Napo; it was the rainy season, and the Napo in flood is a swirling mud-brown torrent, up whose rapids no unpowered boat can make headway. It therefore seems likely that Orellana was indeed swirled away willy-nilly on what was to prove one of the great (if involuntary) voyages in the history of exploration. For the Napo flows into the Solimoes, and the Solimoes flows into the Amazon, and Orellana was the first man to follow this great river from its headwaters to the sea: a 2,000 mile odyssey through a world much of which no white man before had set eyes on.

The Amazon, in the mid-sixteenth century, was more densely populated than it is today, and as Orellana made his way downriver he passed a succession of tribes whose first contact with men from another race was to prove a terrifying experience. Some fled and allowed the Spaniards to ransack their villages at will. Some greeted them with dignity and offered them food and shelter and only turned against them when they began pillaging and looting. Others met them with war-drums and a hail of arrows. One of the tribes who resisted fiercely was said by the Dominican friar Gaspar de Carvajal to have been led by women. 'Ten or twelve of these Amazons were seen fighting in front of the men as female captains. They were tall and white, with long braided hair wound up about their heads, and went naked with only their private parts covered; in their hands they had bows and arrows, and each did as much fighting as ten Indian men.' Other reports would have us believe that these women warriors had no time for men, that they had intercourse only once a year, kept only their female children, and cut off their right breasts to enable them better to draw their bows. In other words they were replicas of the Amazons of Greek legend, and were the product not of eyewitness observation but of subsequent chroniclers with fertile imaginations and a knowledge of the classics. In spite of this, the world's greatest river continues to be named after these mythical women warriors . . . Not far from the mouth of the Amazon, Orellana put ashore to repair his brig and prepare her for the hazards of the open sea. He then succeeded in sailing her north-west along the coast, until, in September 1542, he half drifted, half sailed, into the Island of Margarita, off present-day Venezuela. In the eighteen months since he left Quito he had travelled 400 miles by land and 4,000 miles by river and by sea: a leap into the unknown which has been described as not so much a *tour de force* as a miracle.

Meanwhile, on the opposite side of the continent, Pizarro was in trouble. For several days he laboriously hacked his way downriver, hoping with every step he cleared that he would find Orellana waiting for him with food. By the time he resigned himself to the fact that he could expect no help from Orellana, he and his men were weakened by fever and exhaustion and dying of starvation. They did the only possible thing and turned back in what they hoped was the direction of Quito. It was a nightmare journey. 'To enable us to proceed,' wrote Quesada, 'the youngest and strongest went ahead, opening up a trail with axes and machetes, having always to cut through dense undergrowth so that all could pass.' It rained twenty-four hours a day, the jungle became metamorphosed to swamp, and at times they were wading waist deep in water. They ate the last of their dogs and the last of their horses. 'Then they ate the leather of their saddles and stirrups, first boiled in water then roasted in the ashes of their fires. They became so sick, sore, wan, wretched and afflicted that it was pitiable to look upon them.' If they hadn't by chance stumbled across an abandoned plantation of manioc, they would almost certainly have perished without trace. The manioc saved their lives – at least for the time being. They stayed beside the plantation for several weeks, then set out once again for Quito. 'Most of them,' we are told, 'were by this time naked and barefoot, covered with sores, and having to open up the path ahead with their swords. All the time it rained, so that they never saw the sun and could never get dry.' It would be hard to imagine a more dispiriting ordeal. However, it was not in the conquistadors' nature to give up; and in June 1542, after sixteen months of purgatory, the survivors staggered back into Quito, 'without a single horse, and with nothing left them but the swords in their hands . . . having failed altogether to reach the land [they] had gone to seek'.

Gonzalo Pizarro died a few years later. He died as he had lived, in acrimony and violence. He was made governor of Quito, and attempted to establish a latterday feudal domain, independent of Spain. For a brief spell he enjoyed absolute power and proved a brutal and repressive dictator who, in his own words, was 'wedded to his horses and his lances', who treated the Indians with sickening cruelty, and who lopped off the heads of those Spaniards who were rash enough to oppose him – John Hemming puts the number of his executed fellow-countrymen at 340. Inevitably Spain sent loyalist troops to reassert her supremacy. Inevitably Pizarro was defeated. He was captured one day, beheaded the next.

Almagro, Quesada and Gonzalo Pizarro were typical conquistadors, and their stories encapsulate – from a Spanish viewpoint – the whole story of the post-conquest Andes. It is not so easy to find a typical Inca whose story encapsulates the same period from an Indian viewpoint; for the indigenous people of the Andes had no chronicler to relate their misfortunes, and they have therefore come down to us as statistics rather than characters. The exceptions are the principal members of the Inca dynasty. Their fate was related in some detail by contemporary chroniclers, and the story of one of these Inca rulers, Manco, might be said to epitomize the story of his people as a whole.

Manco Inca was born in Cuzco in about 1516. He was therefore only in his mid-teens when he first made contact with the Spaniards, coming one night into their camp as a fugitive from the armies of the Atahualpan north who were seeking to kill him. It is not therefore surprising that he saw the Spaniards, initially, as friends. For a while the relationship between Manco and the conquistadors was amicable. The Inca was crowned, with much pomp and ceremony, in Cuzco. He was realistic enough to make no protest at the looting of his capital, and when Almagro set out on his expedition to Chile Manco gave him 15,000 of his troops to ensure safe passage. What turned Manco against the conquistadors was partly the way Almagro treated these troops – using them as chain-bound load-carriers and starving them to death – and partly the personal abuse that he suffered at the hands of the young Pizarros. Gonzalo Pizarro forced the Inca, under threat of torture, to hand over vast quantities of his personal treasure; he also lusted after the Inca's Coya Queen, the young and beautiful Cura Ocllo, and demanded that Manco hand her over as well. 'Now, Señor Manco Inca,' Pizarro is reported to have said, 'this gold and silver is all very fine, but let's have the lady Coya. She's what we really want.' In despair Manco persuaded one of Cura Ocllo's companions to dress up as the Coya, 'and when the Spaniards saw her handed over, so well dressed and looking so beautiful, they were all delighted and shouted: "Yes, that's the one! She's the Coya! Weigh her in!"' However, the deception was soon discovered, and Manco wrote bitterly: 'Gonzalo Pizarro took my wife, and still has her.' It was for Cura Ocllo the first in a chain of abuses that make her story one of the most terrible personal indictments of human cruelty.

It may have been the rape of his Coya Queen that finally drove Manco from cooperation to rebellion. Throughout the summer of 1535 stories of the Spaniards' greed and brutality had been percolating through to Cuzco, and Manco was now beginning to realize that his people had escaped the suzerainty of the Quitans only to fall victim to the far more demanding and humiliating suzerainty of the foreign invaders. His advisers begged him to break with the conquistadors: 'We cannot,' they argued, 'spend our lives in misery and bondage. Let us rebel, and, if we have to, die in defence of our freedom and our women and children.' Manco agreed. However, his first attempt to slip away from the capital and raise the standard of rebellion ended in disaster. He was captured, brought back under guard and imprisoned. By all accounts he was brutally treated. According to his son, he was shackled with iron chains about his neck and feet, and burned with a lighted candle. Christobal de Molina wrote: 'They treated him very, very disgracefully, keeping him imprisoned, urinating on him and sleeping with his wives, so that he was deeply distressed.' Manco himself said that the Spaniards called him a dog, struck him and took away his wives and his land. His disillusion with them is summed up in a single sentence: 'When I first met them I believed that they were kind people and, as they claimed, the children of Viracocha; but events didn't take the course I had anticipated, and it is clear from the way they have behaved since they invaded my kingdom that they are not children of Viracocha but rather children of the devil.' Manco's second attempt to leave Cuzco was more carefully orchestrated. In the autumn of 1536, at about the time that the rains were ending and the campaigning season was about to begin, he escaped to the Yucay Valley some 20 miles to the north of Cuzco. Here, in the bleak hills that lie at the heart of the kingdom of the Sun God, Manco presided over a secret assembly of chiefs, military commanders and *orejones*, all of whom drank an oath that they would drive every Christian from their homeland or die in the attempt.

The Inca Empire didn't go under without a struggle. For more than five years Manco led a spirited resistance movement, first hemming in and very nearly obliterating the Spaniards in Cuzco, then waging a guerrilla campaign against them from the mountain fastnesses of Vilcabamba, Ollantaytambo and Machu Picchu. These years of resistance were, for the people of the Andes, a time of confusion and horror. Not only did Indian fight Spaniard, but both the Indians and the Spaniards fought among themselves. Every army that marched against Manco had its quota of anti-Inca levies; every year the pro-Almagro conquistadors and the pro-Pizarro conquistadors were at each other's throats – in 1538 the Pizarros had Almagro publicly garrotted; in 1541 the Almagrists hacked Francisco to death in his palace in Lima. All accounts agree that the war was conducted with a cruelty that has left scars which time has been unable to heal. 'This,' wrote de Guzman, 'was the most cruel and dreadful war the world has ever known. For between Christians and Moors there was at least some fellow-feeling . . . but in this Indian war there is no such feeling on either side, and they give each other the cruellest deaths they can think of.' The Indians hacked off the hands and feet of captured Spaniards and watched them bleed to death. The Spaniards burned, mutilated and impaled captured Indians; they also, as part of a deliberate campaign of terror, murdered and mutilated Indian women. To quote John Hemming: 'Hernando Pizarro ordered his men to kill any women they caught during the fighting. The idea was to deprive the fighting men of the women who did so much to serve and carry for them. "This was done from then onwards, and the stratagem worked admirably and caused much terror; for the Indians feared to lose their wives, and the latter feared to die."' It is perhaps worth making the point that these accusations of cruelty are not the sort of exaggerated propaganda which, in time of war, one combatant often levels against another without justification. They are stories that have come down to us not from the Indians (who, of course, couldn't record them), but from the Spaniards themselves, and are derived not from hearsay but from eyewitness accounts and contemporary records. Perhaps the most terrible of all these stories is that of the treatment meted out to Manco's Coya Queen.

Cura Ocllo had escaped from the Pizarros at the same time as her husband and was with him during most of the great rebellion, first at the siege of Cuzco and subsequently in a succession of mountain hideouts – it is said to have been the Coya Queen herself who first spotted Spanish troops approaching Oncoy and gave the warning that enabled Manco to lay an ambush in which 24 of Pizarro's soldiers were killed. However, in the battle of Chuquillusca (not far from Manco's headquarters at Vilcabama) the Incas were defeated; Manco only escaped by swimming a fast-flowing river, and Cura Ocllo was captured. During the journey back towards Cuzco the Spaniards attempted to rape her; but, we are told, 'she defended herself with great spirit, covering her body with filthy matter so that the men trying to rape her would be nauseated. She did this several times until they reached Ollantaytambo.' Nevertheless, at Ollantaytamo both Francisco Pizarro and his secretary are said to have raped her. Worse was in store for her. In an effort to persuade the Inca to surrender, Pizarro sent him envoys with gifts that included 'a Negro, much silk and a horse'. Manco, however, was in no mood to surrender and killed the entire party. In fury and frustration, Pizarro took his revenge on the Inca's beloved wife. Cura Ocllo was stripped naked, tied to a post in front of the Spanish army, beaten insensible by Canari Indians and finally shot to death with arrows. To add to the horror, her mutilated body was floated downriver in a basket to where Pizarro knew it would be found by the Inca. 'Manco,' we are told, 'was beside himself with despair and grief at the death of his wife. He wept and made great mourning for her, for he had loved her dearly.'

Manco's own death, only a few years later, was almost as tragic as that of his Coya Queen. In 1544 the first Viceroy of Peru arrived from Spain, with promises that the rule of law would be enforced and that the Indians would be given at least some voice in the government of their territory. Manco met the Viceroy's deputies, and had hopes of fashioning with them an Inca-cum-Spanish alliance which would rid the Andes of the Pizarro faction; but before the scheme could get off the ground he was murdered. A few years earlier Manco had saved the lives of a number of Almagrist fugitives. He befriended these men who had been found lost and starving in the rain forest, giving them sanctuary and hospitality – houses to live in and women to prepare meals for them. For two years the Almagrists had lived with the Inca as favoured guests; however, in the hope of ingratiating themselves with the Spanish authorities, seven of them now decided to murder him. It was done during a game of quoits. The leader of the assassins suddenly produced a hidden dagger, jumped on the Inca as he was about to make his throw and stabbed him in the back:

His companions [writes John Hemming] then repeatedly plunged the dagger into Manco in front of his nine-year-old son so that he fell to the ground covered in blood and wounds, and they left him for dead. So ended Manco Inca. The heroic warrior who had so frequently confronted Spanish forces and eluded Spanish pursuers, fell to Spanish treachery. He was stabbed in the back by men whose lives he had spared and who had enjoyed his hospitality for two years . . . His death was a tragic loss for the natives of Peru; for he was the only native prince whose royal lineage and stubborn courage enjoyed the respect of Spaniards and Indians alike.

It would be an exaggeration to say that the treatment of Manco and Cura Ocllo was typical of the treatment meted out to the people of the Andes; nevertheless their story must have had many parallels among the hundreds of thousands of unknown altiplano and forest dwellers who suffered cruelty, abuse and death at the hands of the conquistadors.

In the short term the cruelty of the conquerors led to an escalation of reprisals in which the Indians were as guilty of atrocities as the Spaniards. Many of these atrocities were directed at the Catholic Church. The martyrdom of Father Diego Ortiz is a case in point. Ortiz was an enlightened and progressive Augustinian, who was a close personal friend of the Inca, ran a flourishing church in Vilcabamba and was much respected for his skill in medicine. However, when the Inca Titu Cusi (Manco's son) died unexpectedly in Vilcabamba, the priest was suspected – without the slightest justification – of having poisoned him. He was seized, his hands were tied behind his back with such violence that his wrists were dislocated, and he was stripped naked and left overnight in the open. Next day he was tied to a cross and beaten. The following day a hole was bored through his jaw, a rope passed through the hole and he was led in a macabre procession to the nearby town of Marcanay. According to eyewitnesses he endured his ordeal with great fortitude, 'raising his eyes to heaven and asking God to forgive his tormentors their sins; for this the Indians jeered at him'. His fortitude didn't save him. At Marcanay he was struck repeatedly on the back of the neck with a mace until he died. His body was then laid out on the highway and ritually trampled on; finally it was shovelled into a deep and narrow hole, head first with a spear thrust between the legs; the hole was then filled with filth and saltpetre – the idea being that from such a grave God would be unable to raise him from the dead.

It would be comforting to think that in the long term this sort of violence has had little effect on South American history, that such things don't happen today. Unfortunately this is not the case, for the cruelty of the conquistadors was followed by the cruelty of the *encomenderos* and mine-owners, and their cruelty has been followed in recent years by the cruelty of the land-developers, so that in many parts of South America the relationship between Indians and whites has seldom risen above the nadir that it registered in the sixteenth century. Murders as pointless and as tragic as that of Diego Ortiz are still taking place. Only a few months ago an American relief worker was beaten to death in an obscure Bolivian village. The reason: he was carrying a blood donor card, and the villagers so misunderstood the meaning of this that they thought the man had come to collect Indian blood to take back to American hospitals to save American lives. And so the violence is perpetuated not only generation after generation but century after century.

By the end of the sixteenth century the original conquistador-adventurers had been superseded by new-style government officials often appointed direct from Spain; and now more than ever before there was a dichotomy between intention and achievement. It is a widely held misconception that the Spaniards exploited the Indians without greatly bothering about the rights or wrongs of what they were doing. This idea was popularized by nineteenth-century Protestant historians, who delighted in portraying Catholics with a crucifix in one hand and the impedimenta of Torquemada in the other. However, in reality, both the Spanish Crown and the Catholic Church agonized almost *ad nauseum* over the ethics of conquest. As early as 1511 a Dominican friar told the conquistadors: 'You are in mortal sin because of the cruelty and tyranny you practise in dealing with these innocent people. By what right do you keep them in such cruel and horrible servitude? On what authority have you waged a detestable war against those whose only "crime" was to live quietly and peaceably in their own land?' Such views were by no means uncommon in the sixteenth century; they were held by many distinguished Spaniards – colonists, government officials and churchmen alike – perhaps the best known being Bartholme de las Casas, who devoted his life to championing the cause of the Indians. This pro-Indian lobby was especially strong among members of the court and government, and it was largely as a result of their advocacy that the Council of the Indies produced a spate of extremely enlightened legislation. Serious efforts were made to protect the Indians from exploitation. All forms of slavery were declared illegal; Indians were never to be used as load-carriers, they were to be paid for their labour, their roads and irrigation works were to be left undamaged. Serious efforts were also made to introduce them to what was assumed (however erroneously) to be a higher (i.e., a Spanish) way of life; they were to be allowed to trade, to own property and to take Communion; they were to enjoy the same civil liberties as the Spaniards themselves.

It was, however, one thing to pass laws in Madrid, and another to enforce them in Lima or Quito. The Spanish empire, which in its heyday comprised almost half the known world, was too far-flung, fragmented and diverse to be kept under effective centralized control, and the ideals of the mother country were all too likely to founder when faced with the harsh realities of life in some jungle clearing in a distant land. The basic fact of life in the Spanish domain of the Andes was that Indian labour was passive, plentiful and cheap; the quickest way to grow rich was to exploit this labour, and this is what the Spaniards did. There were two fields in particular in which Indians labour was exploited: mining and coca-growing.

The Spaniards' lust for gold was slaked initially by looting and melting down the Incas' wealth of artefacts. When this source dried up, they turned to mining, and in particular to silver mining. It was the old search for El Dorado in a new guise. In 1545 huge deposits of silver-ore were discovered at Potosi in the Bolivian highlands at an altitude of more than 11,000 feet. A few years later mercury was discovered at nearby Huancavelica. Mercury is an essential ingredient in the efficient refining of silver, and with both metals readily obtainable the Spanish viceroy boasted that he would 'make Potosi and Huancavelica the greatest marriage in the world . . . the twin posts on which this kingdom is supported'. He did exactly that. Within a decade Potosi had mushroomed into the largest town in the New World, with a population of over 120,000, and a weekly output of 175,000 pesos' worth of silver. Indians from all over the Andes were brought to work in the mines.

It was a hard life. The Bolivian altiplano is seared by blinding sun by day and polar cold by night; strong winds whip away the thin dun-coloured soil; violent rains sculpt the landscape into grotesque patterns; the air is thin, and strangers, lungs labouring, suffer both shortness of breath and disorientation; there are no trees and no grass, nothing but mile after 100-square mile of dessicated rock that is veined with silver. Into this rock the reluctant miners were forced to sink tunnels-cum-shafts, some nearly 1,000 feet deep.

The Indians enter these infernal pits by means of leather ropes, like swaying staircases. Once inside they spend the whole week [in a shaft] without emerging, working by candlelight in perpetual darkness in the bowels of the earth, where the air is thick and evil-smelling. Both descent and ascent are highly dangerous, for they come up loaded with their sack of metal tied to their backs, taking fully five hours step by step, and if they make the slightest slip they are likely to fall some 700 feet to their death.

The Indians hated working in the mines, but were obliged to do so because of the prevailing *encomiendas* system of forced labour, a system whereby wealthy Spaniards would be granted a right to the labour of a certain number of Indians in a specific area. Many Indians tried to escape this forced labour by hiding in the mountains or the rain forest; they became fugitives in their own homeland. This led to a decline in the number of those engaged in farming – the occupation on which all else in the Andes has traditionally depended – and this in turn led to privation and depopulation. It has been estimated that in the 100 years between 1550 and 1650 the number of people living in the altiplano declined from over 5 million to under 1 million. Many Spaniards spoke out against the evils of Potosi and Huancavelica: 'It is contrary to divine and natural law,' wrote Domingo de Santo Tomas in 1550, 'that men should be forced to endure such excessive labour, so prejudicial to their health and their lives.' It was largely as a result of this sort of criticism that laws were passed stipulating that the Indians should be fairly paid and well treated. Again, however, these laws proved easier to pass than to enforce. The truth was that both the Spanish settlers and the Spanish Crown derived huge profits from their South American mines.

The other great industry which involved forced labour was coca-growing.

Coca is a plant of the family *erythroxylacaea* which grows on the lower east-facing slopes of the Andes; the plant is about six to eight feet high, and has laurel-like leaves. When chewed, these leaves act as a mild narcotic, deadening pain, hunger and fatigue. Coca had been used in tribal rituals for thousands of years, and the Incas incorporated it into the accoutrements of their religion, making its use a privilege of the élite – during the domination of the Incas, commoners were not allowed to take coca except with the permission of the Inca or his representative. It was because of this tie-up with the Inca religion and not because of any medical concern that the Church condemned the use of coca – 'a plant', according to Diego de Robles, 'that was invented by the devil for the destruction of the Natives'. However, in spite of priestly disapproval, addiction to coca (like addiction to alcohol) increased enormously in the years immediately following the Spanish conquest. There were several reasons for this. The Inca ban limiting its use to the privileged few was rescinded; the introduction of money facilitated its purchase; and, most telling of all, the trauma of their subjugation to an alien race led the Indians to grasp whatever escapist solace was available to them. In the same way that nineteenth-century Australian Aborigines took in despair to alcohol, so seventeenth-century South American Indians took to coca. The contemporary chronicler, Hernando de Santillan, wrote that 'they first became addicted to it soon after the conquest of their country'. The Spaniards were quick to take advantage of this addiction; they fuelled it, and made profit from it.

Large areas on the periphery of the rain forest were planted with coca bushes, and large numbers of Andean Indians were forced to leave the high, cool and dry altiplano and work in these low, hot and humid plantations. It was like being transported to another world. The Indians' respiratory system, developed over many generations to operate in the thin air of 10,000-12,000 feet, was unable to adjust; they died in their thousands of anaemia and the dreadful *mal de los Andes* or uta, which eats away the nose, lips and throat and ends in an agonizing death. It has been estimated that over 40 per cent of the Indians who were drafted to work in the coca fields died, while most of those who managed to struggle back to their mountain villages were left pale, weak and afflicted by a lethargy from which they never recovered. There was, from churchmen in particular, a chorus of protest at these conditions, and a royal decree branded coca 'an illusion of the devil, in the cultivation of which an infinite number of Indians perish through heat and disease'. However, coca-growing, like mining, was big business. An average-sized plantation made 80,000 pesos' profit a year; the traffic with Potosi alone made 500,000 pesos. The result was a powerful coca lobby which managed to block well-intentioned reform and maintain production; de Santillan probably hit the nail on the head when he wrote, 'down there in the coca plantations one disease is worse than all the rest: that is the unrestrained greed of the Spaniards'.

In spite of the good intentions of the Spanish government, it has been reliably estimated that nine million Indians died in the Andean mines and one million in the Andean coca plantations.

Spanish suzerainty over the Andes lasted for some 275 years. These, basically, were years of exploitation, with the Spaniards first divesting the Incas of their treasure and then exploiting their mineral wealth and labour. Moreover, the wealth derived from this exploitation was not ploughed back but was channelled direct to Spain. Spanish trading policy was restrictive and for most of the colonial period the Andes were, to the outside world, a no-go area. Foreigners were prohibited even to set foot in the mountains; trade had to be exclusively with the mother country. The net result was the 'Spanish night' of Pablo Neruda's poetic imagery – '*Lord de mare, nos amarra los suenos la noche espanola*' (Lord of the sea, the Spanish night binds down our dreams) – a situation of poverty in the midst of plenty which for so long has characterized so much of South American history.

Despite this exploitation, the South American Indians fared a good deal better than their counterparts in other colonized countries. In Australia and North America the indigenous population was reduced almost to the point of extermination; in South America the indigenous population is larger today than it was on the eve of the Spanish conquest. In South Africa interracial marriage was, until recently, forbidden by law, and it is still not possible for the partners in such marriages to live together; in South America there is a large and flourishing class of mestizos, and mixed marriages are common. In areas like Polynesia hardly anyone today speaks Polynesian, and the traditional culture has been obliterated; in the Andes the majority of the population still speak Quechua, and the old culture coexists, albeit at times uneasily, with the new. All this is evidence both of the resilience of the Andean people, and of the concern for these people shown by the Spanish government and the Catholic Church.

The role of the Church in helping the Indians adjust to the alien culture that was being imposed on them should not be underestimated. The pre-conquest South American Indians were a deeply spiritual people whose religion was woven inextricably into the fabric of their lives; they venerated holy places, went on pilgrimages, enjoyed seasonal rituals, had a priestly hierarchy and observed a strict moral code. For such a people the transition from their old beliefs to Christianity didn't involve such a leap into the unknown as was demanded, say, of the Polynesians or the Australian Aborigines; they were able to preserve many of their traditional values, beliefs and customs within the structure of the Catholic Church. This is one reason why the Church has been so successful in South America, having now almost 100 million adherents. In the days after the conquest the Church provided the Indian and mestizo elements in its congregation with what might be termed a bridge, a stepping-stone to help them make the transition from the old culture to the new, while in recent years priests are continually speaking out against injustice to the Indians, and have been tortured to death in Chilean prisons and flung to their death from Contra helicopters for their pains.

The story of the Spanish conquest is one of pure brutality and greed. The story of the post-conquest Spanish administration, in contrast, is a story not only of exploitation and repression but also of good intentions, tolerance and concern.

Chapter 7

The Naturalists

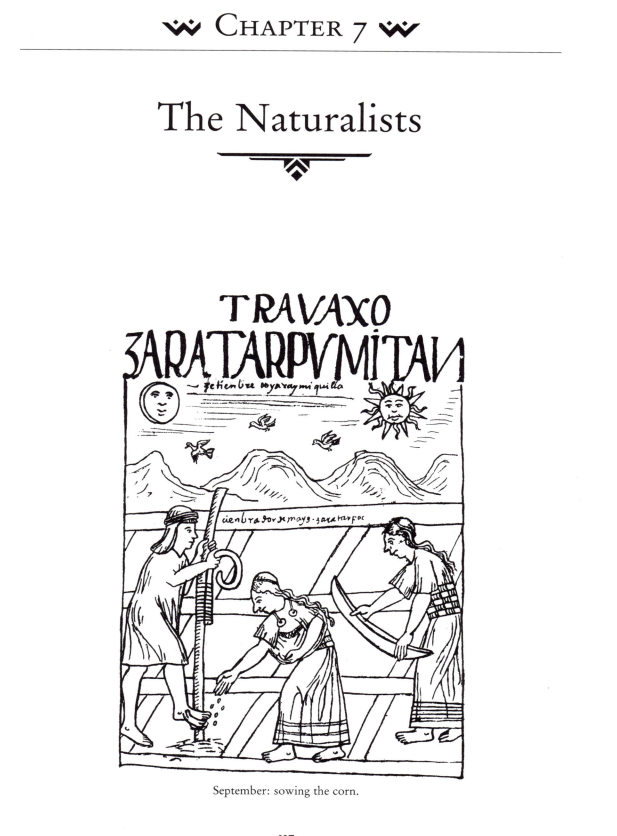

September: sowing the corn.

The seamen whose voyages opened up for Europeans worlds hitherto unknown to them in Africa, Asia and the Americas were almost all Portuguese or Spanish. It was the Portuguese Dias who first rounded the southern tip of Africa, and the Portuguese da Gama who was the first European to reach India by sea; it was under the Spanish flag that Columbus set foot in America and Magellan crossed the Pacific. It is therefore hardly surprising that when a dispute arose as to whom these 'Newfounde Lands of the Worlde' belonged, the Pope, by the Treaty of Tordesillas, divided the earth in half and gave one half to Portugal and one to Spain. The Andes fell to Spain; and for more than 250 years the Spaniards regarded the range as theirs by virtue of discovery, conquest and divine decree. And theirs exclusively. Non-Spaniards, with the exception of mercenaries in their armies, were *persona non grata*.

The leitmotiv of Spanish colonial policy throughout the seventeenth and eighteenth centuries was a determination to preserve this monopoly.

It was a hopeless task, and one which exacerbated ill feeling between the nations of the Iberian peninsula and the rest of Europe: 'I would like to know,' wrote the King of France, 'what clause in Adam's will entitles the kings of Castile and Portugal to divide the earth between them!' Europe suffered a succession of wars which were part dynastic, part religious and part colonial. In the New World the Spaniards were so determined that outsiders should neither enter their territory nor enjoy the fruits of it that they adopted a stultifying policy of secrecy and restriction in an attempt to seal off their South American colonies from the outside world. The result was economic stagnation, and poverty. Instead of ploughing back the gold of the Incas and the silver of Potosi into local industry, farming and trade, the money was channelled back to Spain to pay for the mother country's enormous squadrons of ships and armies of mercenaries. As H.A.L. Fisher put it, 'money was mistaken for wealth, and the true foundation of economic prosperity was ignored'. It is one of the anomalies of history that in spite of the vast quantities of gold and silver which flowed to Spain from her South American colonies, both were almost perpetually bankrupt.

One result of this Spanish policy of secrecy and restriction is that comparatively little is known about life in the Andes in the centuries that immediately followed the conquest. Many reports were sent back to Spain – some by priests, some by administrators and some by specialists in farming or mining – but the majority were suppressed either by the Council of the Indies or by King Philip II himself, on the grounds that they might be useful to those who were ever trying to divest Spain's far-flung empire of its riches. It is another of history's anomalies that Spanish explorers, Spanish administrators and Spanish priests were to achieve considerable success in the New World, only to have their successes deliberately concealed by the Spanish authorities. For by the end of the sixteenth century Spain was sated with discoveries. The last thing she wanted was more new worlds to conquer or new people to subjugate. All her energies were concentrated on husbanding, for her exclusive use, what she already had.

So almost as soon as South America was discovered it became cocooned in a veil of secrecy. Rumours percolated through to Europe of the continent's 'rare and singular vertues, of its divers Herbes, Trees, Plantes, Oyles and precious Stones', but the facts about these wonders were all too often buried in Spanish archives, unknown to the rest of the world. It was rumoured that South America could boast birds enormous as the roc and as long-lived as humans, carnivorous fish which hunted in packs and could devour a human being within seconds, and trees whose magic leaves could stave off fatigue and hunger and make those who chewed them immune to pain. These rumours were true, but it was almost two centuries before evidence to substantiate them was forthcoming; and the men who first provided this evidence, and whose travels made the first inroads into the Spanish 'closed shop' of South America, were the naturalists.

Of the naturalists' many forays into the Andes perhaps the most important were the geodetic expedition organized by the French Académie des Sciences, the plant-collecting expedition of Ruiz and Pavón, the travels of von Humboldt, and the botanical researches of Wallace and Bates.

The French geodetic expedition was led by Louis Godin with the young and flamboyant Charles-Marie de La Condamine as its second-in-command. Godin was one of those dedicated, self-effacing scientists whose work has never been given the recognition it deserves. It was largely due to his expertise and tenacity of purpose that a section of the Andes was for the first time meticulously surveyed. However, once this work had been completed he remained in Peru, published little and disappeared from the limelight. La Condamine, in contrast, was drawn to limelight as a salamander to flame. Aristocratic, brave, highly intelligent and highly efficient, he was one of the eighteenth century's new breed of entrepreneur-cum-scientist, ever eager to discover more about the mysteries of our planet, ever eager too to cash in on his discoveries. Like most of the French petty nobility of his day, as soon as he had completed his education he joined the army where he quickly made his mark as an astronomer. Before he was thirty he was elected to the Académie des Sciences, and became embroiled in the popular scientific dispute of the day: was the earth an oblate spheroid (slightly flattened at the poles) or a prolate spheroid (slightly elongated at the poles)? The former theory was championed by Isaac Newton and the British; the latter theory was championed by Jacques Cassini and the French. The question was more than esoteric, it was of vital importance in map-making and navigation. The only way to decide which theory was right was by on-the-spot investigation – that is to say by measuring the arc of a degree of latitude both in the Arctic and on the equator and comparing results. One expedition headed for Lapland; another, led by Godin, for the Andes.

Godin's expedition had the express approval of Philip V, and this seems to have been the first time that Spain had officially allowed outsiders to set foot in her South American territories. There were several reasons for the concession and several strings attached to it. France and Spain now both had a Bourbon king who favoured family cooperation; the French undertook to meet all the expedition's costs; they also agreed to the appointment of two Spanish naval officers as supernumeraries, and it says much for the tact and good sense of these two Spaniards, Jorge Juan y Santacilia and Antonio de Ulloa, that throughout most of the expedition they remained on good terms with the French while at the same time ensuring that Godin and his team 'kept their eyes on the ground' and made no attempt to unravel the tangled web of Spain's colonial secrets. The expedition left La Rochelle in May 1735, and few imagined as they watched the Isle de Ré disappear into the haze that it would be thirty-eight years before some of them saw their homeland again.

The French and Spanish scientists met for the first time in Cartagena, and established an immediate rapport. All were young (La Condamine 34, Jorge Juan 22, Ulloa no more than 20), all had the same aristocratic/scientific background and all were anxious for their joint venture to be a success. 'There are no problems with our French colleagues,' wrote Ulloa, 'which can not be overcome by goodwill and good humour.' They spent only a couple of weeks in Cartagena; long enough for La Condamine to note the addiction of both men and women to smoking cigars and dancing the 'grossly indecent fandango', and for Juan and Ulloa to start compiling the monumental report which, it now became apparent, was to be a secondary objective of the expedition. For Ulloa had been ordered by Philip V to compile a dossier on the state of Spain's South American possessions, and over the next eight years the young Spaniard pieced together what von Hagen describes as 'the most astute report ever made on a colonial empire', a mass of accurate facts and eminently sensible recommendations for reform.

The scientists left Cartagena in November 1735, having decided to reach their destination, Quito, via the isthmus of Panama and the Pacific. It was to prove a long but not unpleasant journey, always leisurely, often interesting, seldom exciting. Not until March 1736 – almost a year after leaving La Rochelle – did they catch their first glimpse of the Pacific Andes; for during the early stages of their voyage from Panama the words 'fog' or 'mist' had appeared every day in their ship's log. However, on 9 March the mist suddenly lifted, and there in all its splendour lay the Cordillera Occidental, 'seemingly within a stone's throw of our port beam, its lower slopes green with rain forest, its upper white with snow'. They headed towards the little port of Manta.

Here the expedition made a spur-of-the-moment decision to split up, La Condamine and the astronomer Pierre Bouguer staying behind to start surveying, while the rest of the party continued as planned to Guayaquil and thence to Quito. The reason for this decision was that the semi-desert coast to the north of Manta looked ideal terrain for establishing a base-line near the equator on which to build further surveys by triangulation. However, the scientists had reckoned without the *garu*, the mist-cum-fog which hangs like a semi-diaphanous canopy over the Ecuador coast, often obscuring the sun until late afternoon. Having spent several not very profitable weeks enshrouded in the *garu*, La Condamine made another spur-of-the-moment decision. He decided to make the rest of the journey to Quito not by the usual route through Guayaquil, but by striking directly east across the Andes.

His companion in this ambitious venture was Pedro Vincente Maldonado y Sotomayor, the youngest son of an aristocratic Creole family. Maldonado, who had turned up unexpectedly one evening in the French camp, was gifted, energetic and ambitious. At the age of only 27 he had been appointed governor of the province of Esmeraldas, and he hoped to bring prosperity to his newly acquired domain by bringing back into use the old Inca trade route between Quito and the coast via the Rio Esmeraldas. This, he told the scientists, was a far shorter and better route than the established one via Guayaquil, and to prove his point he offered to take them to Quito via the Esmeraldas. The cautious Bouguer declined, and departed for Guayaquil. The more adventurous – or more gullible – La Condamine accepted.

Their journey was not remarkable, but it demonstrates clearly the spectacular diversity of the Andes and the formidable difficulties of travelling through them.

The first part of their route lay over the coastal desert. This was a littoral almost totally devoid of water or vegetation, yet teeming with life. For offshore lay one of the richest fisheries on earth – the breeding-ground of the misnamed Californian sardine and Peruvian anchovy – and these fish attracted birds in their millions: white-breasted cormorants, mottled-grey boobies, raucous gannets, great colonies of nut-brown pelicans and flocks of the graceful Andean flamingo. The rocks above the waterline were white with their skeletons, their droppings and the pulverized remains of sea shells and fish bones, 'so white', wrote La Condamine, 'that from it there emanated a glare as bright as sunlight on snow'.

As the two men approached the mouth of the Esmeraldas the desert was transformed with dramatic swiftness to rain forest. The people here were pure Negroes, descended from the survivors of a wrecked slave ship; they were well disposed towards Maldonado, and ferried the scientists wherever they wanted to go as they mapped the mouth of the river. One day they brought them *caoutchouc*, which La Condamine described as 'a sort of stretchable cloth made out of the coagulated sap from a tree of the genus *hevea*'. La Condamine was fascinated and, finding that the substance was not only stretchable but cushioning and waterproof, he made himself a *caoutchouc* container to house the more delicate of his instruments. It is often claimed that this was the first recorded use by a European of a substance soon to help build empires and revolutionize industry: rubber. In fact several Jesuit priests had a prior knowledge of rubber, and it would be more accurate to say that La Condamine was the first to introduce a rubber-manufactured product to Europe.

When they had finished mapping the mouth of the Esmeraldas the two men were ferried upriver in style in a *pirogue*, a narrow 40-foot canoe. At first the river was wide and slow-flowing, its banks a wall of luxuriant rain forest, from which La Condamine collected a variety of exotic plants and observed an even greater variety of exotic birds: the huge-billed toucan, the orange-feathered trogon, and the iridescent humming-bird, no larger than a moth, which hung suspended in mid-air while it fed. However, the Esmeraldas is a chameleon river; by their third day in the *pirogue* it had narrowed, and was flowing strongly between great walls of rock. Poling became more arduous. Frequent halts were called for, and it was during one of these halts that the Negroes brought La Condamine a substance which looked like an amalgam of mercury and gold. It was only when samples were subsequently analyzed by metallurgists in France that it was realized a new metal had been discovered: platinum.

On their sixth day they came to Puerto de Quito, beyond which the river was no longer navigable. In spite of its grandiloquent name the 'port' consisted of no more than a handful of empty and semiderelict buildings, for Maldonado's dream of opening up the Rio Esmeraldas to commerce was not yet realized. This was as far as the Negroes were willing to take them; they were people of the coast and were ill at ease in the cooler foothills of the Andes. However, no sooner had the scientists' first helpers disappeared downriver, than others materialized from the forest: Colorado Indians: small, near-naked men whose hair and bodies were dyed bright vermillion, and who agreed to carry the scientists' baggage on the next stage of their journey.

They had now covered more than half the distance to Quito, but the most difficult part of their journey, the ascent of the Andes, was still to come. As they began to climb a barely-discernible path it started to rain, and the rain was to continue without respite for the next five days; for they were now entering the cloud forest, that belt of sodden and mist-enveloped woodland which from roughly 3,000 feet to 10,000 feet clings to the west face of the Andes. In spite of the bizarre beauty of the cloud forest with its riot of exotic plants and birds, it was a depressing journey. Their clothes became sodden. The ground became a quagmire of mud – for every step the scientists took forward, they slid half a step back. As they climbed higher the trail steepened, the temperature dropped, and soon to the discomfort of rain and mud was added that of cold. A present-day botanist following much the same trail described his experience as 'the ultimate in masochism'. At 7,000 feet their Colorado helpers had had enough; they turned back, and from now on La Condamine and Maldonado had to rely on the Indians whose villages they passed through to loan them mules. By the time they emerged on to the *paramo* – a boglike grassland carpeted with mosses and lichens – La Condamine was already suffering from dizziness and shortage of breath, and still the snow-capped peaks loomed up ahead of them. By the time they had struggled to the head of a 12,000 foot pass through the cordillera, both men were in the last stages of exhaustion. Around them was a scene of utter desolation, a titanic landscape of naked rock devoid of vegetation or life; but below and ahead, on the far side of the pass, lay the valley of the altiplano, a chequerboard of farmland and scrub half hidden in cloud. A couple of days later they were looking down on their destination, Quito. 'The city,' wrote La Condamine, 'has a most spectacular setting: its white buildings cling to the slopes of a valley which nestles among a veritable tribe of volcanoes.' Encircling the ancient Inca stronghold the travellers could count fifteen great volcanic peaks, many of them active, dominated by the bulk of Chimborazo, then believed to be the highest mountain in the world. Next morning when they rode into Quito they discovered that Juan, Ulloa and the rest of the scientists had arrived a few days earlier.

The geodesists were now ready to start work on measuring a degree of latitude on the equator, and as they studied the encircling cordillera it was obvious this would be no easy task. It was Louis Godin, the astronomer and senior mathematician, who was in charge of surveying. Under his guidance a base-line was established on the plains of Yarqui, about 12 miles north-east of Quito. The surveyors then began to build up by observation, from either end of this line, a series of triangulations which would eventually extend over 3° of latitude, i.e., for a distance of some 200 miles. It was difficult work. In those days surveying instruments – plane tables, measuring-rods, transits, signalling-lamps and quadrants – were nothing like as sophisticated as they were a century later when most other parts of the world were for the first time accurately mapped. Godin and his team were pioneers. They were also working in exceptionally difficult conditions. In the plains the diurnal change in temperature was almost beyond belief: 'in mid-afternoon our mercury records more than 100°; during the night it records well below zero'. In the cordillera whose snow-capped peaks had to be climbed to serve as base-points for triangulation, conditions were even worse, and the surveyors were drenched with rain, battered by hail, lashed by violent winds and storms, and terrified by volcanic eruptions; often for days at a time observations were impossible because of mist and cloud. Their mules and equipment fell into ravines and were lost; their Indian helpers fell ill and left them; one of their scientists, Couplet, died of malaria; one of their botanists, Joseph de Jussier lost his collection of specimens and went out of his mind; their doctor, Jean Senièrgues, was battered to death by an enraged mob – a tragedy which underlines a perennial problem with expeditions: no matter how worthy their aims, they are often misunderstood by the local population. The people of Quito, for example, were convinced that the French scientists' measuring-poles were divining-rods for locating buried gold.

When the survey was about two-thirds finished Juan and Ulloa were summoned to Callao, the port of Lima. Here they were asked to help organize the port's defences against an expected attack by a British fleet commanded by Admiral Anson which was currently circumnavigating the world in a voyage part exploratory, part piratical and wholly disastrous. Anson in fact never attacked Callao – his crews were too decimated by scurvy – but for more than a year Juan and Ulloa were unable to take part in the surveying. In their absence La Condamine ordered a mini-pyramid to be built at either end of their base-line to commemorate the expedition's achievements. Each pyramid was topped by fleur-de-lis and emblazoned with a Latin inscription attributing the survey to La Condamine, Godin and Bouguer. Juan felt, with some justification, that the failure to mention his name and Ulloa's was belittling to Spain, and there began an unedifying and comic-opera dispute, which engendered considerable heat in Europe, where it was felt national honour was at stake. After a spate of litigation and a plethora of orders and counter-orders, the pyramids were demolished.

There followed another and far more serious blow to French pride. The expedition to Lapland, which had been measuring a degree of latitude in the Arctic, completed its survey and announced its findings; and when these were compared with results already ascertained in the Andes, it was realized there was no longer room for controversy. The earth was an oblate spheroid. Newton and the British had been right; Cassini and the French had been wrong. As Voltaire succinctly put it, 'Both the Earth and the Cassinis have been flattened!'

This was a bitter disappointment to Godin and his surveyors. However, greatly to their credit they completed their work, and at the end of eight years of painstaking triangulation produced a survey of a section of the Quitan Andes which was a model of accuracy and precision, and which set a standard of excellence unsurpassed for more than a century.

By December 1743 the final observations had been completed and the expedition began to break up. Godin accepted the position of astromoner-in-chief at the University of Marcos in Lima. Juan and Ulloa spent a further year in present-day Chile, completing their report, then sailed independently for Spain. Ulloa had the misfortune to be captured en route by British privateers; but he was well treated and on his arrival in London he received 'many courtesies' from the Royal Society. His voluminous report was returned to him intact. La Condamine decided to return to France via the Amazon. He didn't get back to Paris until 1745, and spent the rest of his life experimenting with and promoting the use of a wide range of South American produce such as rubber, curare and quinine. He also – several years ahead of Jenner – pioneered the use of vaccination against smallpox, a technique that he had seen used in Amazonia by a Carmelite friar. Few men have done more to make the wonders of South America known to the outside world.

Godin, La Gondamine, Juan and Ulloa had been collectors of facts. The next team of scientists to visit the Andes, Dombey, Ruiz and Pavón, were collectors of plants. In the generation that separates the two expeditions botany had become a science.

Almost as soon as the New World was 'discovered' it was appreciated that its trees, plants and flowers were very different from those of Eurasia. However, hard facts about the flora of the New World were hard to come by. This was because plants don't yield the same quick and obvious profit as precious metals, and therefore less interest initially was taken in them; because distance and time precluded specimens reaching Europe in good condition; and, above all, because there was no generally accepted system of identifying and classifying plants. For botany in the early eighteenth century was still not far removed from the folklore and mystical pharmacy of the Middle Ages. It was the Swede Carl von Linné, generally known as Linnaeus, whose researches at Uppsala resulted in a universally accepted system by which plants could be categorized. Linnaeus's system was based on the fact that all plants have either stamens (pollen-bearing organs) or pistils (pollen-receiving organs) and that the number of these organs is constant in a given species. In his works *System Naturae*, *Genera Plantarum* and *Classes Plantarum* Linnaeus pioneered the concept of classifying plants according to the number of their stamens or pistils. He admitted this was an artificial system; but in spite of its artificiality it worked remarkably well, especially when Linnaeus introduced the refinement that each plant should be given a two-word Latin name, the first for its genus and the second for its species. Once this system was universally accepted, a plant growing in Spanish territory could be found by a French botanist and described in an English textbook, and everyone would know what the plant in question was. On the bedrock of this scientific basis a start was made on cataloguing the earth's flora; and not only cataloguing it but collecting it, propagating it and moving it from place to place. One of the first of the great flora-collecting expeditions was that of Dombey, Ruiz and Pavón.

This was another Franco-Spanish venture, only with the Spaniards this time acting not as observers but as participants; for Spain was now beginning to realize the potential of her South American flora. It is sometimes implied that the Spanish were tardy and reluctant botanists. This is not so; rather, because of their obsession with secrecy, they were tardy and reluctant publishers of botanical findings. By the latter part of the eighteenth century Spain had accepted Linnaeus's system of classification, Charles III was anxious to encourage scientific projects, and botany was regarded by the Church as a useful and acceptable activity – 'the beauty of growing things', wrote Miguel Barnades in *Principios de botánica*, 'demonstrates God's wisdom, their multiplication and renewal demonstrates His power, and their usefulness to man demonstrates His ineffable goodness'. A very different view was to be taken by the Church when Darwin and Wallace began to suggest the mutability of species, but this was a century later; and the little team of scientists who sailed from Cadiz on 19 October 1777 had the full backing of both Church and state.

Once again they were a young team, consisting of one Frenchman, Joseph Dombey (aged 32), and four Spaniards, Hipólito Ruiz (aged 22), José Antonio Pavón (also 22), and the artists Joseph Brunete (31) and Isidro Galvez (23). Dombey was the most senior, most experienced and most accomplished botanist in the party. He was a protégé of the French Minister Jacques Turgot, who had first put forward the idea of the expedition in the hope of stimulating France's economy by introducing new plants from South America – in his instructions Dombey was told to pay particular attention to cinnamon trees, coca bushes and saltpetre (an essential ingredient of gunpowder). A contemporary describes Dombey as 'of a pleasing countenance, well-proportioned and possessed of a strong constitution'. In temperament he was mercurial, full of elation one moment and despair the next: not perhaps the easiest of companions, though in extenuation of his ups and downs it should be said that he was in a difficult position, being both older and better qualified than Ruiz, yet having to work if not under him at least in tandem with him. Hipólito Ruiz, the expedition leader, was born in Burgos and trained as a pharmacist; he had little botanical experience, and seems to have been put in charge of the expedition on the somewhat vague grounds of 'his naturally wise nature and his zeal for the glory of Spain'. His portrait shows us a thickset, slightly florid man who looks (and was to prove) energetic, intelligent and not easily diverted from his purpose. Though his ability and commitment were never in doubt there was an irascible side to his character, and he too was probably not the easiest of companions. It was as well that the third member of the triumvirate was of a more placid disposition. José Antonio Pavón had little botanical knowledge when he joined the expedition, but he was to prove a careful collector and the ideal second-in-command, 'modest, easy-going and of the most affable disposition'. It is typical of the way of the world that whereas there are any number of portraits of Dombey and Ruiz, there isn't one of the engaging and self-effacing Pavón. The artists were men of considerable ability, chosen after competition from a number of applicants. Their work speaks for them; artistic, accurate and painstaking, it was on a par with that of their contemporaries, Forster, Prevost and Parkinson.

The basic objective of the expedition was, in the words of Charles III, 'to examine and identify the natural products of my American dominions . . . in order to promote science, foster commerce and form herbaria and collections'. To this end the naturalists were expected to obtain not only specimens but detailed information about them. From each tree, for example, they were to bring back a sample of its bark, wood, leaves, flowers, fruit, sap and seeds, together with its local name, its history and the uses to which it could be put. All information was to be shared between the three botanists; each discoverer of a plant was to list his discovery in a diary, and whenever possible three speciments of everything were to be collected. It was anticipated that their work would take at least four years.

Ruiz's expedition, through no fault of its participants, was to prove a succession of disasters and near-disasters; and the greatest disaster of all was only avoided by chance before its work even began. The plan had been to land at Buenos Aires and reach Peru by crossing the Andes. A sudden war with Portugal necessitated a change of plan, and the expedition travelled instead via Cape Horn. When they arrived in Peru they heard that a caravan crossing the Andes at precisely the time they had hoped to, had been massacred by the Indians. 'But for the grace of God and war,' wrote Dombey, 'our heads would now be trophies of the *indios bravos*!' It was a foretaste of the hazards that the New World had in store for them.

However, there were no hazards in Lima where the naturalists landed on 8 April 1778, only a seemingly endless round of receptions, meetings and festivals. Lima was then the premier city in the New World, the outlet through whose port, Callao, the exotic produce of South America was shipped to Eurasia. A contemporary of the naturalists, Gregorio de Cangas, waxes eloquent over the city's charms:

The most notable characteristic of Lima is the exceeding kindness of its people to strangers. Commerce flourishes. The women are beautiful, with diminutive feet and long and abundant hair; their clothes, and those of the men, are ostentatious and costly. The academic faculty flourishes . . . Especially notable are the bakeries, the variety and succulence of the fruits, the bronze foundaries, the light construction of the buildings [because of earthquakes] the great multitude of servants available for the house, the grace and beauty of the young people, and the ease and convenience of travel.

Ruiz was more critical. He thought it 'extremely indecent' that the women displayed their legs 'almost up to the calf', and was horrified by their extravagance. When writing of the city's under-privileged, he indulged in all the usual clichés, describing the Indians as 'deceitful and superstitious', the Negroes as 'thieving', the mulattos as 'arrogant', and the Creoles as 'inept'. Ruiz was very much a product of his age and class, and a less discerning observer than Ulloa.

In May 1778 the naturalists started collecting plants in the vicinity of Lima. The locals, with some contempt, dubbed them *brujos yerbeteros* (herb-gathering witch-doctors). 'They were astonished,' writes Dombey, 'to see us crossing the fields on foot carrying plants, and thought that with no carriages or servants we must be poor indeed.' For almost a year Ruiz, Pavón and Dombey remained close to the Peruvian capital, seldom travelling out of sight of the sea. This was a gentle initiation to the more serious work in montana and rain forest that lay ahead – too gentle for Dombey's liking, and there are several references in his diary to 'my indolent companions'. About the only bit of excitement during this first year was when a local bandit attempted to rob them of the three months' wages which they were carrying with them; the attempt misfired. By March 1779 they were back in Callao, loading the fruits of their labours into the *Buen Consejo* for shipment to Europe. The Spanish collection consisted of 275 plants and 242 drawings 'illuminated in their natural colours', the French collection of 284 plants and two boxes of minerals (mainly silver, mercury, platinum and saltpetre). Few of the plants were new to science; by no stretch of the imagination could the naturalists be said to have roughed it, and their work so far had been pedestrian.

However, a couple of months later they were heading into more difficult and more rewarding terrain: the montana, an area of rain forest, cloud forest and grassland which covers the Andes from roughly 3,000 feet to 11,000 feet. This was a very different world to the coastal plains: wilder, wetter, more precipitous and far more sparsely populated. Within a couple of days of leaving Lima the naturalists were losing their mules in steep-sided ravines and swollen rivers, and having to haul themselves in wicker baskets across swaying suspension bridges; a couple of days after that they found themselves gasping for breath as they wound their way between the snow-capped peaks of the cordillera. By the end of May they had struggled through to Tarma, 'a small not unpleasant town set close to the ancient highway of the Incas'. With Tarma and the nearby town of Huanuco as their bases, they spent the next two years collecting the exotic flora of the Andes.

Explorers have a goal to aim for, mountaineers have a summit to attain; their exploits therefore fall into a natural narrative and climax. The early naturalists, in contrast, simply moved from place to place collecting plants literally by the thousand: locating them, removing them from their habitat, studying them, drying them, pressing them, drawing them, classifying, analysing and describing them. They also had to preserve, store and transport those specimens which they hoped to send back to Europe. Their work had no climax and was never finished; it went on and on, with one day very like the next. On the plus side they had the satisfaction of realizing that they were making known to the world a large number of useful (and especially medically useful) plants, and of seeing an abundance of beautiful flowers and scenery. On the minus side they suffered physical hardship, danger and disease.

It is one of Ruiz's more attractive qualities that he was utterly dedicated to his work and had a keen awareness of its importance – witness his comment soon after arriving at Tarma: 'Large numbers of the plants here are new to us. What a wonderful opportunity to enrich Botany and *Materia Medica* for the benefit of mankind!' His *Relación historica . . . del Peru y Chile el botanico* is full not only of detailed descriptions of these plants, but of their medical history. How this plant helps to heal wounds, this to ease childbirth, this to quench thirst, this to remove cataracts; how *Buddleja incona* deadens toothache, coca cures dysentery and diarrhoea, and plants of the genus *Tillandsia*, when used in hot water, are beneficial as a sedative. It is worth making the point that such claims are not old wives' tales, but are the bedrock on which most of our present-day drugs are based. Another of Ruiz's attributes was his awareness of the beauty of nature. This is something the majority of us take for granted today, but it was by no means common among eighteenth-century travellers. Most of the *Relación* consists of matter-of-fact botanical data; but every now and then Ruiz goes into rhapsodies over a waterfall or a bank of flowers:

The gorge was whitened by an almost continuous cascade of water, in some places raging and almost deafening, in others serene and beautiful, appearing from a distance like pure snow, forming the most extraordinary and delicate designs. . . . It seemed as though from the very creation of the world nature had designed this landscape for the orchid. The ground was covered with a great multitude of them, their perpetual fragrance delighting the senses and inviting one to remain in their company for ever. They covered the ground like a mosaic, the varied colours of their strange and precious flowers giving the most beautiful tints to this unusual pavement of nature.

There was, however, another side to the coin. The naturalists found in the Andes not only satisfaction and beauty, but hardship, danger, sickness and death.

During their seven years' botanizing they were only occasionally in danger from their fellow men. There was a certain amount of petty pilfering from their commissariat, a couple of attempts to rob them, and on one occasion their camp was ringed by over a thousand belligerent Chuncho Indians – although it was the naturalists' baggage and not their heads that the latter had set their sights on. They were in more danger from natural hazards: precipitous tracks, falling trees, flash floods and extremes of climate. Ruiz had one lucky escape when the mule he was riding slipped and fell over a precipice; luckily the animal was tied to a horse, and Ruiz escaped with a badly cut face from the horse's hooves. He also had a frightening experience when he was forced to spend a night in the snow without shelter: 'I thought I was going to die', he wrote, 'in that uninhabited place for lack of warm nourishment and on account of the cold.' But their greatest danger was disease. Cloud and rain forests are not the healthiest environment; the stranger in particular, who lacks immunity, is liable to infection from a wide variety of poisonous thorns, venomous bites and stings, and parasites that enter the bloodstream undetected. All these took their toll of the naturalists. On more than one occasion they were short of food, and by the end of their third year Dombey in particular was showing all the classic symptoms of scurvy – loss of appetite, loose teeth, bleeding gums and melancholia. Both Ruiz and Pavón suffered agonies from skin disease. 'Our legs,' wrote Ruiz, 'became covered with a rash of pimples which itched so abominably that we could not contain ourselves and spent half the night scratching until our skin was raw.' In addition, Pavón was afflicted with *mayco*: a skin disease in which the hands, buttocks and neck are covered with pus-filled papules. At times they were so weak and run down that even a comparatively minor mishap was a potential disaster. The artist Joseph Brunete fell from his mule; he seemed to have suffered no great injury, yet he grew progressively weaker and within a month of the accident he was dead. Dombey too might have died if he hadn't quit. His hearing and eyesight deteriorated alarmingly, and, in his own words, '[he] seemed altogether to lose [his] old vigour'. In 1784 he loaded 73 cases of specimens aboard the *El Peruano* and sailed for Cadiz.

The loss of their most experienced botanist and artist was not as serious a blow to the expedition as might have been expected. Ruiz and Pavón had grown in confidence during their two years in and around Tarma, and they continued plant-hunting successfully both in the Cordillera Blanca of Peru and the more spectacular cordillera of Chile. Brunete was replaced by a local artist, Francisco Pulgar, who suffered from ill-health and a disputatious disposition but was an excellent botanical painter.

By 1782 the expedition was nearing the end of its anticipated four years in the Andes. However, the long-standing war between England and Spain still made it hazardous for the naturalists to return home, and since they had not yet done any plant-collecting in Chile, they moved south and set up a new base in Concepcion.

Ruiz and Pavón were enchanted with Chile. 'It is an earthly paradise,' wrote the former, 'one of the most enviable countries in the world . . . and its people are kind and generous.' It was a paradise in particular for botanists, and the Spaniards spent the better part of two years collecting and cataloguing the multitudinous flora of the southern Andes. They were especially interested in the huge Chilean pines, *Araucania araucana*, better known today as the 'monkey puzzle'; for they were quick to see that its straight and durable trunk would be excellent for ship-building. A random sample from the *Relación* shows the sort of detail that was completed for each specimen collected:

PEUMUS BOLDUS: This small tree grows to a height of 18 to 24 feet, is evergreen, and very luxurious, the density of its branches – which emit a pleasant fragrance rather like cinnamon – providing excellent shade. The natives use the pulverized leaves of this tree to relieve pain. The juice of the leaves mixed with water is used to cure earache; to cure colds in the head they parboil the leaves, crush them and sprinkle them with wine. Hot baths, taken in water impregnated with the leaves, help to relieve rheumatism and dropsy. The fruits, when ripe, are small but sweet and tasty; when young they are used like olives, and are delicious when pickled. The pips of the ripened fruit are made into rosary beads. The wood is much used in building, when burned it gives off a pleasant fragrance, and barrels made from it improve the quality of wine. In short this is a small tree worthy of propagation and being grown in gardens; and among its attributes, an infusion of its leaves can be used in place of tea. [*Peumus* is still preferred in many Chilean homes today as an alternative to after-dinner coffee.]

By early 1784 the botanists were back in Lima and their collection of plants was being loaded aboard the *San Pedro de Alcantara*. The specimans were carefully crated and stowed: '31 tubs of living trees including Chilean pines, bananas, avocados, guavas, cocoa, myrrh, ginger, quina quinca and walnuts; 53 cases of dried plants, seeds, preserved birds, animals and fish etc., and 1013 plant drawings including 800 of new species.' Ruiz had been given special funds to ensure that the packaging was done properly; even so the botanists must have had qualms as they saw the fruits of five years labour being consigned to the leaking hold of a ship of the line whose captain clearly valued the gold, silver, copper and quinine in his cargo more highly than the plants.

Ruiz and Pavón were now anxious to return to Spain. However, it was learned that many of the specimens which they had sent back earlier had been either damaged or lost en route; it was therefore decided that they should pay one last visit to the Andes east of Huanuco to obtain duplicates, enlarge on their original descriptions and train their successors.

This final phase of the expedition was not a success. There were new plants in abundance, and Ruiz was eager to add them to his collection. However, the weather was bad; the terrain was difficult and sparsely populated – one village they worked in was so isolated that the local priest came only once a year when he had to celebrate all the holy days together in a single Mass – and the new artists proved inexpert and contentious. When Ruiz reprimanded them for the lack of accuracy in their drawings, they answered that they 'did not know how to do better'; eventually they said they were too ill to work and returned to the comforts of Lima. Worse – much worse – was to follow. It was August, and the local Indians had been burning undergrowth to clear ground for the sowing of next year's crops. One evening while Ruiz was away collecting specimens, the fires got out of control and set light to their hacienda. Within minutes the building was engulfed in flames. Pavón saved what little he could, and got badly burned in the process; but the bulk of the botanists' recent plant collection, together with their diaries and all their folios of drawings were lost. When Ruiz returned he found the hacienda 'a still smouldering volcano. I thought', he wrote, 'that I would go out of my mind. I tried to force my way into the building where I knew my papers to be; but the heat was too great,. and I could save nothing. I felt like killing myself. It was midnight before, overcome by exhaustion and despair I fell unconscious to the ground.' Next morning the botanists raked disconsolate through the ashes, but all they found were a few fragments of fused metal – the remains of Ruiz's silver tableware, chamber pot and spurs. Gone were twenty boxes of specimens, their diaries for the past three years, and, most tragic loss of all, three large folios of detailed and recently updated botanical description covering more than 600 plants.

Ruiz and Pavón did the only thing possible. They set to work collecting more specimens and rewriting their descriptions, but the heart had gone out of them. Returning in 1786 to Lima, they became embroiled in a succession of not very savoury financial and botanical disputes and lawsuits. And it was now, as they were awaiting King Charles's permission to return to Spain, that they heard of a disaster greater even than the fire that consumed their hacienda.

The hold of the *San Pedro de Alcantara* had been ankle-deep in water while the ship was lying at anchor in Callao. Soon after sailing she ran into a succession of storms, and the botanists' '31 tubs of living trees' were swept overboard. Near-foundering, the *San Pedro* staggered round the Horn and into Rio de Janeiro. By this time most of her crew were either drowned, dead from scurvy or had deserted. However, a new crew were signed on, the ship was patched up, and against the advice of the Rio de Janeiro harbour-master she headed for Europe. On 2 February 1786 she sighted the coast of Portugal and her troubles seemed to be over; but unaccountably during the night she steered the wrong course and was wrecked on the cliffs of Peniche, a little to the north of Lisbon. She sank within minutes, with the loss of 39 men, women and children, some 2 million pesos' worth of gold and 6 million pesos' worth of silver, together with all the plants, seeds, drawings and botanical descriptions which it had taken Ruiz and Pavón five years to collect.

Luckily a fair number of the plants, drawings and descriptions had been duplicated. Nevertheless this was a terrible loss, and one which highlights the problem Spain had in communicating effectively with her Andean territories. Exact figures are hard to arrive at, but it seems probable that out of every three plants which had been collected in South America, only one reached Europe safely. The wonder, therefore, is not that Ruiz's *Relación* and the herbarium which he helped to establish in Madrid were incomplete, but that they included as many species as they did – an inventory made some years after his return suggests that Ruiz succeeded in bringing back 2,980 dried plants, 2,264 illustrations of these plants and between 250 and 300 living specimens; he also completed 120,000 folio pages of writing, including a wealth of botanical descriptions. This was a magnificent achievement; although once the expedition was back in Europe, the bitter disputes and long delay over publishing its findings must have been heartbreaking, considering the hardships Ruiz and his fellow-botanists had to endure. Ruiz recalled:

For nearly eleven years we travelled through deserted and trackless terrain, suffering from heat, fatigue, hunger, thirst, near-nakedness, want, storms, earthquakes, swarms of mosquitoes and other insects, the danger of being devoured by jaguars and other wild beasts, plots of thieves, disloyal Indians, falls from precipices and the branches of great trees, fording of rivers and torrents, the fire at Macora, the death of the artist Brunete, the wreck of the San Pedro de Alcantara, the separation from Dombey, and the loss of many of our plants and manuscripts . . . When our labours at last came to an end I was thankful to deposit the crates containing our plants in the [king's] Botanical Gardens.

Ruiz's expedition was important both for what it achieved and the precedent it set: the precedent of a team of naturalists studying the earth's phenomena in pursuit not of gain but of knowledge.

The next important study of the Andes was made not by an expedition but by an individual: an individual whose research-work embraced – in addition to botany – geology, zoology, anthropology, geomorthology, seismology, oceanography, astronomy, meteorology and geomagnetism. Alexander von Humboldt made valuable contributions to each of these. Yet the sum of his achievements was even greater than the sum of its parts, for by integrating his work in these very different fields, he originated the concept of an entirely new science – geography.

Alexander, Baron von Humboldt was born in Berlin, in those days a small provincial town, on 14 September 1769. His father was an officer in the Prussian army who died when Alexander was only eleven; his mother was a highly intelligent cosmopolitan Huguenot who seems to have given her two sons an excellent education but not much in the way of maternal love. Alexander and his brother Wilhelm were educated at home by a succession of private tutors. The first of these, Joachim Campe, had recently translated *Robinson Crusoe* into German, and it is tempting to think that it might have been Campe who first instilled into his young pupil that love of adventure and out-of-the-way places which characterized his later life. However, the probability is that Humboldt's future was shaped by more potent forces. He was born the same year as Napoleon, and was a child of that intellectual revolution soon to reach its physical apogee in the storming of the Bastille. His teachers and friends were cosmopolitan and progressive; and although most of them were far from being active revolutionists, they were sympathetic to the new ideas currently challenging the privileges and prejudices of the Middle Ages. Humbolt therefore studied not only classical Latin and Greek, but also mathematics and the 'new' sciences. He first became interested in botany at the age of 16 when he met Karl Willdenow, the author of *The Flora of Berlin*, who classified specimens the young von Humboldt collected. This interest quickened when Humboldt met Georg Forster, the naturalist who had sailed with Cook on the second of his expeditions to the Pacific, and whose *Voyage Round the World* had recently introduced the German-reading public to the wonders of the Pacific islands. The two men embarked on a field trip together, collecting rock samples in the Rhine Valley; and Humboldt subsequently wrote, 'it was Georg Forster who first awakened in me an inextinguishable longing to visit the tropics'. It was, however, to be many years before this longing was fulfilled.

In 1791 Humboldt entered the Academy in Freiburg, where he took what would nowadays be called a crash course in mining. A year later he was appointed assessor to the Smelting Department in Berlin, and a year after that became Director General of Mines in Franconia. Not much is known about his four-year career in the mining industry, but he seems to have tackled his work with the same common sense, conscientiousness and thoroughness which were later to characterize his achievements in the field of geography; and it was while working in Franconia that he published his first major work, *Florae fibergensis specimen* (a study of underground plants) – an indication perhaps that although he made his livelihood from mining his true interests lay elsewhere. It was the death of his mother in 1796 which enabled him to pursue these interests. She left him a very considerable fortune, and he at once quit his job and travelled to Paris, then the rallying point of the intelligentsia of Europe. His two years in Paris were to prove both frustrating and rewarding. Frustrating because he was invited to join a number of major expeditions – among them Baudin's to the Pacific and Lord Bristol's to the Nile – but in every case the expedition failed to get off the ground because of the Napoleonic Wars. Rewarding because he was able to meet and draw inspiration from the élite of Europe's philosophers, scientists and explorers. This was the era in which Rousseau was proclaiming in *Du Contrat Social*, 'man is born free, yet everywhere he is in chains'; the astronomer Laplace was boasting, 'my solar system works perfectly without the need of a God'; and Wordsworth was writing: 'Bliss was it in that dawn to be alive, But to be young was very heaven!' Darwin was young – no more than 27 – and as he witnessed his fellow scientists 'battering down the walls of superstition which medieval ignorance had built', Humboldt must have longed to make his own contribution to replacing popular misconception with scientific fact.

It was, ironically, Charles IV of Spain who gave him the opportunity he longed for. Humboldt was carrying out experiments on the Castillian plateau with the French botanist Aimé Bonpland when he was persuaded to petition the King for permission to travel in his South American territories. He wrote a memoir, outlining the benefits that might accrue from a scientific study of Spanish America, was granted a royal audience, and in a surprisingly short time received permission to 'execute all such operations . . . in my American dominions . . . as may be judged useful for the advancement of the sciences'. It was, for Humboldt, a dream come true. 'Never before,' he wrote, 'had so comprehensive a brief been granted to any traveller, and never before had a foreigner been honoured with such confidence.' Humboldt never betrayed this confidence. Yet the irony is that he probably did more than anyone to bring about the collapse of Charles's South American empire. For he opened a window through which Europeans got their first comprehensive view of South America, and South Americans heard for the first time the strains of that revolutionary music which was currently sweeping Europe.

Humboldt and Bonpland arrived in the Venezuelan port of Cumana on 16 July 1799. According to his letters of introduction Humboldt was '29 years old, five foot eight inches in height;[he had] light brown hair, grey eyes, a somewhat larger than average nose and mouth, and a face slightly marked with the scars of smallpox . . . [He was] travelling for the acquisition of knowledge.' And what a cornucopia of knowledge he managed to amass during his four years in South America. No traveller before or since ever observed and recorded such an abundance of minutiae in such a wide range of subjects. Not surprisingly, it took 32 years and 30 bulky volumes to publish the results of his labours. From such a glut of material it is not easy to select highlights. However, three achievements in three very different fields might be said to epitomize his travels: his survey of the link between the Amazon and the Orinoco; his attempt to climb Chimborazo; and his study of the Peruvian Current.

When Humboldt arrived in South America, parts of the continent were still unexplored; the Vichala-Guainia basin in particular (at the junction of present-day Colombia, Venezuela and Brazil) was *terra incognita*. This was the setting for Conan Doyle's *The Lost World*, and the graveyard for 312 out of 325 Spanish explorers who had attempted to unravel its secrets in the 1750s. So little was known of the area that the world's greatest map-maker, Aaron Arrowsmith, placed a huge lake at the centre of it; a lake which, he suggested, provided feeders to both the Amazon and the Orinoco. Almost the only Europeans to live in the area were Capuchin Friars. They said there was no lake, but that there *was* a waterway connecting the two great rivers; and to prove or disprove the existence of such a waterway was Humboldt's objective.

In the autumn of 1799 he and Bonpland headed into the llanos, those vast and featureless plains which fringe the eastern slopes of the Andes. No one ever described them better than Humboldt:

On leaving the mountain valleys of Caracas, the traveller sees before him the Llanos or steppe receding until they merge into the far horizon; neither hill nor cliff breaks the uniformity of this boundless plain, only the occasional broken strata of limestone . . . Like the greater part of the Sahara, the Llanos are in the torrid zone: during one half of the year they are desolate as the sands of Libya, during the other half they resemble a grassy plain like the steppe of Central Asia . . . They are well suited to the rearing of cattle, and numerous herds (estimated at the time of my journey to number some one-and-a-half-million) roam the steppe. The great increase in the number of these animals is the more remarkable from the variety of dangers with which they have to contend.

Under the vertical rays of the sun, the charred turf crumbles to dust, and the hardened soil cracks as from the shock of an earthquake. If at such a time two opposing currents of air come into contact with the ground, the plain assumes a singular aspect. In cone-shaped clouds whose lower extremities reach down to the earth, the sand rises into the air in the electrically-charged centre of a whirling current, producing an effect like the waterspout so dreaded by mariners. The lowering sky diffuses a dim straw-coloured light over the plain. The horizon draws nearer; the steppe seems to contract, and with it the heart of the traveller. The hot, dusty particles which fill the air increase its suffocating heat, and the east wind blowing over the heated soil brings no refreshment but a still-more burning aridity. The pools begin to disappear. As in the north the animals become torpid with cold, so here under the influence of the parching drought, the crocodile and the boa fall asleep, buried deep in the dry mud. Everywhere the death-threatening drought prevails; and yet by the play of refracted light, the thirsty traveller is pursued by the phenomenon of mirages – the illusive image of a cool rippling sheet of water; and the distant palms, apparently raised by the unequally heated and therefore unequally dense strata of air, hover above the ground from which they are separated by a narrow intervening margin. Half hidden by clouds of dust, restless with pain and thirst, the herds roam round and round; the cattle lowing dismally, and the horses stretching out their long necks and snuffing the wind as if by chance a moister current might betray the location of a not-entirely-dried-up pool. Shrewder and more adaptable, the mule has found a way of alleviating his thirst. The ribbed melon-cactus conceals beneath its prickly skin a watery pith. The mule dislodges the prickles with his forefeet, and cautiously drinks the cooling juice. Even when the heat of day is superseded by the coolness of night, the animals cannot rest. Huge bats suck their blood like vampires while they sleep, attaching themselves to their backs and causing festering wounds in which settle mosquitoes and a host of parasitic insects.

But at last comes the welcome season of the rains, and then how suddenly and dramatically the scene is changed! The deep blue of the hitherto cloudless sky becomes lighter; the stars lose their brilliance; a single cloud appears in the south, like a distant mountain, rising perpendicular from the horizon. Gradually an ever-thickening vapour spreads mist-like over the sky, and soon a distant thunder ushers in the life-restoring rain. Hardly has the earth received this refreshing moisture than the previously barren steppe emits a sweet smell and begins to clothe itself with grasses. The herbaceous mimosas unfold their drooping leaves to greet the sun . . . Soon the cattle are grazing contentedly. And tall springing grasses hide the beautifully-mottled jaguar who, lurking in safe concealment and measuring carefully the distance of a single bound, springs catlike as the Asiatic tiger on his passing prey.

Humboldt's account of their journey is full of such fine descriptive passages, as well as observations on rocks, plants, animals, fish, people, climate and terrestrial magnetism. One day the travellers would be studying the symbiosis of ants and fungus, next day they would be dissecting electric eels, and the day after that observing the infanticide rituals of the Orinoco Indians. No phenomenon escaped them. Their interest and their curiosity encompassed every facet of nature.

It took them a couple of months to cross the llanos, and a couple more to ascend the Orinoco in a *lancha*, a large unwieldy craft with oxhide benches for'd and a palm-thatched cabin aft. Once the *lancha* capsized, and Humboldt and Bonpland were lucky to right it before the river's many crocodiles took advantage of their predicament. Their hosts now were Capuchin Friars, whose missions were dotted at strategic intervals along the riverbank, and who were unfailingly helpful to Humboldt despite the fact that he was not a Catholic. 'You will want for nothing at my mission,' Father Cerasco told him, 'and the longer you stay the better I shall be pleased.' The travellers, however, were anxious to settle the mystery of the confluence of the Orinoco and the Amazon. They stayed only a couple of days with the Capuchins, then, following their directions, headed south down one of the Orinoco's tributaries, the Atabapo. At a spot where the Atabapo begins to fan out into a series of rivulets, they made a short portage, dragging their canoe through swampland until they came to a stream called the Cano Pamichin. This, they found, soon joined the Rio Negro, one of the major feeders of the Amazon. A week later they discovered that another river, the Casiquiare, also linked the two major waterways. 'Thus,' wrote Humboldt, 'we find that the great lake, supposed to be over 160 miles in length, does not exist and must be reduced to an area of swampland no more than two or three miles in circumference.' He mapped the area with pin-point accuracy, and surveyed the route for a canal, which, he suggested, 'might be dug in the position where we made our portage, so as to facilitate trade'.

This may not have been a major feat of exploration; but it clarified an issue which had been in doubt for centuries, and it alone would have made Humboldt's and Bonpland's journey worthwhile. They themselves, however, regarded their collection of scientific data as of far greater importance. On the journey back to the coast their *lancha* was like an overcrowded ark. For Humboldt had accumulated a large number of birds and animals - manakins, toucans, marmosets and monkeys – from which he was loth to part. He had also accumulated over 16,000 pressed plants and an unspecified number of skins, barks and geological specimens. These were given pride of place in the cabin, while the explorers found what shelter they could on the open deck. Unfortunately for them it rained without respite – for 13 days at a stretch on the Atabapo – and Bonpland's health began to deteriorate. Racked alternatively with chills and fever, he was unable to keep down food. Humboldt thought he had typhus (though more probably it was malaria) and was beside himself with anxiety, for he and Bonpland had formed a friendship which was to last for life. Eventually the Frenchman became too ill to travel, and they sought shelter in a mission. Here the Capuchins prescribed a remedy of honey mixed with the bark of angostura and quinine, which almost certainly saved his life.

While waiting for his companion to recover, Humboldt had a chance to study the customs of the local Indians. He appraised them with the same logical, unprejudiced and meticulous attention to detail that he lavished on natural phenomena. Some writers (like Ruiz) condemned the Indians out of hand as deceiptful, superstitious and good for nothing. Others (like Bougainville and Commerson) depicted them as Noble Savages, devoid of sin. Humboldt stood up for their rights and spoke out against their slavery and oppression; but he was under no illusion as to the squalor and brutality of many aspects of their lives. If twins were born, one was instantly killed, since it was believed that two children born at the same time couldn't have the same father; children who were too weak to keep up with the tribe's peripatetic life-style were also put to death, and young married women were encouraged to have abortions on the grounds that they could then concentrate better on their domestic duties. 'So much,' wrote Humboldt, 'for the boasted happiness of man in the state of nature!'

Although Bonpland soon recovered sufficiently to travel to the coast, it was some time before he and Humboldt were fit to embark on another major journey. In the intervening months the Frenchman had a whirlwind romance with a beautiful *samba* (a girl of mixed white and Indian origin), while Humboldt, en route for Cuba, was first captured by a pirate and then rescued by a British man-of-war – his four years in South America were certainly not lacking in incident.

Not until April 1801 were the two friends again on the trail together, travelling this time from Cartagena to Lima via the Andes and making en route a study of the range's volcanic origins. As a bonus, they hoped to meet in Bogota the legendary Father Mutis, the priest, physician and pioneer-botanist who had devoted the greater part of his life to collecting and studying the flora of the Andes.

The first part of their journey, being poled up the slow-flowing Magdalena, was on the face of it unremarkable; it had been done many times before. It was, however, perhaps the greatest of all Humboldt's attributes that wherever he travelled he added, by meticulous observation, to our understanding of our planet. During their 45 days on the Magdalena the travellers kept a precise record of the river's direction, width, temperature and velocity. By the time they exchanged their flat-bottomed dug-out for horses and mules on which to ascend the Andes, they had produced a map of the final 300 miles of the river which included a wealth of accurate and hitherto unrecorded detail.

After a hair-raising climb – in places the path they followed consisted of steps only 20 inches wide cut into a vertical rockface – they reached Santa Fe de Bogota. The former capital of the Muisca Empire was now a prosperous market town with more than 30,000 inhabitants and many magnificent baroque churches. Here the travellers were met by the archbishop's carriage, lodged in the most luxurious residence and entertained by the viceroy. This was typical of the welcome accorded to Humboldt throughout the Andes. 'The people,' he wrote, 'are warm, convivial, and of great simplicity of manner and likeable candour . . . wherever I went I was received with great kindness and without a hint of suspicion.'

Yet the members of the establishment who welcomed Humboldt with such courtesy were to find him a cuckoo in the nest; for inevitably an intellectual from Paris who might be said to epitomize the new scientific spirit of the age had about him the aura of a revolutionary. And in Colombia and to a lesser degree in Peru the tinder for revolution needed only a spark to set it ablaze. Men like Antonio Narino, who had translated the

Rights of Man into Spanish, had been imprisoned; men like Bernardo Zea, a brilliant botanist who championed Indian rights, had been sent to Spain for execution; and the intelligentsia (especially the Creole intelligentsia) were longing to prove in Bogota and Lima the theories which had been successfully put to the test in Paris. Humboldt and Bonpland did their best to eschew politics; but by their mere presence they fanned the winds of change. Bonpland, in his cups, was rash enough to admit that he believed in 'the reproductive capacity of revolution', and the catch-phrase reverberated the length of the Andes. Humboldt was rash enough, on rare occasions, to protest against some particularly harsh injustice. On their journey from Bogota to Quito, for example, on a path which even sure-footed mules were unable to climb, the travellers were offered a ride on the backs of *caballitos* (little horses), mountain Indians who, for a pittance, were forced to carry white men up the most arduous part of the ascent. 'It makes one's blood boil,' wrote Humboldt, 'to hear human beings described in the same terms as a horse or a mule.' Nearly all those who helped Humboldt and Bonpland in their research work were liberal-minded; many were revolution-minded. Mutis, for example, asked if his most promising pupil, Jose de Caldas, might travel with the botanists to Quito. Caldas was a brilliant scientist – the man who pioneered the technique of determining altitude by the temperature at which water boils – and he and Humboldt became not only colleagues but friends. This didn't save Caldas a few years later. As he stood blindfold facing a firing-squad he was told 'Spain has no need of men of learning'. In more ways than one the Andes in the 1800s could be described as eruptive.

For more than a year, from November 1801 to January 1803, Humboldt studied the volcanology of the cordillera around Quito, where, in an area of some 100 square miles, more than a dozen great cones were intermittently active. It was dangerous work. Only a few years earlier much of Quito had been destroyed and over 40,000 people had been killed in a violent earth tremor, and as Humboldt climbed volcano after volcano, usually to the very lip of the crater, he found few Indians willing to carry his scientific equipment. Rather than resort to coercion, he carried it himself. His best known feat is probably his attempt to climb Chimborazo, then believed to be the highest mountain in the world. Without oxygen and for most of the climb without porters, he struggled to 19,170 feet, only to find a huge crevasse barring the way to the summit. Suffering from nausea and bleeding from both nose and mouth, he was forced to give up; but it is possible that no man (at that time) had ever climbed higher.

Some of his other climbs were even more hazardous:

Twice on 26th and 28th May (1802) I climbed to the crater of Pichincha, the volcano overlooking Quito. As far as I know only Condamine had been there before me, and he arrived without instruments and could not endure the cold for more than 15 minutes. I managed to take my instruments with me, and was able to carry out observations and collect samples of air for analysis. The first ascent I made with a single Indian companion. Knowing that Condamine had approached the crater over the snow-slopes that led up to its rim, we decided to follow the same route. This was nearly the end of us! The Indian suddenly disappeared up to his chest, and we realized to our horror that we were on a snow bridge – only a few feet from where we were standing we could see daylight through the holes. Without realizing it, we had ventured on to the vaults overhanging the crater. Frightened but undeterred, I tried another approach. On the rim of

Opposite Contemporary illustrations of life in eighteenth-century Peru: *clockwise* preparing food; taking hallucinatory drugs; cutting maize; ploughing with oxen and making chica.

E. 58

Omeco-machacuai   EST. Nº LXXXIII

E. 63

E. 70.

An Aymara Indian in his reed-boat on Lake Titicaca, the setting for the Incas' myth of creation.

Above The two men who did most to free the people of South America from Spanish suzerainty: *left* the passionate idealist Simon Bolivar (1781-1830); *right* the practical soldier José de San Martin (1778-1850).

Below Chimborazo, painted by Alexander von Humboldt, whose travels in South America helped fan the winds of change which led to the revolutionary wars.

the crater were three rocky pinnacles, free of snow because it is melted by the steam rising out of the fumerole. I climbed one of these pinnacles, and found close to the top a shelf of rock, projecting like a balcony over the abyss. Here I set up my instruments. The rock, which was about 12 feet long, and 6 feet wide was shaken by constant earth tremors – we counted 18 in less than half-an-hour. If we lay down we could get a perfect view of the crater. It would be difficult to imagine anything more sinister. The vent consists of a circular hole . . . its circumference covered with snow, its centre dull black. Its depth appears limitless . . . I'm afraid we are going to have to tell the people of Quito the bad news that their volcano is active – possibly its fires have been rekindled by the catastrophe of 1797. There were bluish flames flickering in its depths, and we felt violent tremors every two or three minutes. These made the whole rim of the crater tremble, but were barely noticeable at a distance of 200 yards . . .

It was for adventures such as these that Humboldt became a household name. It has been claimed – probably with some exaggeration – that in the early nineteenth century he was the best-known man in Europe apart from Napoleon. Nowadays his climbing prowess if forgotten, and it is his scientific achievements that are remembered: how he established the magnetic theory of volcanism; became the first man to suggest the linear distribution of volcanoes along lines of weakness in the earth's crust; invented the use of isothermal lines; pioneered the drawing of cross-sections of land-forms; and originated the concept of relating flora to zones of altitude and temperature. And all this he achieved before he even set eyes on the Pacific and the great cold-water current which is the most famous of the many natural phenomena that today bear his name. (Fourteen towns in the United States alone are named after him; also mountains in North America and South America, Australia, New Zealand and New Caledonia, glaciers in Greenland and Antarctica, rivers, bays and forests too numerous to mention, and even a *mare* – 'a sea' – on the moon.)

It always embarrassed Humboldt that the Peruvian Current was named after him. 'I only measured the temperature of it,' he wrote. 'I didn't discover it.' It is true that local fishermen had known of and exploited the current for at least 3,000 years before Humboldt set eyes on it. It is also true that Humboldt spent comparatively little time studying the Current; he recorded its temperature no more than a dozen times in less than half-a-dozen places. Yet the conclusions he arrived at were definitive. He discovered that along most of the Pacific coast of South America the temperature of the water was a uniform 60°, and the temperature of the land a near-uniform 73° – a reversal of the usual ratio. He deduced from this that when air from the Pacific moved inland its temperature must be raised and its moisture-carrying capacity increased. So instead of voiding moisture *onto* the land, the clouds sucked moisture *out of* the land. 'It is this,' he wrote, 'which explains the abundance of mist on the Pacific seaboard and the total absence of rain.' He accounts for the Atacama so logically that one can only wonder no one had been able to account for it before.

A couple of years later he was back in Paris, planning his *Kosmos*, the gargantuan work expounding his belief in 'the harmony of nature' which he always regarded as his *magnum opus*. It was 40 years before the appearance of his first volume, and Humboldt died at the age of 90 before the appearance of the last.

Humboldt received many accolades. Darwin called him 'the greatest scientific traveller who ever lived'; Goethe said simply 'he was a genius'; and he has been dubbed 'the father of modern geography' and 'the first ecologist'. As an authority on South America he is not perhaps so well known. Yet he had a profound love of the continent – both its natural phenomena and its people - and Simon Bolivar's tribute would have pleased him: 'Baron von Humboldt did more for South America than all the conquistadors put together.'

In Humboldt's footsteps came a whole spate of travellers: men who were animated by the same spirit of scientific curiosity but who were specialists rather than encyclopaedists: palaeontologists like D'Orbigny, zoologists like Spix, and ento-mologists likes Bates and Wallace. Of these the last-mentioned is perhaps the most interesting, both as a person and a scientist.

If you mention evolution most people today at once think of Darwin and the Galapagos. Yet if the brig *Helen* hadn't been unlucky enough to catch fire in mid-Atlantic, the word 'evolution' might for most people today conjure up a picture of Wallace and the Amazon.

Alfred Russel Wallace was born in Usk, Monmouthshire on 8 January 1823, one of seven children of a not very successful lawyer. There was insufficient money for him to complete his education and he left school at the age of 13 and was employed first as an apprentice-carpenter then as a surveyor. He seems to have been a kind, shy and self-effacing young man, with a mind of his own and radical views – an Owenite in politics, an agnostic in religion, more a pacifist than a patriot, and one of the few early explorer-scientists who was wholly without racial prejudice. Carpentry and surveying may not sound ideal occupations for an embryo entomologist. However, the former taught him practical skills which later helped him to survive in the rain forests of South America and Indonesia, while the latter took him into the beautiful countryside of the Welsh border, where he gradually developed an affinity with and a love of nature. He began to collect first rocks, then plants, then beetles. It wasn't long before he became intrigued by the extraordinary diversity of the beetle family, the huge number of different species which existed within the same habitat. 'If I had been asked,' he wrote, 'how many different kinds of beetle were to be found in any small district, I should have guessed fifty or at the most a hundred. Now I learnt that there were more than a thousand.' Why, he wondered, were the beetles so diverse? And surely Noah couldn't have taken a pair of *every* species into the Ark?

When Wallace was in his early twenties there occurred two events which were to shape his life. He met Henry Bates, and he read *Vestiges of the Natural History of Creation*. Bates was about the same age as Wallace, and better educated. He had been collecting beetles for years, and lent Wallace a book which contained descriptions of more than 3,000 British species. If there were that many in the British Isles, Wallace asked himself, how many must there be in the world? As well as showing his new friend his book on beetles, Bates also showed him a copy of *Vestiges*. This was a curate's egg of a book, published (very wisely!) under a pseudonym, but we now know that it was written by Robert Chambers (the founder of *Chamber's Journal*). Most of it was a farrago of nonsense: 'animals that are yellow in colour and have stripes are always the most evil members of their group. Is this not true of tigers, and are not zebras the most spiteful and untameable of their class?' Yet sandwiched between such rubbish were passages of rare discernment. In particular Chambers stated categorically that neither the Creation nor the immutability of species should be regarded as proven fact; and he asked, very pertinently, why adaptive development should not be part of God's plan? Also – and this in the early nineteenth century was an exceedingly brave thing to do – he included Man as a creature of the natural world. Wallace was fascinated by these ideas; but he saw very clearly where the weakness of *Vestiges* lay: Chambers produced hardly a shred of evidence to substantiate his theories.

It would be wrong to say that the idea of collecting such evidence sprang instantly to Wallace's mind, but it was almost certainly at the back of his mind; and when in 1847 he became disenchanted with the social injustice and financial insecurity of life in Victorian England, he wrote to Bates and suggested that the two of them should embark on an expedition to the headwaters of the Amazon to collect (and later sell) natural history specimens. Rather to his surprise Bates accepted with enthusiasm.

The two men could raise no more than £100 between them and both subsequently referred to the expedition as their 'rash adventure'. There was, however, nothing rash or improvident about their preparations. They made contact with the most prestigious scientists, museums, gardens and research establishments of the day, and arranged for whatever specimens they collected to be shipped back to England, delivered to the right authorities, and, most importantly, paid for; in this essential facet of their work they were greatly indebted to the efforts of their agent, Samuel Stevens.

They arrived at Para near the mouth of the Amazon in May 1848 and were, between them, to spend the next 15 years collecting entomological specimens – principally moths, butterflies and beetles.

The collecting began almost as soon as they stepped ashore, and in one of the earliest of his many letters home Wallace paints an evocative picture of the environment in which he was to work for the next four years:

I could only marvel at the sombre shade [of the rain forest], scarce illuminated by a single direct ray of the sun, the enormous size and height of the trees, most of which rise in huge columns a hundred feet or more without throwing out a single branch , the strange buttresses around the base of some, the spiny or furrowed stems of others, the extraordinary creepers and climbers which wind around them, hanging in long festoons from branch to branch, sometimes curling and twisting on the ground like great serpents, then mounting to the very tops of the trees, thence throwing down roots and fibres which hang waving in the air, or twisting round each other to form ropes and cables of every variety and size . . . On my first walk into this forest I looked about, expecting to see monkeys as plentiful as at the Zoological Gardens, with humming birds and parrots in profusion. But for several days I did not see a single monkey, and hardly a bird of any kind, and I began to think that these must be much scarcer than they are represented to be by travellers. However, I soon found that the creatures are plentiful enough as soon as I knew where and how to look for them.

Judged by the tenets of the previous century Wallace was an unlikely explorer. One wonders what La Condamine or Ruiz would have made of him: a mild-mannered, middle-class myopic who financed his travels by selling beetles at sixpence a pair! Yet the contribution he made to our knowledge of the earth was far greater than that of his aristocratic predecessors. Indeed Tom Sterling in *The Amazon* claims with some truth that the 'four years Wallace spent in the Amazon were as productive in terms of man's knowledge of nature as any four years in the history of science.'

To start with the Amazon was kind to the explorer-entomologists. They rented a house on the outskirts of Para, and quickly established a routine of field work, collecting ornithological specimens in the early morning (when the birds were most active) and entomological specimens in mid-afternoon (when the insects were most active.) In the evenings they mounted and preserved their specimens, and made copious notes and drawings. It soon became apparent that they had stumbled across a naturalist's Aladdin's Cave, a treasure-trove in which huge and beautiful beetles, butterflies and moths were not only multitudinous but amazingly diverse. Literally every other insect they saw seemed to be of a different species; witness the entry in Bates's *Journal*: 'On Tuesday collected 46 specimens of 39 species. On Wednesday collected 37 specimens of 33 species, 27 of which are different from those taken on the preceding day.'

This was rewarding work: rewarding financially because Stevens had guaranteed them 3d. a specimen, and at the end of three months they had collected 3,635; rewarding scientifically because the insects they collected represented no fewer than 1,300 species, more than half of which were previously unknown; rewarding spiritually because both Wallace and Bates, freed from the restrictions of middle-class Victorian England, blossomed out into likeable if somewhat eccentric characters. It is not the least of their achievements that they got on famously both with their fellow entomologists and with the exceedingly varied indigenous population. At a time when explorers in other parts of the world were all too often berating their native helpers, there is, in all Wallace's and Bates's diaries hardly an angry or a derogatory word.

At the end of four months in Para they were tempted to move further afield; for, they asked themselves, if the environs of a city yielded such treasures, what would they find in the depths of the rain forest? The idyll was about to end, the heartache about to begin.

The upper reaches of the Amazon are not the easiest place in which to survive. Amabel Williams-Ellis, a recent biographer of Wallace, writes of the area:

Let no-one, reading this in civilized surroundings, think of the miseries and dangers as trivial. A friend of the present writer has just returned from this part of the world. He is a skilled mountaineer, has done first ascents in South America, knows the wild places of Africa, and is, in short, difficult to daunt. Yet on his return he declared that even today, with helicopters above the trees, outboard engines clapped to the canoes, new roads and even the occasional bus, it is still exceptionally difficult country. Penetrating heat, heavy dampness, twilit forest, rocks, rapids, ferocious insects, leeches and a general absence of anything eatable, all have to be taken into account.

And Williams-Ellis doesn't mention the greatest advantage of all enjoyed by the modern traveller: immunization from what used to be fatal diseases such as typhus and malaria. Both Wallace and Bates are restrained writers who play down the difficulties and dangers that beset them; but without doubt they had an extremely hard time of it.

At the end of six months they split up. The parting seems to have been entirely amicable, and they remained friends for the rest of their lives; but for the next few years each ploughed his own idiosyncratic furrow through the vaulted world of the Amazon.

No one has summarized Bates's exploits better than Tom Sterling:

The sprightly little ex-hosier's apprentice travelled tirelessly up and down the river and through the surrounding forests, fortified by an almost childish love of nature and a belief that nothing would happen to him. His adventures were seldom heroic, but they were charged with his own strong sense of humanity which he extended, somehow, to all creature-life . . . He crawls through the jungle litter looking for blind ants; anacondas wake him in the middle of the night, arousing no emotion but curiosity; he is sympathetic to bats; he tracks down enormous spiders and poisonous wasps; he takes baths with alligators. Somehow he makes one feel that these activities were not only normal, but humdrum.

Over a period of eleven years Bates collected specimens of 14,712 different species of insect, of which more than 8,000 were previously unknown. No one ever did more to advance entomological knowledge.

Wallace's exploits are not so easy to summarize; nor, for reasons soon to be apparent, is it possible to say exactly how many specimens of how many species he collected. Towards the end of 1848 he was joined by his brother Herbert, who seems to have been one of life's good-natured but chronic failures – having failed at whatever he turned his hand to in England, he came to South America with the idea of working with his brother as a collector of insects. However, he found the Amazon too much for him, and castigated the river in execrable verse:

> By many an Indian cottage,
> By many a village green,
> Where naked little urchins
> Are fishing in the stream,
> With days of sunny pleasure,
> But, oh, what weary nights,
> For here upon the Amazon
> The dread mosquito bites –
> Inflames the blood with fever,
> And murders gentle sleep,
> Till weary grown and peevish
> We've half a mind to weep!

When his brother, who was made of sterner stuff, set off for the headwaters of the Rio Negro, Herbert retreated to Para, only to find the city in the throes of yellow fever and smallpox. According to contemporary records 12,000 out of Para's 16,000 inhabitants contracted one disease or the other. Bates (who happened to be passing through the city) caught yellow fever. 'I was in hopes,' he wrote, 'that I should escape, but it seems to spare no newcomer. At the time I became ill every medical man in the place was worked to the utmost attending victims of the other disease [smallpox] so I was obliged to be my own doctor.' Another newcomer to succumb was Herbert Wallace. He complained of high temperature, giddiness and pulsating headaches, and developed the sickly pallor which gives the disease its name. Bates did all he could to nurse him, 'but on the 5th day of his sickness Herbert was taken with the black vomit and within hours was dead'.

It was a couple of years before Alfred Wallace, returning from the rain forest, heard of his brother's death. He felt responsible. He was in poor health himself – 'whenever I attempted to walk, the exertion brought on shivering and sickness' – and Para, in mourning for its dead, was a depressing environment. He decided to cut short his botanizing and return to England.

He arranged for his collection – the fruits of four years' research-work – to be loaded into the brig *Helen* which was about to sail for Southampton, and on the morning of 12 July 1852 was carried aboard himself, 'being too weak to walk'. It would be difficult to overstate the importance of the items which Wallace had collected in the approaches to the Andes and which he now consigned to the hold of the *Helen*: case after case of hitherto unknown butterflies, moths and beetles, each meticulously mounted and labelled; sheet after sheet of accurate and beautifully coloured botanical drawings, and page after page of notes on each specimen's appearance, habitat, diet and characteristics. There was also a herboria of dried plants, and a 'variety of living creatures . . . parrots, parrakeets, uncommon monkeys and a forest wild-dog'. In financial terms the collection was worth a great deal more that the £200 for which it was insured; in scientific terms it was priceless, for it contained the facts with which Wallace, in mid-century, was already groping towards the theory of evolution by means of natural selection.

The commercial cargo carried by the *Helen* was rubber, cocoa and *Copaifera officinalis* – a resinous substance used in the manufacture of varnish and lacquer. *Copaifera officinalis* was known to be volatile, so the kegs containing it were packed in damp sand. However, as the brig was about to sail, a last-minute consignment was hoisted aboard, and since there was no sand left in which to pack the kegs, the *Helen*'s captain, Captain Turner, ordered them to be bedded in rice chaff . . . Three weeks later, when the *Helen* was some 700 miles north-east of Bermuda, Turner knocked on the door of Wallace's cabin. 'I'm afraid,' he said, in the best tradition of naval sang-froid, 'the ship is on fire. Come and see what you think of it.'

Wallace's diary chronicles the highlights of the ensuing tragedy:

A thick vapour was coming out of the forecastle, which we both thought was more like steam than smoke. The fore hatchway was opened to try and ascertain the origin of the vapour, and a quantity of cargo was thrown out. We then went to the after hatchway.

This was a mistake. The opening of the after hatchway produced a through draught, and both vapour and heat increased.

The carpenter was told to cut a hole in the deck through which water might be poured, but the planks proved too thick and the smoke became unbearable. All hands who were not firefighting were ordered to get out the boats and assemble in them such necessities as we should want in the event of our being obliged to take to them . . . I went down to my cabin, now suffocatingly hot and full of smoke, to see what I could save. I got my watch and some notebooks with drawings of plants and animals. My clothes and my large portfolio of sketches I was obliged to leave . . . Soon the fire burst through the cabin floor, and consuming the dry pine-wood, flared up through the skylight. There was now a scorching heat on the quarterdeck, and we saw all hope was over. The captain ordered us into the boats, and was himself the last to leave.

When the boats had pulled away, the men, resting on their oars, watched helplessly as their vessel was gutted to the waterline.

The flames soon caught the shrouds and sails, making a magnificent conflagration up to the very peaks, for the royals were set at the time. The vessel, having now no sails to steady her, rolled heavily, and the masts, no longer supported, bent and creaked, threatening to go overboard any minute.

Efforts to save Wallace's 'variety of living creatures' were useless:

The poor things would not attempt to reach us, but retreated to the bowsprit, where the flames finally got to them.

With the coming of night, the *Helen* seemed to burn even more fiercely.

If for an instant we dozed off into forgetfulness, we were soon woken again to the reality of our position by the red glare which our burning vessel cast over us. The ship was now a magnificent if terrifying spectacle, for the decks were completely burnt away, and as it heaved and rolled with the swell, it presented its interior towards us filled with liquid flame – a fiery furnace tossing restlessly upon the ocean.

By dawn the *Helen* was little more than a charred and disintegrating hulk; there was no point in staying beside her, and the ship's boats got under way for the nearest land, Bermuda. It would be wrong to describe what happened next as an epic of the sea, but the next ten days were, for the crew of the *Helen*, a decidedly unpleasant and frightening experience. The boats, overloaded, had only a few inches of freeboard, and rode the huge Atlantic swell uneasily. The crew, constantly drenched with spray, were soon suffering from sunburn and dehydration. They were short of water. Contrary winds prevented their making the hoped-for progress towards Bermuda. They might not have survived if on 15 August they hadn't been sighted and picked up by the *Jordeson*, en route from Havana to London with a cargo of mahogany.

Wallace, to quote his own words, 'had lost almost all the rewards for [his] four years of privation and danger'; and it says much for his physical and mental toughness that as soon as he got back to England he set about picking up the pieces of his career without self-pity. He was determined to continue insect-collecting; and this was not simply because he appreciated the scientific and commercial value of each new species he discovered, but because he felt that only by studying and comparing a multiplicity of species could he hope to find the facts which would substantiate his embryo theory of evolution. The trouble was that he had no money; and it was fortunate for him that at this crisis in his career he found a sponsor, the Royal Geographical Society. It was due to the support of the Society in general and its president Sir Roderick Murchison in particular that Wallace, in 1854, was able to set sail for Malaysia.

Four years later, while recuperating from malaria on the island of Ternate, he had his inspirational 'flash of light' which enabled him, at the same time as Darwin, to arrive at the theory that different species of creatures evolved by natural selection.

In the event, it was Darwin, the respected establishment figure who had already been working on his *Origin of Species* for twenty years, rather than Wallace, the outsider, who got the credit for this momentous theory. But it is interesting to speculate on what might have happened if Wallace's Amazon collection hadn't gone down with the *Helen*. Quite possibly, on his return to England, he would have made the sort of comprehensive study of his specimens which can't be made in the field, and come to the conclusion that as early as 1854 he had sufficient evidence to publish his own definitive paper on evolution. If *Copaifera officinalis* had been less volatile, the name conjured up by the theory of evolution might be that of Wallace rather than Darwin.

Reading the journals and biographies of Humboldt, Darwin, Wallace and Bates one is struck by what pleasant characters they were. They lived contented family lives, and behaved impeccably towards both the indigenous peoples and their colleagues-cum-rivals; even Bates's secret marriage to a girl who was illiterate and little more than half his age seems to have been idyllically happy. And as well as being commendable men, the explorer-naturalists did highly commendable work which has enormously increased our knowledge and understanding of our planet. This may seem a simplistic point to make, yet exploration in other fields has not always been either so altruistic or so beneficial. Much polar exploration, for example, was tainted by self-aggrandizement and jingoism; much African exploration was fuelled by the love of hunting and the hope of commerical exploitation, and much oceanic exploration has been motivated by the wish to establish strategic bases, trade-routes and fisheries. The great naturalists are almost unique in that their work seems to have been wholly on the side of the angels; and this aura of integrity has been heightened in recent years by the support given by modern naturalists to the causes of human rights and conservation.

Nowhere has this support been more in evidence than in South America, where throughout the present century men like Rondon, the Villas Boas brothers and the American-born Posey have worked tirelessly not only to advance botany and ethnology, but to advance also the cause of the indigenous people.

It was in 1907 that Candido Rondon was appointed to supervise the building of a telegraph line through the Mato Grosso. The appointment turned out to be an inspired one, for Rondon was to prove a competent surveyor, an excellent engineer and (unusual in those days) a staunch advocate of Indian rights. 'He penetrated this vast and little-known area,' his citation tells us, 'and by his fearlessness, resolution and force of personality, succeeded in making friends with the Indians . . . Eventually he persuaded them not to destroy the newly erected telegraph posts, but to guard them.' It was during these negotiations that Rondon coined the phrase which was to be his motto for the rest of his life: 'Die if need be; but kill never'. Subsequently, he accompanied Theodore Roosevelt on his expedition up the Rio Pilcomayo, an arduous, dangerous and not unimportant feat of exploration. He also helped to found Brazil's first Indian protection agency.

The humanitarian approach favoured by Rondon in the Mato Grosso was extended by Claudio, Leonardo and Orlando Villas Boas to the Amazon. From the 1940s to the 1970s these three dedicated brothers devoted the better part of their lives to seeking out and making contact with the remote and often unfriendly tribes of the Amazon basin, many of whom had never seen a *civilazado*. It was delicate and dangerous work: the leaving of gifts, the patient waiting, arrows scything unexpectedly through the trees, more gifts and more waiting, the momentary glimpse of a half-seen figure, and at last the first wary encounter – the first touch and the first halting attempts at communication. Few men have done more than the Villas Boas brothers to bridge the gap between peoples of divergent culture.

Tribes who were visited yesterday by the Villas Boas are being studied today by teams of ethnobiologists. One such team, led by Darrell Posey, has for several years been studying the Kayapo Indians in the headwaters of the Xingu. Posey and his fellow-scientists are examining the resources of Amazonia through Indian eyes: that is to say they are learning how the Kayapo manage to live perfectly happily in the rain forest by making use of its natural resources: how, for example, they cure headaches with the wax of pink bees and burns with the wax of black ones, and how they mulch some plants with the detritus of termite nests and protect others by guarding them with transported colonies of *aztecas* (ants). This is rewarding work, for as Posey says, 'while it is good to save plants and animals, it is better still to acquire the knowledge of how to use them'. Such knowledge, accumulated over millennia by the Indians, is one of Amazonia's most valuable treasures.

CHAPTER 8

The Red Flag of Freedom

October: guarding the young corn shoots.

The revolutionary wars which, in the early nineteenth century, finally freed the people of the Andes from Spanish suzerainty were a *mélange* of bitter fighting, daring strategy, amazing feats of heroism and endurance, and sickening atrocities. One episode encapsulates the improbable spirit in which they were fought. Bolivar's patriot army had just made a spectacular crossing of the northern cordillera when they were attacked by a larger and better-equipped force of Spaniards. In the battle that followed a patriot officer had his arm blown off. Seizing the severed limb in his other hand, he waved it in the air with a shout of 'Long live the fatherland!'. This incident is well known. What is not so well known is that the officer in question was no South American patriot, but an Irish mercenary, and that when asked 'which fatherland?' he replied: 'England or Ireland. Whichever will give me burial.'

The war had many causes, both external and internal. Externally, the last decades of the eighteenth century has seen the defeat of the established order in several parts of the world. In North America the colonists had successfully rebelled against Great Britain. In Europe the radicals had rebelled – again successfully – against the *ancien régime* of France. In both the New World and the Old the concept of freedom had been metamorphosed, apparently against all the odds, from dream to reality. The people of South America began to ask themselves if what had happened in Boston and Paris might not happen also in Cartagena, Buenos Aires and Lima.

Internally, the war was brought about by the exasperation of the Creoles (native-born Americans of Spanish descent) with the repressive policy of the mother country. In his book *The New Conquistadors* Jan Read makes this point very clearly: 'The creoles bitterly resented a state of affairs in which *peninsulares* were always sent from Europe to occupy key positions ... Countries, like children, grow up and finally jib at outside control, and the grievances of the Spanish colonists sprang from the attempts of the mother country to impose strict control long after it was in a position to do so.' There were three spheres in particular in which this outside control was resented: administration, agriculture and trade.

The vast Spanish domains in South America were divided into eight administrative districts: the Viceroyalty of New Granada (consisting of the Captaincy-General of Venezuela, the Audiencia of Santa Fe and the Presidency of Quito), the Viceroyalty of Peru (including the Audiencia of Lima and the Captaincy-General of Chile) and the Viceroyalty of La Plata. Each of these districts was governed by officials appointed from Madrid who usually knew little about the New World yet monopolized all the key positions. The manifesto of 1816 in which the people of La Plata declared their independence complained specifically of this anomaly: 'Public offices are held exclusively by Spaniards, and although Americans are equally qualified to hold them by law, yet they are appointed only in rare instances, and then not until they have sated the cupidity of the courts by handing over vast sums of money. Of the 170 Viceroys who have governed this country only 4 have been Americans; of the 610 Captains-general only 14 have been Americans; even among the common clerks it is rare to find an American.' What was true of La Plata was true of the other Vice Royalties.

In the field of agriculture the Spaniards never realized the full potential of the Andes. The Incas' magnificent irrigation channels and terraces were allowed to fall into disrepair, and the Indians themselves were forced to work not on the land but beneath it – at the turn of the eighteenth century there were more than 1,400 mines in Peru alone, and according to the reliable John Miller (in his *Memoirs of General Miller in the service of the Republic of Peru*) more than 8¼ million Indians had died while working in them. The flocks of llama, vicuña and alpaca dwindled; the growing of some crops (such as tobacco) was made a government monopoly, and the growing of other crops (such as flax, hemp, saffron, olives and grapes) was expressly forbidden. In 1803, for example, orders were received from Spain to root up all vines in the northern provinces of South America; this was because the Cadiz merchants had complained of a decrease in the consumption of home-grown Spanish wine. All this was, to say the least, frustrating for the many dedicated and intelligent South Americans who saw all too clearly that the mother country instead of suckling her colonies was being suckled by them.

The most detested restrictions of all were those of trade. Although Spain was unable herself either to meet the growing demands of the colonists for manufactured goods or to purchase all the raw materials that the colonists produced, she forbade them to trade elsewhere. 'No South American,' wrote Captain Hall of the Royal Navy in 1818, 'could own a ship, nor could a cargo be consigned to him; no foreigner was allowed to reside in South America unless born in Spain, and no non-Spanish capital could be (put to use) in the colonies. Orders were given that no foreign ship should touch at a South American port; even ships in distress were not received with common hospitality, but were seized as prizes and the crew imprisoned.' To cap it all a punitive purchase tax, the detested *aleavala*, was levied on every transfer of goods.

The inflexibility of the Spanish colonial administration, and in particular its embargo on trade, led to widespread and highly organized smuggling. Again, Captain Hall wrote:

The South Americans, finding that the Spaniards could not or would not furnish them with adequate supplies, invited the assistance of other nations. To this call the other nations were not slow to listen; and soon there was established one of the most extraordinary systems of organized smuggling which the world ever saw. This was known as contraband, and was carried out in armed vessels, well-manned and prepared to fight their way to the coast and to resist the blockade of the Spanish. This singular system of warlike commerce was conducted by the Dutch, Portuguese, French, English and latterly by the North Americans.

The result was that when the revolution finally erupted it had a host of ready-made allies: soldiers and seamen who had served in the Napoleonic Wars who, with the coming of peace, found themselves at a loose end, who were not averse to risk and hardship provided the financial rewards were high, and who could by no stretch of the imagination be described as friends of the Spanish colonial regime.

It would, however, be wrong to infer that it was for financial reward alone that so many foreigners took part in the South American Wars of Independence. Most of the Creoles and many of the mercenaries who fought in the revolutionary armies were inspired by a genuine wish to see liberty and justice (the ideals of the French and American revolutions) take root in South America. They were not fighting a patriotic war, for the disparate vice royalties didn't as yet consider themselves as countries; they were not fighting a class war, for aristocrats and peasants fought with equal dedication on both sides; and they were not taking part in a rebellion of the masses against an élite, for the

Indians and mestizos were for the most part passive spectators. The war was essentially one of ideas, with the status quo – represented by the Spanish hierarchy, bureaucracy and army – coming under attack from the seekers of change – represented by Creole intellectuals and mercenary freedom-fighters.

In the final analysis the seekers of change were to prove more successful in war than in peace. Yet the chaos into which South America was plunged after the revolution should not be allowed to obscure the fact that its principle aims were idealistic and were achieved. The Spanish yoke *was* broken. Freedom of a sort *did* come to the people of the Andes. Unhappily, in the words of the greatest of all the revolutionaries, Simon Bolivar, 'although South America won freedom she lost almost everything else'.

The revolution, which at last hesitantly erupted in the early 1800s, could hardly be called unexpected, for throughout the previous century discontent had been simmering in South America like magma beneath a volcano. In 1692, after a widespread failure of crops, rioters had rampaged through the streets of Mexico City and Lima shouting 'death to the Spaniards who are eating our maize'. In 1730 more than 2,000 mestizos staged an armed protest against the hated Peruvian *aleavala*; and in 1749 Venezuelan Creoles sacked the offices of a monopolistic trading company in Caracas. Then, from the Spanish point of view, came the most terrifying insurrection of all. In 1780 José Condorcanqui led an uprising of more than 60,000 Quechua-speaking Indians who massacred every Spaniard in sight and managed to gain control of almost the whole of the central Andes. Condorcanqui, the illegitimate son of a Spanish friar and a mestizo, was well educated, brave and idealistic; but his solution to every problem was violence. He assumed the old Inca name of Tupac Amaru (the gifted one) and appealed to the Creoles to join his Indians in 'killing every one of the Spaniards, thus freeing all of us who suffer from the tyranny of Europeans'. The Creoles, however, appalled by the violence of the uprising, made common cause with the Spaniards suppressing it. After six months of bitter campaigning the brave but ill-armed Indians were defeated – as they had been defeated so often before – by Spanish cavalry, and Condorcanqui was captured. Reprisals were savage. The Indians' villages were razed to the ground, their crops were burned and their flocks slaughtered. Condorcanqui was forced to watch the execution of his wife and children; then his tongue was cut out, and his body torn limb from limb by horses.

Terrifying as the 1780 insurrection had been it had never in fact posed a serious threat to the Spaniards, for the Indians had been disunited, poorly armed and bereft of foreign support. A far greater threat was posed by the Creole intellectuals – men like Baquijano, Narino, Unanue, Rodrigues and Miranda – who were united, intelligent and able to drum up a great deal of foreign support, especially from Great Britain. Of these precursors of revolution the greatest was Miranda.

Francisco de Miranda was born in Caracas in 1750, the son of wealthy Creole merchants. He had a first-class education at the universities of Santa Rosa and Caracas, then, like many young men of his day who were uncertain what career to follow, he joined the army. At the age of twenty-one he was drafted to North Africa, where he quickly discovered that he wasn't cut out to be a soldier; indeed, the atrocities he witnessed in Morocco gave him a horror of bloodshed which, in later years, was to diminish his effectiveness as a revolutionary. In 1783 he left the army, and began travelling the world in an effort to whip up support for the concept of Creole independence. He won the backing (in principle if not always in practice) of such diverse and influential figures as John Quincy Adams, Thomas Jefferson, Catherine the Great of Russia, Napoleon and William Pitt, and came to the conclusion that the country most likely to help his cause was Great Britain. In 1784, on the first of his many visits to London, he founded the Gran Reunion Americana, a society which was later to provide the revolution not only with financial support and arms but with some of its greatest leaders. Throughout the 1780s and 1790s Miranda submitted a spate of proposals to the British government, urging them to 'help the people of South America in their efforts to resist the oppressive authority of Spain'. The British blew hot and cold. When England and Spain were at war, Miranda's proposals more than once came within an ace of being implemented; when England and Spain were at peace Miranda had to be content with the filibustering exploits of men like Popham, Beresford and Cochrane – adventurous serving officers whose relations with their government were strained to, and sometimes beyond, breaking point. It was due in large part to Miranda's machinations that at the turn of the century a number of these filibustering expeditions landed in South America, their tatterdemalion supporters all anxious to drive a nail into the Spanish coffin – some in the name of liberty, some in the hope of wealth, and some in the expectation of personal aggrandizement. None was successful in the long term, but between them they helped to establish what became an almost accepted pattern for armed intervention in Spanish colonial territory; and in 1806 Miranda himself, at the head of a group of somewhat naive 'liberators', landed in Venezuela. This, he hoped, would be his great moment. Right from the start, however, things went wrong, largely because Miranda had been abroad for so long that he had lost touch with the climate of opinion in his homeland. Much to his consternation he found himself greeted not with enthusiasm but with suspicion, and was obliged to beat an ignominious retreat to the islands of the Caribbean. A few years later he tried again, this time with better planning and more success, and in 1811 Venezuela declared independence.

Miranda, however, soon found himself facing what was to prove a perennial problem for the liberators. Exactly who were they trying to liberate from whom?

Miranda wanted to get rid of the Spaniards – on that he was unequivocal – but he wanted to replace them not with a broad-based amalgamation of all the South American peoples, but with a Creole aristocracy – with his fellow radicals, intellectuals, merchants, bankers and professional classes, who, he felt sure, would be able to turn South America into a better and more prosperous place. What Miranda did *not* want was to free his country from the restrictive *peninsulares* only to see it taken over by the anarchic *pardos* (poor whites and freed slaves) who were also eager for revolution but were not averse to the sweeping away and massacre of Spaniards and Creoles alike. As a result of this dilemma he was unwilling to promise too much in the way of freedom to too many people. In consequence the revolution, as he envisaged it, lacked popular appeal. It also lacked fire in the belly, for Miranda's aversion to bloodshed made him extremely reluctant to use force. Time and time again he allowed his adversaries to retreat or negotiate their way out of trouble. The culmination to a succession of setbacks came on 26 March 1812 when an earthquake struck Caracas. 'There was,' wrote an eyewitness, 'a devastating roar, followed by the silence of the grave.' More than 20,000 people were killed, most of them revolutionaries; for as chance would have it the royalist section of the city escaped unscathed, whereas the revolutionary section was reduced to ruins. The story goes that as the young Simon Bolivar dragged victims out of the rubble, he was heard to shout: 'No matter if Nature opposes us. We will fight it too!'

Whether the story is true of apocryphal, it pinpoints a major difference between Bolivar and Miranda. Bolivar, in the face of disaster, was belligerent and defiant. Only a few months after the earthquake he issued his famous manifesto, in which he declared: 'Our tolerance is exhausted, our hatred is implacable; the war will be to the death . . . Any Spaniard who does not work for us will be considered a traitor and shot.' Miranda, in contrast, was appalled by the suffering that the revolution was causing his countrymen, whom he saw 'being massacred one moment by the inhuman and atrocious Negro slaves,' and killed next moment by 'the unprincipled and oppressive royalists'. For him the earthquake was the last straw. Convinced, in his own words, that 'an honourable reconciliation was preferable to the hazards of a devastating civil war,' he opened negotiations with the royalist commander, Juan Monteverde, and on 25 July 1812, much to the fury of his fellow-revolutionaries, he capitulated.

He had been promised that patriot lives and property would be spared. This promise was instantly broken. Patriot leaders were hunted down and shot, and Miranda himself was first imprisoned and then sent in chains to Cadiz where, broken-hearted, he died of typhus: a tragic end for a man who may at times have seemed vain and excessively preoccupied with soliciting foreign aid, but whose devotion to the cause of revolution never wavered and whose failures were brought about by his determination to cause the minimum of bloodshed and never to impose on his people liberties which they hadn't chosen freely for themselves.

His contemporaries were critical of his 'softness'. Posterity has judged him more kindly – and more fairly. Today he is known simply as *El Precursor*: the initiator of independence.

In the north the flames of revolution flickered and subsided. In the south they flickered, took hold and spread: spread from the fulcrum of Buenos Aires across the pampas and into the Andes.

Here, among the towering peaks of the cordillera, in one of the most spectacular campaigns in history, the destiny of a continent was decided.

On 8 June 1806, at much the same time as Miranda was making his first abortive landing in Venezuela, a British fleet sailed into the estuary of the River Plate, and, in spite of the fact that Great Britain and Spain were at peace, bombarded and captured Buenos Aires. The perpetrator of this act of piracy was Admiral Sir Home Rigg Popham, an unscrupulous adventurer who, having helped himself to treasure worth some £300,000 from the coffers of Buenos Aires, wrote to a friend in England that 'the conquest of this place opens up an extensive channel for the manufacturers of Great Britain'. It is typical of this sort of filibustering expedition that Popham was driven out of Buenos Aires within six months, that he went on to capture Montevideo, that he was then called home to face a court martial for having embroiled his country in a war that was entirely of his own making, but that the treasure he brought back was paraded in triumph through the streets of London to the tune of 'Rule Britannia'. Though the British government officially deplored such excesses, the British public loved them; and without doubt freebooters like Popham played a not inconsiderable role in weakening Spanish authority and advancing the cause of revolution.

Even more injurious to Spain were the contraband-runners. Throughout the early years of the century foreign ships in general and British ships in particular engaged in a widespread, illicit and highly lucrative trade with the Atlantic ports of South America, bringing the colonists not only the cotton, woollen, iron and china products of the Industrial Revolution, but also such bizarre items as chandeliers, warming-pans, stays, coffins and ice-skates.

One of the most successful of these traders was William Brown, who began his naval career as cabin-boy in a New England whaler, and ended it as commander-in-chief of the Argentine navy. Brown was typical of the many flamboyant adventurers who risked their lives in the service of the revolution, while at the same time advancing their financial and personal status. Historians yesterday tended to depict these adventurers as romantic lovers of freedom; historians today tend to depict them as mercenaries. The truth lies somewhere between these extreme views; for although without doubt there were rogues, con-men and profiteers among the freedom-fighters, there were also many others who had a genuine empathy with the Spanish colonists and who supported their cause not only because it was profitable for them to do so, but because they believed it to be both noble and just. It is interesting to record that shortly before Brown died he had a most friendly reunion with his old sparring partner, the royalist Admiral Norton, with whom, decades earlier, he had exchanged broadsides on the estuary of the River Plate. 'If you had served an Empire instead of a Republic,' Norton is reputed to have said to him, 'you would now be a duke with a handsome pension.' To which Brown replied simply: 'But I like to think that Buenos Aires will remember my services.'

As well as being harassed by filibusters and contraband-runners from outside their territory, the Spanish in La Plata had to face a succession of insurrections from within. In 1808 Montevideo repudiated viceregal authority; Chuquisaca did the same in 1809 and Asuncion in 1810. These rebellions were, after bitter fighting, crushed, with the result that a whole generation of Argentine revolutionaries was virtually wiped out. Others, however, soon came forward, including the key members of Miranda's London-based Gran Reunion Americana: among them the man who in terms of fighting was to do more than anyone to win the war for the revolutionaries, José de San Martin.

San Martin was a brilliant strategist and a compelling, if very private, personality. The son of a Spanish cavalry officer, he was born in 1778 in Yapeyu in north Argentina. He completed his education at a military academy in Spain, and because the turn of the century was, in Europe, a time of almost continuous warfare, he saw in his early years a good deal of action; by the time he was thirty-three he was a lieutenant-colonel. One incident seems to have made a lasting impression on him. He was guarding a palace in Madrid when it was attacked by a mob; the doors were blown in, and the unfortunate Captain-General of Andalucia, who was the object of the mob's fury, fled in terror over the roof-tops, where he was hunted down, trapped and savagely butchered. Ever after, San Martin had a horror of mobs and of unnecessary violence; like Miranda, he was in many ways an unlikely revolutionary leader.

Yet he became a highly effective one. In 1811 he was posted to London, where he joined and quickly became a leading member of the Gran Reunion Americana. A year later he returned to the Argentine, determined, in his own words, 'to bring independence and happiness to the people of Spanish America'.

It seemed an impossible dream. In the north the revolution had collapsed. In the south the Spaniards in La Plata were apparently in a strong position, having crushed every insurrection that had taken place in the last decade. The revolutionaries, in contrast, were in disarray: disheartened by failure, divided by local jealousies, hampered by the difficulty in coordinating their movements in so vast a battlefield, and uncertain whether they wanted foreign aid – one reason for Popham's failure to hold Buenos Aires had been that 'its people made it abundantly clear they were in no mood to exchange the repression of Charles IV [of Spain] for the sovereignty of George III [of Great Britain]'. San Martin now gave evidence of one of his greatest virtues: patience. Ignoring the pleas of his fellow revolutionaries for action, he set about building up a clandestine army of the élite. 'In my regiment,' he wrote, 'I want only lions.' Each man was recruited secretly and interviewed personally; he had to be tall, strong, brave, intelligent and of good character – that is to say his private life had to be (as was San Martin's) beyond reproach. Training was long and arduous. Fair-weather revolutionaries failed to last the course; but those who came through were welded into a force to be reckoned with.

In 1813 the revolutionaries enjoyed a major political success; in elections in Buenos Aires a popular 'people's assembly' was returned to power. This assembly promptly abolished the Inquisition, the nobility, royal symbols, forced labour, tithes and judicial torture; it also took steps to end slavery. This was throwing down the gauntlet. Opinion for and against the revolution polarized, and renewed fighting broke out all over the Viceroyalty of La Plata. The revolutionaries (or patriots) held Buenos Aires, one or two university cities, and one or two remote country districts which were dominated by the sort of bandit-extremists whom the Creoles always regarded as dubious allies. The Spaniards (or royalists) held Montevideo and most of the interior. In particular they were strongly entrenched along the only road which linked Buenos Aires to Lima: the much-used trade route via the River Parana, the *pampas* and the mining districts of present-day Bolivia. Both sides, initially, regarded this road as the key to success; for both sides realized that the heart of the struggle would lie in Peru. Peru was the most stable, the most prosperous, the most conservative and the most heavily garrisoned of the Spanish viceroyalties. To the patriots it was a bastion which would eventually have to be stormed; to the royalists it was a bastion from whose centrally placed garrisons they could reinforce their peripheral viceroyalties. It was therefore to the River Parana that San Martin and his regiment were sent.

Here the patriot forces, known as the Army of the North, were led by General Manuel Belgrano, an extremely competent commander who found himself faced with a difficult (if not impossible) task. Every time Belgrano won a victory – and much against the odds he was to win several – the royalists simply brought up reinforcements from Peru. Two other factors worked against him. The local gauchos wanted peace more than they wanted freedom, and were reluctant to help the patriots; those who *did* help them and were caught had their heads impaled on spikes and their families sold as slaves. Also the patriot forces were poorly equipped and seldom paid. For more than a year San Martin and his regiment were embroiled in a costly and unproductive campaign which culminated in royalist victories at Vilcapugio and Ayohuma, the resignation of General Belgrano, and the reduction of the Army of the North from over 4,000 to less than 2,000. This, San Martin decided, was not the way to win independence for the people of South America. On taking over from Belgrano, he retreated westward, established a holding line in the foothills of the Andes, and settled down to regroup and, above all, to rethink.

The idea he came up with involved such risks it was initially condemned as 'lunatic' by the patriot junta in Buenos Aires. Nevertheless San Martin went ahead with preparations to put it into effect. He asked to be appointed governor of Cuyo: a vast, bleak and sparsely populated province which in those days formed a sort of Andean no man's land between Argentina and Chile. Here he began a slow, methodical build-up towards what has been called 'one of the most remarkable exploits in military history'. For San Martin's plan was to strike at Peru not by land via the trade-route up the Parana, but by sea via the coast of Chile. To do this he had first to liberate Chile, and to liberate Chile he had to take his army over the Andes – which everyone told him was impossible.

The Andes had, it is true, been crossed twice before by armies: by the Incas under Topa Yupanqui and by the Spaniards under Almagro. Both these crossings, however, had been made comparatively close to the equator; and Almagro had lost two men out of three. San Martin's projected route late farther to the south, through an even more formidable section of the Andes, close to the giant peak of Aconcagua, at 22,834 feet the highest point in the Americas. This is magnificent but terrifying terrain: an uninhabited wilderness of jagged, near-unclimbable peaks, foamwhite rivers fed by melted snow, and narrow valleys twisted and fissured by volcanic upheaval. The cold is so intense that steel shatters like glass, the wind has a touch of death, and almost the only living creatures are condors, soaring on unseen air-currents over the slopes of ice-coated scree. Human beings are made to feel intruders. No wonder San Martin confided in a friend, 'It is not the strength of the enemy that keeps me awake at night, it is how to cross those enormous mountains'.

Yet there *were* passes even through this part of the Andes: little-known and little-used tracks, where in the height of summer muleteers in single file hacked their way through the snow with their merchandise of flour, dried fruit and wine. On the south-west border of Cuyo lay the lowest and most easily crossed of these passes, the Planchon; on the north-west border lay two higher and more difficult passes, the Los Patos and the Uspallata, winding one either side of Aconcagua. San Martin's first priority was to reconnoitre these passes, a task for which he needed the cooperation of the local gauchos. This was given with unexpected enthusiasm.

There must have been something truly remarkable about San Martin's achievements during his three years in Cuyo; for in the words of his biographer Bartolmé Mitre, 'from this sparsely populated province alone he raised an invincible army which was to free two republics and spread the principles of the revolution throughout the entire continent'. How, one wonders, did this formal, uncharismatic man transform what was essentially a sleepy backwater into the powerhouse of the revolution, a fulcrum in which *everyone* – peasants, farmers, Indians, aristocrats and even foreign residents – became so enamoured with the patriot cause that they gave it their time, their labour, their money and in many instances their lives? He was certainly helped by the brutality of the royalists, whose atrocities turned the local people against them. He was helped too by a small circle of eccentric disciples: his aide-de-camp John Thomand O'Brien, a 6½-foot Irishman who declared himself willing to follow his leader 'if need be to hell'; James Paroissen, a dedicated Huguenot doctor whom San Martin subsequently decorated 'for his humanity and devotion to the wounded'; and Luis Beltran, a robust mendicant friar, able to turn his hand with equal facility to carpentry, horse-shoeing and the design and repair of gun-carriages. But what seems to have won the hearts of the people of Cuyo is that San Martin assumed the role of a sort of biblical patriarch: 'He achieved cooperation', writes Irene Nicholson,

by caring for the health and welfare of his people, by improving education, introducing vaccination, and irrigating farmlands. Soon the people began to regard him as a father whom they loved. Very much alone – for though he was surrounded by friends he had no close confidant – he looked after everything himself with the help of one secretary and two clerks. He was an austere figure, symbolizing a kind of paternal despotism, which was wholly acceptable under the pressures of war, but which was to prove a handicap once the mood of corporate sacrifice to an ideal had passed.

Enthusiasm for the revolution seemed, in those early days, to know no bounds. Agricultural production was stepped up, arms foundries worked twenty-four hours a day, landowners offered free pasture to the army's horses and mules, the ladies of Mendoza threw their jewels into the revolutionary coffers and made uniforms for the revolutionary troops, while foreign residents 'offered to shed their last drop of blood in the cause of independence'.

These preparations obviously didn't escape the notice of the Spaniards. However, San Martin had a remarkably efficient intelligence network, and his agents infiltrated into Chile where they managed to spread false information about the patriots' intentions. In particular they managed to convince the Spanish that San Martin was planning to cross the Andes via the southern (Planchon) pass. To heighten this impression San Martin invited the Pehuenche Indians, who lived at the approaches to the pass, to a *fiesta* where he loaded them with gifts and asked for permission to cross their land; this information was then leaked to the royalists.

On the afternoon of 17 January 1817, in the town square of Mendoza, San Martin unveiled a flag 'woven by the ladies of the revolution'. 'Soldiers,' he is reported to have cried, 'this is the first independent flag to be blessed and raised in South America. I swear to defend it or die for it. Will you do the same?'

'There was,' writes Mitre, 'a great shout of *Vive la Patria!*' – though whether 'La Patria' was Argentina, Chile or the revolutionary cause is not clear, and the incident sounds out of character (San Martin hated mobs and mob-oratory) and may by apocryphal. What is true, however, is that over the next few days patriot agents throughout Chile were visited by itinerant vendors who offered them 'fat hens for sale': San Martin's code-message that the crossing of Andes was under way.

We know more about the preparations for the crossing than about the crossing itself.

San Martin's army seems to have been small: about 3,000 infantry, 700 cavalry, 250 artillerymen, 1,200 irregulars, and an unspecified number of muleteers and artisans. Prerequisites of success would have been speed and a first-class commissariat, and the key to both of these were mules – well over 10,000 of the patient, sure-footed animals accompanied the army, some ridden by the troops, others loaded with equipment and supplies. Provisions were carried for twenty days. The basic ration was *charquican* (dried beef ground to a powder and mixed with chilli and fat). This was a compact and nutritious diet; and as well as his rifle and bayonet, each soldier carried a knapsack containing sufficient *charquican* and water for eight days. Keeping pace with the troops was a baggage-train, bringing carefully tested ropes, cables, anchors, ladders and portable bridges to help with the crossing of mountain torrents and snowfields. On the morning of 18 January a diversionary column set out for the Planchon, its thirty horsemen creating as much dust as possible to give the impression that a large force was heading south; and at nightfall the two main columns (commanded by Miguel Soler and Bernardo O'Higgins) set out in secret for the Los Patos and the Uspallata. Each column had a precise timetable to keep to and a precise tactical plan to follow, and these, in spite of apparently insuperable difficulties, were strictly adhered to. In this respect San Martin's conquest of the Andes has much in common with Amundsen's conquest of the Pole: both achieved success by meticulous planning, keeping to an exact timetable, and the sacrifice of their animals. The South Americans, however, were not nearly so well equipped to face cold as the Norwegians; and no one will ever know how many died during the crossing, some, like the Incas before them, probably frozen solid to the rocks as they leaned against them. San Martin in his diary says simply:

The army had 10,600 saddle and pack mules, 1,500 horses and 700 head of cattle. Despite the most scrupulous care there arrived in Chile no more than 4,300 mules and 511 horses, all in very bad condition. Food for the 20 days that the march was expected to last was taken on mule-back; this was necessary because there was no house, let alone a town or village, between Mendoza and Chile, and five huge and uninhabited ranges had to be crossed. The army suffered greatly from lack of oxygen, as a result of which many soldiers died. Others succumbed to the intense cold.

Soon to the hazards of altitude were added those of battle; for no sooner had San Martin's troops debouched from the passes than they were attacked by the royalists.

The Spanish commander, Marco de Ponte, had not been altogether deceived by San Martin's feint towards the Planchon; he was, however, in a difficult position. With the knowledge of hindsight it is obvious that he would have been well advised to concentrate his troops (which would then have greatly outnumbered San Martin's) around Santiago; but this, his senior officers pointed out, was a passive strategy. His best plan, they argued, was to attack the patriots the moment they emerged from the cordillera, while they were still physically weak and before they could pick up local support. De Ponte therefore divided his forces, and sent about 3,000 men to guard each pass.

As San Martin's columns emerged from the Los Patos there took place a succession of skirmishes, with the royalists first attacking then falling back, surprised by the number and *élan* of the patriots. The decisive encounter took place on 12 February at Chacabuco. The battle was like a small-scale Waterloo: the artillery menacing but ineffective in the background, a muddy stream and a couple of farmhouses at the heart of the defence, troops advancing in thin blue and red lines then falling back to form defensive squares, positions captured 'at the point of the bayonet'. It was also one of the last battles to be won by a cavalry charge. For more than a thousand years, in terrain as disparate as the steppe of Mongolia, the plateau of Castilla and the plains of Texas, the horse had reigned supreme as a weapon of war. This era was coming to an end. But now in the high reaches of the Andes the horse had a last moment of glory as Soler's 511 cavalry, with sabre and lance, shattered de Ponte's squares and pursued the demoralized royalists down the road to Santiago. It was a decisive victory.

Chacabuco was only a small-scale battle – royalist losses were no more than 500 killed and 600 taken prisoner, while patriot losses may have been a low as 200 – yet its consequences were out of all proportion to its size. It has been claimed that it 'altered the face of a continent'; and this is no exaggeration. For the royalists in the south never recovered confidence; before the battle the tide had run with them, after the battle it ran against them, and Chile soon became not only the first viceroyalty to achieve effective independence but also the springboard from which the other viceroyalties were in turn invaded and liberated.

None of this, however, happened easily or overnight, and almost ten years of fluctuating fighting were to separate San Martin's crossing of the Andes from the final surrender of the Spanish in Callao in 1826. There were several reasons why the war dragged on for so long. The royalists had competent generals and loyal troops; they were not prepared to give in easily. The Indians never accorded the revolution the sort of wholehearted support which might have turned it into a popular uprising; used and abused by both armies, they regarded their so-called liberators as little more than the same rider on a different mule. Another factor to prolong the war was that the patriots were frequently at loggerheads among themselves. This was partly because the various viceroyalties were so disparate. The two fulcrums of revolution, for example – Chile and Venezuela – were not only 3,000 miles apart in distance, they were a world apart in character: the one a fishing, mining and crop-growing community oriented to the Pacific, the other a cattle-grazing community oriented to the Atlantic. Other viceroyalties were equally dissimilar. It is therefore not to be wondered at that in different parts of South America the revolution was fuelled by different hopes, raised different questions and needed different answers. Visionaries like Bolivar and San Martin may have dreamed of creating a Grand Confederation of the Andes – a sort of latterday Inca Empire comprising all the viceroyalties and ruled by enlightened European radicals – and if they had succeeded South America today might be a more stable place; but with the character of both the country and the people against them, one wonders if their dream was not an impossible one.

Another reason for patriot disharmony was that their leaders were men of such widely different nationality, religion, background and temperament. The three men who did most to liberate Chile – San Martin, O'Higgins and Cochrane – are a case in point. San Martin was the son of a Spanish soldier and a devout Catholic; he was born in Argentina and educated in Spain. O'Higgins was the natural son of an Irish soldier and a Creole; he was born in Chile and educated in England. Cochrane was the son of a Scottish peer; he was born in Lanarkshire and served in the Royal Navy.

Cochrane's role in the liberation of South America demonstrates very clearly both the enormous debt that the revolution owed to its foreign freedom-fighters and the enormous problems some of these men created.

Thomas Cochrane, the Tenth Earl of Dundonald, was born in 1775. At the age of seventeen he joined the Royal Navy, and at once found his *métier*, serving with distinction throughout the latter part of the Napoleonic Wars. His best-known exploits were probably the defence of Rosas, where his ship's company held almost an entire French army at bay (a feat immortalized by Marryat in *Peter Simple*), and the battle of the Aix Roads, where his ship's company, again almost single-handed, destroyed the better part of a French fleet with fire ships (a feat which earned him the grudging congratulations of Napoleon). He was a brave and inspired fighter of all types of naval engagement. However, he was also intolerant, hot-headed, and outspoken – 'All the Cochranes,' wrote Admiral of the Fleet Lord Saint Vincent, 'are mad, romantic, money-getting and not truth-telling.' The young firebrand made a host of enemies in high places. These enemies had their revenge when Cochrane became involved in a sensational stock-exchange scandal; he was found guilty of 'infamous conduct' and stripped of his honours, his family banner was thrown out of Westminster Abbey and his name removed from the Navy list. At this nadir in his fortunes he was approached by the Chilean envoy in London with the proposition that he should take command of the embryo patriot navy. The idea appealed to Cochrane on several counts; it appealed to his love of naval warfare, his love of making money, and his love of liberty and liberalism; and in the autumn of 1819 he arrived in Valparaiso, together with his wife and two young children. (Lady Cochrane, according to contemporaries, was 'young, fascinating and highly gifted'. Her husband had first seen her at the age of sixteen, walking in Hyde Park in a school crocodile, and had promptly eloped with her.) In many ways Cochrane was to prove an ideal choice to built up and lead the patriot navy, and during his five years as 'Vice-Admiral of Chile [and] Admiral and Commander-in-Chief of the Naval Forces of the Republic' he repeatedly carried out attacks on Spanish ships and Spanish ports which, for audacity and effectiveness, have never been surpassed in the history of naval warfare. His most important coup was the capture of Valdivia.

Valdivia in southern Chile has been described as 'the Gibraltar of South America'. It is a superb natural harbour, ringed by dense forests of *nothofaguas* and near-perpendicular cliffs. Into the cliffs were cut nine castles and batteries with a fire-power of 128 guns. The stronghold was garrisoned by close on 1,000 troops, and was considered impregnable.

One evening, on the quarterdeck of his flagship the *O'Higgins*, Cochrane said casually to the officer commanding his marines, 'What do you think people would say if with this one ship I tried to take Valdivia?'

When the officer didn't answer, Cochrane went on, 'They would call me a lunatic. But I tell you, operations which the enemy doesn't expect are always likely to succeed . . . And the best answer to a charge of rashness is victory.'

In fact, a few months after this conversation, Cochrane found himself not with one ship but three; for the diminutive *Montezuma* and *Intrépido* were loaned to him by the Governor of Concepcion, together with 250 Chilean troops. On 18 January 1820 the *O'Higgins*, flying the Spanish flag, sailed boldly into Valdivia harbour, dropped anchor under the guns of the batteries and signalled for a pilot. Believing the *O'Higgins* must be the *Potrillo* (a galleon due to arrive any moment with the garrison's pay) the Spanish sent out a longboat with a pilot and a guard-of-honour. Cochrane, meanwhile, had embarked in his gig and was making an inspection of the harbour defences; by the time the Spaniards realized they had been duped, he had the information he needed and was under way. A couple of days later, having in the interval captured the *Potrillo* and her treasure of 20,000 gold doubloons, he was back. This time it was the *Montezuma* and *Intrépido* who flew Spanish flags and asked for pilots. The garrison, however, were not deceived a second time and opened fire. Although hampered by heavy swell and a scum of seaweed which 'loaded the oars at every stroke', Cochrane launched his ships' boats and made a frontal attack on Fort Ingles, where the heaviest royalist fire was coming from. His seamen had to 'advance in single fire along a narrow track, rendered slippery by spray from the surf which dashed with deafening roar upon the rocks'; nevertheless they succeeded in driving the Spaniards back into the fort. This, however, looked like being the extent of their success; for the Spaniards in retreat simply 'drew up the ladders leading to the ramparts and reckoned themselves safe'. They had, however, reckoned without the cunning of *El Diablo Cockrane*, who before the main action started had secretly landed his Chileans farther down the coast. These troops were now approaching the back of the fortress unseen. Under cover of darkness and in the confusion caused by the frontal attack, they gained entry by swinging Tarzanlike from trees to ramparts; they then attacked the garrison unexpectedly from the rear. Half the Spaniards in Fort Ingles were butchered, the other half fled, taking with them in the confusion a force of 300 who were just arriving to reinforce them. Before the royalist troops had a chance to regroup or to discover how small a force was attacking them, all the forts and batteries along the west shore of the harbour had been one by one stormed and captured. By dawn Cochrane was in a commanding position, looking down on the town of Valdivia where the demoralized royalists had taken refuge. In fact he would have been hard put to it to launch an attack on the town, because the *O'Higgins* was leaking so badly she had been run aground, and the *Intrépido* had hit a sandbar and broken up. However, such was the terror inspired by *El Diablo*, that the Spanish commander surrendered; the remaining forts and much booty fell into patriot hands, and in less than twenty-four hours' fighting the royalists lost a stronghold which had been thought impregnable and which was of the greatest strategic importance (while a Spanish fleet in Valdivia still threatened Chile in the south there could be no question of the patriots launching an attack on Peru in the north).

If the capture of this 'Spanish Gibraltar' was Cochrane's most important achievement, his most spectacular was the cutting out of the *Esmeralda*.

The *Esmeralda*, a 54-gun frigate, was the flagship of the Peruvian navy. On the night of 5 November 1820 she was lying in Callao harbour, guarded by 27 gunboats, over 250 shore-based guns, and an intricate network of booms; she was manned by 'close on 400 of the best seamen and marines of the Spanish Navy, who slept every night at quarters'. Cochrane, with 240 hand-picked volunteers, planned to cut her out: that is to board her, capture her, and sail her or tow her out of harbour. This was a desperate undertaking: a night for blackened faces, muffled oars, whispered passwords, and the swift and silent capture of the gunboat guarding the entrance between the booms (Cochrane threatened to cut the Spanish crews' throats if they made a sound). With his usual flair for the unexpected he had planned his attack to coincide with a banquet being held aboard the *Esmeralda*, an occasion which he knew would lead to the presence of more Spaniards, but also to more noise and more wine. His men, armed only with cutlasses, managed to reach the flagship without being spotted. They boarded her from either quarter, simultaneously. Cochrane, one of the first over the side, was knocked back into the longboat by a Spanish sentry. He fell awkwardly on to the rowlocks, injuring a vertebra in his spine. Undeterred, he clawed his way back, only to be shot through the thigh. Still undeterred, he bound up the wound with his handkerchief, and directed the attack sitting astride one of the *Esmeralda's* guns, his 'leg held high in an effort to stop the bleeding'. The Spaniards fought bravely, but many were cut down before they had a chance to arm. About 160 were killed or drowned, and while the remainder were being battened down under the hatches the British seamen hoisted sail. By now the harbour was in uproar. Some of the Spanish gunboats tried to grapple with and board the *Esmeralda*, but with the wind in her sails she shook herself free. The shore batteries then tried to open fire on her, but the congestion of shipping in the harbour impeded their shot. The Spaniards had agreed that in the event of a night attack, neutral ships were to hoist coloured lights to identify themselves. The *Hyperium* and the *Macedonina*, which were anchored close to the flagship, obeyed these instructions; whereupon Cochrane (who knew all about the Spanish contingency plans) hoisted similar lights, and in the ensuing confusion managed to work his way out of harbour. A contemporary, Captain Hall, wrote: 'The loss of the *Esmeralda* was a death blow to the Spanish naval forces in that quarter of the world; for although there were still 2 Spanish frigates and some smaller vessels left in the Pacific, they never afterwards ventured to shew themselves, but left Cochrane undisputed master of the coast.'

Peru lay open to invasion.

Another incident in Cochrane's career shows how deeply some of the foreign freedom-fighters became involved in the revolution on a personal level. It was a few months after the family had arrived in Valparaiso, and the Commander-in-Chief of the Naval Forces of the Republic was about to put to sea in his flagship the *O'Higgins*, when his wife was horrified to see their little boy, aged five, rush down the beach shouting 'Viva la patria!' At the water's edge the boy was picked up by Cochrane's flag-lieutenant, and ferried out to the *O'Higgins* which was now under way. As Cochrane himself tells us it wasn't long before his son saw action.

When the firing commenced, I placed him in my after-cabin, locking the door; but not liking the restriction, he contrived to get through the quarter-gallery window and join me on deck. As I could not attend to him, he was permitted to remain. Soon, in a miniature mid-shipman's uniform which the seamen had made for him, he was handing powder to the gunners. Whilst thus employed a round shot took off the head of a marine standing beside him, scattering the unlucky man's brains all over his face. I was spell-bound with agony, believing him killed, but he ran up to me exclaiming, 'I am not hurt, papa; the shot did not touch me.' I ordered him to be carried below; but since he resisted with all his might, he was permitted to remain on deck during the rest of the action.

It is difficult to see how the patriots, who had little expertise in naval matters, could have won command of the sea without the help of Cochrane. Yet his very success led to jealousy, and to problems which were exacerbated by his mercurial temperament. Even his friends admitted he was 'touchy'; his enemies claimed he was 'impossible'; a balanced view would probably be that he was irascible. In Chile, as in England, he made enemies in high places, and in particular he made an enemy of San Martin.

On a personal level the two were antipathetic: the modest, careful, austere and slightly intovert Spaniard, and the ostentatious, venturesome, flamboyant and decidedly extrovert Scotsman; about the only characteristic they had in common was pride. Yet there was a great deal more to their running feud than a clash of personalities. Cochrane saw things always in terms of how-to-defeat-the-Spaniards; his solution to every problem was military. San Martin saw things in terms of how-to-rule-the-people-of-the-Andes-once-they-had-been-liberated; his solution to every problem was political. Cochrane is reported to have said that if he were given a thousand men and a free hand he would conquer Peru in a week. San Martin put his point of view equally forcefully:

Peruvians, do not think we shall treat you as a conquered people. We aspire only to see you free and happy. You yourselves will choose and form your own government, so that you can become a nation as free and independent as ourselves ... People ask why I do not march on Lima immediately. I could, if I wanted to. But I do not seek military glory, nor do I want to be known as the conqueror of Peru – I wish only to see it free from oppression. What good would Lima do me if its people were hostile politically?

Another reason why San Martin was forever holding back is that he saw, more clearly than Cochrane, the need to coordinate patriot strategy on a continental scale. Like most members of the Gran Reunion Americana, he envisaged the war ending with a pincer-movement on Peru. In the south everything was ready by 1818 for such a movement. However, in the north Bolivar had become bogged down in the llanos of Venezuela, and it was not until May 1819 – two and a half years later than San Martin – that his army crossed the Andes. In the interval San Martin procrastinated, drawing on himself the scorn of his contemporaries and the undeserved condemnation of historians.

While for a couple of years the revolution hung fire in the south, it engulfed the viceroyalties of the north with terrifying violence.

Here the man who sustained it and imbued it with at least a patina of his vision and idealism was Simon Bolivar.

He was born in Caracas in 1781, youngest son of one of the wealthiest families in Venezuela who christened him Simon José Antonio de la Santisima Trinidad Bolivar y Palacio. In both appearance and personality he was like a chameleon, an amalgam of contradictions. He was a small man, no more than 5 feet 6 inches, with a narrow tubercular chest and delicate hands and feet; yet he was capable of driving his whipcord body to amazing feats of endurance. He had dark eyes, curly hair, the nose of a patrician and the lips of a Negro. It was said by his contemporaries that women found him irresistible. In character he gave the impression of being vain, dressing extravagantly and spending lavishly. In temperament he was mercurial and emotional. Two qualities which even his enemies admitted he had in abundance were intelligence and courage. And he was an idealist: unswervingly devoted throughout his life to the cause of freeing South

America from Spanish suzerainty, and filling the resulting vacuum with a federation of Creole aristocracy.

Bolivar took over as leader of the Venezuelan patriots from the luckless Miranda, and at once stepped up the stakes and the fighting.

Venezuela at the time of the revolution has been described as 'part-plantation part-ranch'. In the coastal valleys were huge fields of tobacco, cotton, coffee and, in particular, cacao, owned by aristocratic landowners and worked by tied or manumitted slaves. In the hinterland lay a vast and featureless expanse of grassland, scorched by sun in the dry season and turned into a near-impenetrable swamp in the wet; this was home to literally millions of cattle, and to the *llaneros* – a wild and warlike race, part-Indian, part-white and part-Negro, who had been hardened (some would say brutalized) by their challenging surroundings, and were among the finest horsemen in the world. Here was the tinder of anarchy and the sort of war in which no prisoners are taken.

At first the patriots tried to enlist the help of both slaves and *llaneros*. They soon found, however, that they had a tiger by the tail, for their 'allies' showed a propensity for massacring *all* whites, be they patriot or royalist, with equal enthusiasm. Before long *peninsulares* and Creoles forgot their differences and made common cause to crush an embryo slave-revolution. The royalists never forgave their fellow-whites for exposing them to the threat of massacre by black mobs, while the slaves and *llaneros* never forgave the patriots for turning against them. So began an appalling cycle of reprisal and counter-reprisal, atrocity and counter-atrocity.

One should beware of accepting atrocity stories at face value. Some are propaganda, others clearly become exaggerated in the telling. However, eyewitness and impartial accounts indicate that, in Venezuela, royalists, patriots and *llaneros* were all guilty of appalling cruelty.

The royalists offered a price [about £2 a pair] for patriot ears, and in some cases are known to have decorated their homes with these trophies . . . In Caracas after they had raped the women, they tied them in hammocks and burnt them to death . . . They peeled the skin off the feet of patriot prisoners and forced them to walk over hot coals.

The patriots replied in kind:

Bolivar, fearing that the very large number of Spanish prisoners in La Guaira and Caracas might rise and join his enemies, ordered that all prisoners – even those sick in hospital - were to be killed. In three days eight hundred people, many of whom were innocent of any crime against the revolution, were massacred. British officers who had arrived to help the Liberator were appalled to see the prisoners stripped naked, bound, then stabbed in the back of the neck until they died.

Any *llaneros*, we are told, who collected twenty Spanish heads (age and sex immaterial) was rewarded with officer status. No prisoners were allowed to live. 'Their leader [Boves] moved among them, personally supervising the killing of some 40 men, women and children who were hacked to death with sabres.' A British officer serving with the *llaneros* writes:

The Spaniards had no sooner surrendered when the natives began their murderous work, and it was continued without intermission until every individual of the entire 1300 [prisoners] was despatched. The British kept aloof from this spectacle as much as possible . . . And afterwards I received a severe reprimand for not having taken an active part in the slaughter. General Urdenetta informed us that since we had entered the service of Venezuela, we were expected to conform to its usages, and in future they insisted on our personal share of putting prisoners to death. We made no reply; but I believe that all inwardly resolved never to obey such an order.

For almost a decade Venezuela was ravaged by a war that was civil, revolutionary and total, its antagonisms sharpened by differences of colour, race, creed and social status. The combatants were evenly matched, with the royalists able to draw on reinforcements from Spain, and the patriots drawing on the many groups who were dissatisfied with the rule of the *peninsulares*. Initially the patriots prospered: 'In his first campaign as a general, Bolivar [his biographer Thomas Rourke tells us] marched 1,200 kilometres over primitive mountain country, fought six battles, destroyed five armies, and conquered the whole western part of Venezuela – all in the space of ninety days.' However, in 1815 an army of almost 10,000 Spaniards, led by the more than competent General Morillo, arrived from Cadiz. A force of this size proved decisive, for in the northern Andes, as in the southern, the number of troops engaged in any one battle was small. Within a year patriot forces had been routed, Creole property(including over 300 haciendas) had been sequestrated, and Bolivar had been driven into exile first in Jamaica then in Haiti. It says much for his resilience that within a year he was back, this time with a new ally and a new strategy.

His ally was Alexandre Pétion, president of the black republic of Haiti, who promised Bolivar troops on the understanding that if he gained control of Venezuela he would free the slaves. This, in fact, had always been Bolivar's intention. 'It is madness,' he had written years earlier, 'that a revolution for liberty should try to maintain slavery'; he had already freed the slaves on his own haciendas, and he now made a determined effort to broaden the base of the revolution and to win back the support of the slaves and *llaneros*. He had most success with the latter, for he decided to set up his headquarters in their territory. Early in 1817 he led his men south into what is now Guyana. This was a new and visionary strategy – to base the revolution not among the cities of the coast, but deep in the hinterland, among the great plains of the Orinoco which were a barrier against defeat, a springboard for attack, and a source of sustenance and wealth in their rich reserves of livestock.

At first he had to fight both royalists and *llaneros*. However, he gradually won the support of the latter by offering them not freedom – they had no interest in so intangible a concept – but plunder in the shape of cattle and land. He never understood the *llaneros*, being too cerebral to have much empathy with an earthbound people whose lives were an unremitting physical battle with their environment; but he did strike up an understanding with their leader, José Antonio Paez. Paez, a giant of a man accompanied always by an even more gigantic Negro bodyguard, was cunning, brave and a guerrilla leader *par excellence*. He welded the *llaneros* into a savage but disciplined force of cavalry – by far the most feared component of the patriot army – and handed them over to Bolivar on the understanding that the latter would distribute the conquered land and the cattle that grazed it among his troops. It was the start of a fruitful if uneasy alliance.

The revolution in the north now ground to a stalemate. Morillo and his royalists were not strong enough to pursue Bolivar into the hinterland and conduct a campaign far from their bases and in different terrain where their opponents had local support. Bolivar and his patriots were never able to persuade the *llaneros* to operate outside their homeland, so whenever they advanced into the coastal hills they found themselves outnumbered and repulsed. In other words Bolivar in Venezuela in 1819 found himself facing much the same problem as San Martin had faced in Argentina in 1815; he was bogged down in an unproductive war which he could see little hope of winning.

He came up with the same solution. He would find a new theatre of war. He too would lead his army across the Andes.

Bolivar's crossing of the Andes was easier than San Martin's in that the northern cordillera were lower than the southern – their peaks at 18,000 feet rather than 22,000 and their passes at 12,000 feet rather than 14,000; also, since they were closer to the equator, the cold was less intense. It was more difficult in that the approach had to be made through harsher terrain, the cordillera were wider, and Bolivar deliberately chose to cross them by an 'impossible' route and at an 'impossible' time of year in order the achieve surprise. It is not known exactly how many troops Bolivar took with him. Contemporary records say only that 'on May 26th [1819] there set out from the Arauca River four infantry battalions, one rifle battalion, the *Bravos* of Paez, the British legion, and cavalry.' Estimates as to how many men this involved vary from 1,500 infantry and 700 cavalry, to 2,000 infantry and 1,000 cavalry. Whichever figures one accepts, and even allowing for the fact that accompanying the army were an unspecified number of mules and muleteers, cattle and cattle-drivers, and at least 250 women, this was a small force with which to try to conquer the most powerful of the Spanish viceroyalties.

Because both the crossing of the Andes and its aftermath were successful it is difficult to realize what a hazardous, not to say forlorn, venture it must have seemed at the time as Bolivar's army set out that summer by canoe and raft up the Arauca River. It rained nonstop for the eight days it took them to reach Gausdualito. Here, as the river became unnavigable, they caught their first glimpse of the Andes, 'rising like grey spectres out of a canopy of cloud'. The moment they saw the mountains, Paez's *llaneros* deserted. The rest of the army plodded on, in single file, through plains which, at the height of the wet season, were a kaleidescope of overflowing river, reed-fringed lake and fever-generating swamp. The men had to hold their muskets above their heads, for the water was often waist-deep and at times shoulder-deep.

This was the sort of terrain in which foreign freedom-fighters in general and the British Legion in particular suffered heavy casualties. An anonymous British soldier (in his *Recollections of a Service of Three Years during the War-of-Extermination in the Republics of Venezuela and Colombia*) has left an account of the Legion's exploits. Most of those who volunteered to serve the revolution had no idea what they were letting themselves in for. They expected to fight a gentleman's war in eighteenth-century European style, and their attitude is summed up in the words of one of the first to enlist: 'Now, boys, for South America: flags, banners, glory and riches.' This roseate image was fostered by European recruiting agencies. Plausible Irishmen like 'General' John Devereux (who had never seen a battlefield in his life) became millionaires by selling spurious commissions in the revolutionary army. Firms like Thompson and Mackintosh (overstocked at the end of the Napoleonic Wars with surplus equipment) made a fortune by selling uniforms more suited to comic opera than the rain forest of the Amazon.

We were told that the uniform of the regiment was a dark green jacket with scarlet collar, lapels and cuff, with an ornamental Austrian knot on the arm, a laced girdle round the waist, and two small gold epaulettes; dark green trousers, edged with gold lace . . . Undress uniform – dark green jacket with red cuffs and collar, trimmed with black lacing, crimson sashes, black leather belts, sabre sash etc . . . the only addition thought necessary for the officer, a blue camelot cloak, lined with red baize.

Many of those recruited never even reached South America. In 1816 a regiment of lancers raised by Colonel Skeene embarked in an ex-frigate, the *Indian*. En route for Venezuela the *Indian* foundered; there were no survivors. Those who did arrive soon found that the fantasy-world of the recruiting agencies bore little resemblance to the real world of disease-ridden swamps, atrocities they were expected both the endure and to perpetrate, and the inability of the revolutionary government to pay them. What happened to McGregor's regiment was typical. Sir Gregor McGregor (who astonished the Creoles by habitually wearing a kilt and having his men piped into battle) commanded a force of 400 lancers. In three years' fighting in the coastal plains his regiment took part in many engagements and greatly distinguished themselves; but in 1817 they were captured. They were forced to walk in chains across the isthmus of Panama; then the officers, still in chains, were put to work filling in an unhealthy swamp; 'after two months, under pretext they had attempted to escape, they were all most barbarously shot'. No wonder the author of *Recollections* describes the war as a '*War of Extermination*'. He gives a good account of the march to and over the Andes.

All descriptions of the dreadful sufferings we endured must fall far short of the reality. First, we had to cross rivers so swollen and fast-flowing that in fording them many were unable to bear up against the flood and were swept away, their bodies dashed against stumps of trees and rocks until life was extinct . . . Others succumbed to a species of fish called raya (a species of piranha) which seized the thighs and calves of their legs and tore large pieces from them.

The men were never dry; their clothes rotted on their bodies, and their shoes disintegrated.

Then our naked feet were invaded by myriads of insects named chegoes. These tormenting creatures penetrated the skin, breeding under it to such an extent that unless they were speedily removed they produced mortification . . . Many who tried to quench their thirst from the pools of brackish water were later found dead, for these were the home of snakes of the most poisonous description.

Four hundred of the British Legion died before even reaching the Andes.

By late June the army had struggled through to the foothills and made contact with the patriot forces under Francisco de Paula Santander who had been waging a guerrilla campaign against the Spaniards in the mountainous borders of present-day Venezuela and Colombia. For a couple of days the combined force, now totalling some 3,500, recuperated in the town of Maturin, so often sacked by the Spaniards that it consisted of nothing but irregular rows of mud-built huts. Then they began the ascent.

The first casualties were the horses. 'The surface of the mountains was composed of small sharp-pointed stones, resembling broken Scotch granite, and every bit as hard'; most horses were unshod; one by one the unfortunate animals went lame; by the end of the second day 75 per cent of Bolivar's cavalry were without a mount. As the trail climbed higher so it grew steeper. In some places, half washed away by torrential rain, it skirted the lip of terrifying precipices. In other places it zig-zagged up rocks so sheer that the men, hands and feet bleeding, were hard put to it to claw their way from one precarious foothold to the next. Those who lost their balance lost their life. In yet other places it crossed mountain torrents which had to be bridged with tree-trunks and cables, while the animals were slung over in baskets of plaited vines. 'Bolivar,' we are told, 'was to be seen everywhere, now exhorting us "only a little farther", now carrying over the weak, the injured and the women.' Soon they were faced with new adversaries: cold and the thinness of the air. The crossing was being made via the remote Paramo de Pisba. This, at 13,000 feet, was the highest and most difficult route over the cordillera; even those who lived in the mountains fought shy of crossing it out of season; for those who had spent their lives in the plains the crossing was purgatory. The cold for many was beyond endurance. The lack of oxygen caused nausea, heart-pounding, bleeding from the nose and ears, and eventually the stupor that leads to death. The men had to belabour one another to ward off a drowsiness that was fatal. Those who stopped to rest, died. The night of 4 July was spent at 11,000 feet on the *paramo*. By now there were neither mules, horses nor cattle left. There was no wood for fires. The wind moaned over the frozen scree. 'The stars,' one of the soldiers wrote, 'shone with a metallic luster. They looked very bright and very far away.' All over the *paramo* men and women lay huddled together that night, trying not to sleep, dying of cold and exposure.

The next day those who had survived struggled through to the west-facing slopes of the Andes. And a couple of days after that the remnants of the army stood looking down on the high green valley of the Sogamoso, its meadows bright with flowers. 'Three-thousand-two-hundred men,' Bolivar's biographer writes, 'had set out to cross the Andes. Now, one-thousand-two-hundred half-naked scarecrows came staggering into the village of Socha.'

One wouldn't have thought they stood much chance of liberating half a continent.

But that is what they did.

It would be wrong to give the impression that as many as 2,000 of Bolivar's troops died while crossing the Paramo de Pisba; for over the next few days stragglers continued to trickle in. However, records indicate that the British Legion lost almost a quarter of its troops, and if we accept this loss as average then casualties for the whole army would have been little under a thousand. Not one of the cattle and not one of the horses survived – even Bolivar, when he struggled through to the Sogamoso, was on foot.

Bolivar was anxious to strike at the royalists before they could concentrate, and it says much for the resilience of his troops that within three days of crossing the Andes they were advancing on Bogota; it says much too for the popularity of his cause that during those three days he was reinforced by 800 guerrillas and, more importantly, 1,000 horses.

The two armies met in mid-July in the wilderness of swamps, rugged hills and narrow defiles at the approaches to the Cordillera Orientale. They were roughly equal in number, but the royalists were better armed and a great deal better equipped – indeed the royalist general, José Maria Barreira, was so shocked by the near-naked state of the patriot troops that he protested he didn't want to fight beggars.

In spite of the eulogies heaped on him by many South American historians, Bolivar doesn't seem to have been the most inspired of generals – Paez once said to him, 'When I am in command we never lose a battle, when you are in command we never win one!' – and after several days of jockeying for position he found himself outmanoeuvred and hemmed in in a gorge surrounded by royalists. He called up his last squadron of cavalry: 'Colonel,' he said simply, 'save the cause of the revolution!' The cavalry charged, and at the same moment the British Legion made a frontal attack on a key height. For several minutes the fighting was fierce and the issues in doubt. Then, suddenly, the Spaniards broke and retreated, if not in panic at least in disorder. Commenting afterwards, Barreira wrote: 'The destruction of the rebel army seemed inevitable and should have been so complete that hardly a man would have escaped death. But desperation inspired in them resolution without parallel. Their infantry and cavalry, surging from those chasms in which they were trapped, hurled themselves against the heights with the utmost fury. Our infantry, confused by their excessive ardour, could not contain them.'

A week later the armies met again, at Boyaca; and again Bolivar was victorious, taking 1,600 prisoners, including the unfortunate Barreira who was promptly shot. The road to Bogota lay open, and on 11 August the patriots entered the city. 'They came,' wrote a contemporary, 'in rags and as spectres. But these were spectres strong in body and soul, because the weak remained in the snow of the mountain-tops where there was no air for the lungs.'

Boyaca was to the northern campaigns what Charabuco was to the southern: a watershed. Before the battle the revolutionary star had been on the wane: afterwards it was in the ascendant. There were, however, many years of bitter and indeed fluctuating fighting ahead, and it was not until June 1821 that the Spaniards suffered what is usually regarded as their decisive defeat. This was at Carabobo, in the shadow of the Venezuelan Andes.

The battle was a microcosm of the war as a whole, encapsulating its confusion, ferocity and heroism. An officer of the British Legion has left an eyewitness account:

We halted at dusk on the 23rd at the foot of the ridge. The rain fell in torrents and reminded us of the night before Waterloo. Next morning the sky was cloudless when we stood to arms, and presently Bolivar sent us the order to advance. We were moving to get round the enemy's right flank, where his guns and infantry were partly hidden by trees and broken ground. Bolivar, after reconnoitring, ordered us to attack by a deep ravine between the Spanish infantry and artillery. The enemy's guns opened fire and our men began to fall. Meanwhile the Bravos de Apure had advanced to within pistol-shot of the Spaniards, but received such a murderous volley from 3,000 muskets that they broke and fled back in disorder upon us.

It was a critical moment, but we managed to keep our ground till the fugitives had got through our ranks, then our grenadier company formed up and poured in their fire upon the Spaniards who were only a few paces from them. Checked by this volley, the enemy fell back a little, while our men pressing eagerly on, formed and delivered their fire, company after company.

Receding before our fire and the long line of British bayonets, the Spaniards fell back to the

Opposite (clockwise) Orchid (*Bletia repanda*), *Coreopsis purpurea*, Rhatany (*Krameria triandra*), Coca Tree (*Erythroxylon coca*). These illustrations are taken from the Ruiz and Pavón Collection. Their plant-collecting expedition in 1778 was one of the first and most important undertaken.

The Amazon rain forest, Colombia.

The Upsala Glacier in Argentina.

Quechua Indian with her llama outside the ruined walls of Sacsahuaman.

position from which they had rushed out in pursuit of the Apure Bravos. From here they kept up a tremendous fire upon us, which we returned as rapidly as we could. Since they outnumbered us four to one, and were strongly posted and supported by guns, we waited for reinforcements before storming their positions. Not a man, however, came to help us, and after about an hour our ammunition failed . . . The curses of our men were loud and deep, but seeing they would not get any help, they made up their minds to carry the enemy's position or perish. Out of 900 men we had not above 600 left, and the colours of the regiment had seven times changed hands, and had been literally cut to ribands and dyed red with the blood of the gallant fellows who carried them. The word was passed to charge with the bayonet; and on we went, keeping our line as steady as on a parade day, until with a loud 'hurrah' we were upon them. I must do the Spaniards justice and say they met us most gallantly, and the struggle for a time was fierce and the outcome doubtful. But the bayonet in the hands of British soldiers, especially on such a forlorn hope as ours, is irresistible. The Spaniards, five to one as they were, began to give ground, and at last they broke and fled.

Then it was that our cavalry, hitherto of little use, fiercely pursued the retreating enemy . . . What happened next I tell you on heresay from others, for I was now stretched out on the field with two balls through my body. I know, however, that the famous battalion of royalists called 'Valence' covered the enemy's retreat, and was never broken. Again and again this noble regiment turned on its pursuers and successfully repulsed the attacks of both our cavalry and infantry.

As for our regiment, it had been too severely handled to join in the pursuit with much vigour. Two men out of every three were killed or wounded . . . So the remainder of the corps passed before the Liberator with trailed arms, and received with a cheer his words 'Salvadores de mi patria!'

Royalist losses at Carabobo were substantially over 3,000, a very high figure indeed considering that, as always in the battles that decided the Wars of Independence, the total number of combatants was small. A month later Bolivar entered Caracas in triumph, and a month after that New Granada and Venezuela jointly proclaimed independence by promulgating the Constitution of Gran Colombia, with Bolivar as president and Santander as vice-president.

It was now, with the war to all intents and purposes won, that the revolutionaries' troubles started. Why, one wonders, were they more successful in war than in peace? Why did the various viceroyalties, once liberated, so swiftly degenerate into a rabble of petty dictatorships, ever at loggerheads both with their own dissidents and each other?

The basic cause of disunity was that during the war the patriots had been united only by their determination to free themselves from the suzerainty of Spain. Once this common objective had been achieved, they quickly discovered they had little in common and less to hold them together.

Another cause of chaos was that in every viceroyalty the pre-revolution *peninsulares* had enjoyed absolute control over every facet of government – 'even among the common clerks it [had been] rare to find an American'. Once these *peninsulares* had been defeated and had returned to Spain, the Creoles found themselves left in a vacuum, with no experience in governing and, more importantly, no bureaucracy to rely on for the running of everyday affairs. Such vacuums invited dictatorships.

This predilection for dictatorship was heightened by the fact that at the end of the war each viceroyalty was controlled by a revolutionary army led by a popular military hero –

O'Higgins in Chile, San Martin in Peru, Santander in Colombia, Sucre (probably the most brilliant in military terms of all the patriot generals) in Bolivia, and Bolivar himself in Venezuela. These first revolutionary leaders were high minded, liberal in outlook and well intentioned; they didn't want to be dictators – Bolivar time and again refused the sweeping powers that were offered him, San Martin even before war was over went to live in voluntary exile in Europe – but with a successful army at their beck and call and with no machinery of government to enforce the rule of law, they found themselves obliged, in spite of their qualms, to assume dictatorial powers. Their successors, all too often, were lesser men whose only qualifications for holding office were military expertise and ambition.

Thus was spawned a progeny of petty tyrants, who, over the last 150 years, have held the people of the Andes in almost medieval thraldom. What happened in Bolivia is typical. In 1825 the newly created republic was given a constitution by Bolivar himself who became its first president. Hopes for an era of enlightenment were high. Yet within the span of a single generation Bolivia had fallen into the hands of the ignorant and bloodthirsty General Mariano Melgarejo, whose exploits might be thought apocryphal if they were not well documented. When a foreign diplomat questioned the loyalty of his troops, he made a whole company of them march at the double out of a second-storey window in his palace. When told of the Franco-Prussian War, he roared drunkenly for his army to mobilize, and set out at the head of them to march overland to the aid of France. His morals were as suspect as his geography – he was murdered in bed by the brother of one of his many mistresses. In its first century of independence Bolivia suffered 187 revolutions.

A final reason for the chaos that followed the war is that it left so many people, particularly the Indians and peasant-farmers, dissatisfied. The leaders of the revolution were all men of liberal and indeed exceptionally advanced views, who wanted the fruits of the revolution – liberty – to be shared by all the people of the Andes. When O'Higgins took control of Chile, he freed the slaves and offered the Indians full citizenship. 'If they will not be happy by their own efforts,' he wrote, 'they shall be made happy by force. By God, they *shall* be happy!' When San Martin took control of Peru, he abolished slavery, the *mita* (the old Inca law by which subject peoples were expected periodically to do a stint of forced labour) and all forms of compulsory labour. 'Henceforth,' he proclaimed, 'the indigenous people are not to be called Indians; they are children and citizens of Peru and shall be known as Peruvians . . . this is their country.' When Bolivar took control of Venezuela, he also freed the slaves and offered land to the *llaneros*. 'Are you not now free?' he exhorted them. 'Are you not now equal, independent and happy?' The revolutionary leaders were almost desperately anxious for the people of the Andes to be happy.

What happened to the dream?

A short answer is that the dream – liberty – was the desideratum of only a small Creole minority. It was an intellectual European concept which had little meaning to an earthbound American people – especially when these people were being constantly reminded of the fact that liberty was a fruit which they were unlikely to taste. For in spite of the good intentions of the revolutionary leaders, the fact is that when it came to practicalities the Indians were treated equally badly during the war by both patriots and royalists – witness Lynch, Nicholson and Miller:

It was the Indians who suffered most from the war. They were plundered by every army, and as the war swept back and forth were seized by one side as auxiliaries or beasts of burden, and then suffered reprisals when the other side came back . . . Both royalists and patriots treated them as serfs, labourers and miners, transferring the personal services demanded of them in time of peace into military service in time of war . . . Every military detachment that halted unavoidably destroyed the crops, and often stole their sheep, goats or poultry . . . It was the practice of both royalists and patriots to lay hold of the first Indian they met and compel him to clean out their quarters, to fetch wood and water, and perform the most menial offices. Habit had familiarized them to this custom. It was a habit of mind among the whites to treat the Indians as inferior beings, and this could not be eradicated overnight by legislation.

It is hardly surprising that the people of the Andes looked at their 'liberators' and saw only the same rider on a different mule.

Indeed it is possible to argue that most Indians were better off before the revolution than after it. Under the Spaniards they had at least lived in peace under the rule of law. After the revolution, under a succession of unstable dictatorships, they had to endure a plethora of wars and coups during which law and order went by the board. Under the Spaniards, they may have been slaves, but at least the authorities had been, in theory, solicitous for their well-being. Under the new dictatorships, they became servile labourers, bonded by poverty to the owners of haciendas and mines who exploited them unshackled by government restrictions. As Lynch succinctly puts it, 'The fruits of revolution were not all sweet and not all shared.'

The Revolutionary Wars of Independence touched the lives of almost all the people of South America, but they touched the hearts of only a few – the Creoles and the freedom-fighters. By the time the war ended, the fabric of Spanish government had been swept violently away, but the roots of Spanish colonial society remained. The war liberated the people of the Andes from Spain, but it didn't liberate them from repression and exploitation. That need is still unfulfilled.

CHAPTER 9

The Mountaineers

November: watering the crops.

They felt certain that the mountain whose summit they were clambering on to had never before been climbed.

It was not so much its height (19,455 feet) which made the dormant volcano of Licancabur so 'impossible' (according to mountaineers) to scale, it was the fact that its summit-cone consisted of nearly 5,000 feet of steep, highly unstable shale: 'Rocks shudder, move and start to slide,' wrote the expedition leader, 'as soon as one steps on them.' Yet when, on 22 November 1953, a team of six climbers led by Henning Kristensen stood triumphant on the summit of Licancabur, they found to their amazement that someone had been there before them.

'A little below the rim of the crater,' wrote Kristensen, 'we found the remains of three stone shelters, the largest about 15 feet long and 6 feet wide, their wall-construction being of the *pirca* type, the unworked stones fitting snugly together without mortar. Beside the ruins was a pile of wood, about 10 feet across, much weathered and fragmented.' It seems that the Atacama Indians must have used this formidable and so-called 'unclimbable' peak as a watchtower, lighting beacons on its summit to give warning of an approaching enemy – very much as the Atacaman shepherds today light bonfires to give warning that they are driving their flocks from one pasture to another.

What happened on Licancabur was by no means an isolated incident. Europeans making what they thought were first ascents during the nineteenth and twentieth centuries, found time and again that they were not in fact standing on a virgin summit. For a surprisingly large number of the major Andean peaks were climbed by indigenous pre-Colombian people long before a European set foot in South America. To give only a few examples: the first Europeans to climb Chuculai (17,782 feet) found on the summit an Indian copper knife that was at least 400 years old; the first Europeans to climb Liullaillaio (22,057 feet) found on the summit the remains of Nazca stonework; on the summit of Pular (20,423 feet) was found the remains of an Inca altar; on the summit of Cerro del Toro (20,951 feet) was found the mummified body of a young Inca man who had apparently been sacrificed; on the summit of Cerro El Potro (19,127 feet) was found the stick of an Inca courier; on the summit of Acaramachi (19,829 feet) were found gold Inca artefacts; on the summit of Paniri (19,554 feet) were found 'very extensive Inca ruins'; on the summit of Miniques (19,390 feet) were found a rock-platform (possibly an altar) of Inca construction and bundles of firewood; on the summit of Nevado (16,407 feet) was found the remains of an Inca body. In her source book *Mountaineering in the Andes* Jill Neate lists more than fifty major peaks which are known to have been climbed by the pre-Colombians. Among these are twelve peaks of over 20,000 feet. Indeed it is quite likely that the greatest Andean peak of all, Aconcagua (22,835 feet), was climbed long before its usually accepted 'first' ascent in 1897. For in the 1940s two climbers, Thomas Kopp and Lothar Heroldd, while making a traverse of the summit-ridge, came across the almost perfectly preserved carcass of a guanaco. There is no way that a guanaco could reach such a height of its own volition; it must, therefore, presumably have been carried there, either for food or for sacrifice by the Incas.

Long before the people of Europe had climbed the 16,000-foot Alps, the people of South America had climbed the 20,000-foot Andes. The idea that mountaineering began in Europe a couple of centuries ago is a myth.

It is, however, impossible to reconstruct the story of the early ascents in the Andes in detail. Since the Incas had no written language, there is no documentation of them; and since the Incas have always been reluctant to talk of them, there is little in the way of an oral tradition. Indeed the Incas' attitude to their mountains might be described as secretive and ambivalent; at times they venerated them as gods, at other times they propitiated them as demons. The reason for this is that the Andean people have always been aware that their mountains are both bringers of life in that their snows provide water, and bringers of death in that they include the world's most active volcanoes. They climbed them only rarely, and always for some specific purpose – to build an altar, to make a sacrifice, to establish a lookout position. The rest of the time they regarded them as *wak'as*, sacred placed identified with a particular god. When travelling through the homeland of these gods they left presents for them – a stone, a piece of clothing or at times something as personal as an eyelash. These were carefully placed in mounds known as *apachita*, set at strategic places like the head of a pass. The Indians had no comprehension of the Europeans' wish to 'conquer' the peaks or study them scientifically; and this is why they have usually been reluctant porters, showing little of the *élan* of the Himalayan Sherpas. Von Humboldt, it will be remembered, carried his own equipment up Chimborazo; and present-day climbers who respect the Indians' traditions do likewise.

Modern climbing, as distinct from pre-Colombian climbing, began in the Andes in the sixteenth century, and has been concentrated mainly in four areas: the volcanic cordillera of northern Equador, the beautiful Cordillera Blanca and Cordillera Occidental of Peru, the Aconcagua massif on the Chile/Argentine border, and the spectacular and heavily forested cordillera of Patagonia.

The Andes of northern Ecuador consist of two massive near-parallel ranges, the Cordilleras Occidental and Orientale, which include the world's greatest concentration of active volcanoes. In the Cordillera Occidental are Chimborazo (20,700 feet), the Incas' 'Watchtower of the Universe', which was at one time believed to be the highest mountain in the world, and whose summit (since the earth is an oblate spheroid) is indeed the point farthest from the centre of the earth; and Pinchincha (15,718 feet), 'the boiling mountain' overlooking Quito, which is probably the first major peak in the world to be climbed by Europeans. In the Cordillera Orientale are Cotopaxi (19,347 feet), the highest active volcano in the world; Cayambe (18,993 feet) on whose slopes is the highest point on the equator; and Sangay (17,454 feet), reputedly the world's most active volcano and the scene of more than one major mountaineering disaster. Between these cordilleras, at a height of roughly 8,500 feet, lies the altiplano, an agricultural-cum-savannah terrain in the centre of which lies the ancient Inca capital of Quito.

This today is not one of the main climbing areas in the Andes. The Cordillera Blanca of Peru, the Cordillera Real of Bolivia and the Aconcagua massif all provide a more spectacular and less daunting locale. It was, however, the scene of some of the earliest climbs ever made by Europeans.

Claims to be first on a summit need to be looked at with a critical eye. However, there seems no doubt that in the summer of 1582 a small team of Spaniards led by Toribio de Ortiguera were the first Europeans to climb Pinchincha. The interesting thing about this is the date. It is a widely held view that the history of mountaineering began in 1786 with the ascent of Mont Blanc. Yet here were the conquistadors 200 years earlier climbing nearly 1,000 feet higher! An examination of Spanish archives reveals that de Ortiguera's ascent was by no means the only early conquest of an Andean peak. In the same cordillera, for example, there were the fully documented climbs of the expedition led by Godin, of which Jill Neate writes:

Many high signal stations were used [for triangulation] including the summit of Pinchincha, where members of the party spent 23 days in 1737, roasting by day and freezing by night, and living on rice and fowls bought up by relays of Indians, their work hampered by drifting fog-banks. La Condamine and Bouguer surveyed the flanks of Cotopaxi during an eruption, reached a height of 4,745m on Chimborazo and climbed Corazon (4,791m) which was covered with permanent snow. They were encamped for 28 days on the mountain, probably on the eastern side.

Even allowing for the fact that these ascents were made not from love of the mountains but for a specific purpose, there is a case for arguing that the cradle of mountaineering was not the Alps but the Andes.

It was not, however, until 1879 that a major expedition tackled the great peaks of the Cordilleras Occidental and Orientale. Then one of the most famous of all mountaineers, Edward Whymper, arrived in South America.

Whymper, in 1865, had led what is perhaps the most famous, tragic and fiercely debated climb in history: the first ascent of the Matterhorn. The Matterhorn (14,689 feet) is a beautiful and dramatic peak rising like a cathedral-spire above the Swiss village of Zermatt. Whymper had been trying to climb it for years. In July 1865 he at last succeeded; but on the way down four out of the seven members of his team fell to their death. He wrote: 'There was a terrific jerk. Then nothing. The rope had parted . . . We saw our unfortunate companions sliding downwards on their backs and spreading out their hands endeavouring to save themselves. They passed from our sight, uninjured, disappeared one by one, and fell from precipice to precipice on to the Matterhorn Glacier below, a distance of nearly 4,000 feet.' The question was had the rope broken or had it been cut? The people of Zermatt and Chamonix, well into this century, were convinced there had been treachery: that Whymper or one of his companions, in order to save himself, had deliberately cut the rope. No evidence of this, however, was ever brought forward; and two facts would seem to exonerate Whymper: it was subsequently found that the rope they were using was an old one and had only been taken with them for use in emergency; and two Swiss guides, the cousins Jean-Antoine and Louis Carrel, who had climbed with Whymper in the Alps subsequently came with him to the Andes – which they would hardly have done if they had thought him a mountaineer not to be trusted.

Whymper and the Carrels arrived in Equador in December 1879, and within a few days of landing at Guayaquil had set out for their first objective, the unclimbed Chimborazo. After a week of urging their mules through dense and humid rain forest, Whymper noted in his diary: 'We are now on the slopes of the Andes, yet the mountains are invisible. Everything is enveloped in mist, and a few hundred yards is the most we can see in any direction.' The track they were following became first a rut, then a sea of mud into which the mules sank up to their knees. At last, however, they came to a pass through the cordillera, and stood looking down on the altiplano, 'an open plain that looked as dry as the Sahara'.

They caught their first glimpse of Chimborazo on 21 December. Whymper's initial impression was of surprise that it had not one but two summits and was heavily glaciated: 'Its upper slopes consisted of great walls of ice cascading down from the [summit] domes over near-perpendicular precipices of rock.' The ice-walls looked unclimbable, except in one place where there was an obvious flaw in their defences – 'a very long snow-slope which seemed remarkably free from impediments and appeared to stretch continuously from the snow-line to the western dome'. This, Whymper decided, must be the route by which Humboldt had attempted the summit, and they would do the same.

After checking their equipment (and in particular their temperamental aneroid barometers) and signing on Indians as porters, they set out, having been blessed by the local priest and exhorted by the local officials. 'We understand, señors,' the latter told them, 'that it is necessary for you to *say* you intend to climb Chimborazo – although everyone knows such a thing is impossible. But *we* know very well that you intend to discover the Treasure that is buried there, and we hope that when you have found it you will not forget us.'

Their track to start with lay over a barren plain, the Arenal. This they crossed without incident, and were soon, at a height of a little under 14,000 feet, on the lower slopes of the mountain.

We camped under a moonlit sky by the side of a tiny stream. The night was still and cold, and at mealtime we all – mountaineers, *arrieros* and Indians – sat together round a blazing fire in the centre of the encampment. The temperature fell unexpectedly low. Although we were almost on the equator, the minimum thermometer registered 21°F, and our little stream became a mass of solid ice . . . Next morning five of the Indians and five of our mules had disappeared.

This was aggravating but not disastrous, and over the next couple of days the expedition climbed steadily and without a great deal of difficulty to 16,000 feet. Here they encountered what was to prove the only major obstacle to their ascent: altitude sickness.

So much is known today about the physiological problems of climbing at high altitudes that it is difficult for us to realize what a frightening phenomenon altitude sickness must have been for Whymper and the Carrels. Few people in those days had climbed higher than 16,000 feet (the height above which the problem usually becomes serious); the summit of Chimborazo was known to be over 20,000 feet, and for all the climbers knew they might be trying to scale heights at which human beings were unable to survive. So when, on the evening of 27 December, they were suddenly taken ill, they were to some extent facing the unknown.

Neither of the two Carrels nor I myself, [wrote Whymper] had ever experienced mountain sickness. When we arrived at Camp II we were in good condition, yet within the hour we were all lying on our backs *hors de combat*. We were feverish, had intense headaches and were unable to satisfy our desire for air, except by breathing with open mouths. This parched our throats, and produced a craving for drink, which we were unable to satisfy, from the difficulty we had in swallowing . . . I was greatly surprised at the suddenness with which we were overtaken, and the fact that we succumbed almost simultaneously. It would be scarcely an exaggeration to say that one hour we were all right and the next all wrong. Our symptoms were threefold: headache, disturbance of the natural manner of respiration, and feverishness. Headache with all three of us was intense, and rendered us almost crazy with pain. Mine continued acute until the 30th, then gradually disappeared. With the others it did not last quite so long. The interference with our respiration was even more troublesome. To talk or drink was difficult. We could only gasp a few words at a time, interspersed with irrepressible spasmodic gulps. We were all feverish – on the night of the 28th my temperature was 100.4°. It will be understood that our incapacity was not due to exhaustion, mountaineering difficulties or want of food, but solely to the rarity of the air.

It is interesting to note that the three members of the climbing party who to outward appearances were the most robust (Whymper and the Carrels) were badly affected by altitude sickness, whereas the fourth member who was to outward appearances the weakest (a Mr Perring who had joined the expedition as an interpreter) was hardly affected at all. Whymper writes – rather unkindly – of Perring that he was 'a somewhat debilitated man, who could scarcely walk 100 yards or traverse a snow-slope without wanting to sit down'. Yet reading between the lines Perring seems to have been the unsung hero of the climbing team. Without his unobtrusive work organizing the porters, keeping the fire going, cooking, collecting and melting snow for drinking, and ministering to the invalids, Whymper and the Carrels might well have been forced off the mountain.

As it was, as soon as they had become acclimatized and their altitude sickness had receded, the last 5,000 feet of Chimborazo presented relatively few problems. There was only one place, on the ice-walls above Camp III, where the Carrels' expertise was called on. There, for almost 1,000 feet, steps had to be cut up a 50° slope, before the climbers emerged on to the arête which led to the twin summits. By midday on 4 January these summits looked to be within easy walking distance, and it seemed that success was assured. Then the sky clouded over, the wind rose and they entered a field of exceptionally soft snow.

This could not be traversed in the ordinary way. The leading man went in literally up to his neck, almost out of sight, and had to be hauled out by those behind. Imagining we had got into a labyrinth of crevasses, we cast about right and left to try to extricate ourselves; but discovering everywhere was alike, we found the only possible way to proceed was to trample down every yard then crawl forward on all fours; even then one or another of us was frequently submerged and disappeared.

After they had been floundering about for more than three hours Whymper asked the Carrels if they thought it would be prudent to give up. 'When you tell us to turn back we will turn back,' the elder told him. 'Until then we go on.'

They reached the top of the western dome a little before 4.00 p.m., only to discover it was lower than the eastern. It took them another hour to reach the summit proper. 'The wind blew hard from the north-east, and drove the snow before it viciously. We were wet, wretched and laden with instruments. With much trouble the mercurial barometer was set up [and they made observations from which they subsequently calculated the height of Chimborazo to be 20,608 feet] . . . Then, planting our flag on the apex of the dome, we turned to depart, enveloped in driving clouds which entirely concealed the surrounding country.'

Light was now draining out of a sky that was already dark with cloud. It took them an hour to extricate themselves from the morass of soft snow; then, to quote Whymper, they 'ran for [their] lives', knowing that if they didn't negotiate the ice-wall while it was still light they would be obliged to spend the night on the mountain with neither tents nor sleeping-bags. They made it, with only minutes to spare, then continued the descent in 'a night so dark we could neither see our feet nor tell, except by touch, whether we were on rock or snow'. They stumbled into their camp, completely exhausted, a little after 9.00 p.m., having been climbing almost continuously for sixteen hours, the last two in total darkness.

No one, at the time, had climbed higher and brought back a fully documented record of their achievement.

Whymper now turned his attention to the other great peaks of Ecuador, and embarked on a series of first ascents: Sinocholagua, Antisana, Cayambe, Sara Urco and Cotocachi; he also spent a night on the rim of the crater of Cotopaxi – an escapade which underlines the fact that in this part of the Andes the most daunting hazard is not technical difficulty, but volcanism. Whymper's description of the eruption of Cotopaxi is evidence that this hazard was not to be taken lightly.

On June 25th an immense black column was flung almost 20,000 feet into the air; this was accompanied by a tremendous subterranean bellowing. That night the whole summit seemed aglow, and early next morning another enormous column rose out of the crater. The ejected matter spread out in a huge cloud. In Quito it grew dark at 8 a.m., and the darkness increased in intensity until mid-day when it was like night. One man informed me that he wished to return home but could not perceive his front door even when he was standing next to it; another man said he could not see his hand when he held it close to his face. At daybreak some inhabitants saw molten lava pouring through gaps in the lip of the crater, bubbling and smoking like the froth of a pot that boils over . . . Suddenly out of the darkness arose a moaning which grew into a roar, and down rushed a deluge of water, ice, mud and rock, sweeping away everything in its course and leaving a desert in its wake. It is estimated that it travelled as far as Latacunga at the rate of 50 miles an hour . . . The scene as lava poured out of the crater must have surpassed anything ever witnessed by man. Molten rock filled the crater to overflowing. Its weight must be reckoned at hundreds of millions of tons; its heat at thousand of degrees Fahrenheit, and where it poured out in cascades on to the surrounding slopes of snow ice and glacier, much of it must have been blown into the air and falling again upon the cone, bounded down in furious leaps ploughing into the mountain like cannon-shot. Parts of the glaciers, detached by the enormous augmentation of heat, fell away bodily, and partly rolling, partly borne down by the flood, arrived at the bottom a mass of shattered blocks . . . The flood swept away arrieros and their animals, erased houses, farms and factories and destroyed every bridge in its course. When I [later] passed this way I found the country a wilderness.

Whymper, in the spring of 1880, spent several weeks studying the cone of Cotopaxi through his telescope, and managed to convince himself that there was less volcanic activity by night that by day. He decided to spend a night on the lip of the crater. It is difficult to say what his motive was; perhaps it was part scientific, part bravado. His leadership on Chimborazo had shown that he had a proclivity to take risks; and one wonders if, subconsciously, he was trying to prove his courage which had been doubted on the Matterhorn.

He had some difficulty persuading porters to accompany him, but by mid-February his team were ready to set out for the mountain. Only five days later they were putting up their tent in the shadow of the crater, for the ascent turned out to be 'not much more than a walk'. There was only one place where they needed to rope-up or cut steps, and the only difficult part of the climb was the final 800 feet – a great 40° slope of ash 'composed of particles which were being daily, indeed hourly, ejected out of the crater'. There were, however, other problems. It took them five hours to pitch and secure their tent, for it proved impossible to excavate a level platform on the ash-slope; the debris could neither be flattened down nor dug out – as soon as a shovelful was removed, more ash simply slid down and filled up the hole; nor was there anything solid on to which the guy ropes could be tied. When the tent was at last erected, 'a fierce wind sprang up, threatening to blow it and everyone in it off the face of the mountain'. When the climbers lay down to rest, they were nauseated by the stench of rubber; the ground sheet forming the 'floor' of their tent was melting. Outside, the temperature was 13° F; inside on the floor of the tent it was 110°F. It must have been almost a relief when it was time to make their reconnaissance.

The night was cool [writes Whymper]. From time to time we could hear the roar of the steam-blasts escaping from the crater. Grasping the rope, I made my way upwards, prepared for something dramatic, for a fierce glow on the under-sides of the steam-clouds indicated that there was fire below. Crawling up to the lip, with Carrel behind holding on to my legs, I leaned eagerly forward to peer into the unknown.

The vapours, though still drifting about, didn't conceal any part of the vast crater. What I saw was an amphitheatre about 2,300 feet from north to south and 1,600 feet from east to west, with an irregular crest, notched and cracked; surrounded by cliffs, by perpendicular and even overhanging precipices, mixed with steep slopes, all encrusted with sulphur. Cavernous recesses belched forth smoke; the sides of the cracks and chasms shone with ruddy light; and so it continued on all sides, right down to the bottom, precipice alternating with slope, and the fiery fissures becoming more numerous as the bottom was approached. At the bottom, probably about 1,200 feet below us, there was a roughly circular spot, about one-tenth of the diameter of the crater, the pipe of the volcano, its channel of communication with the lower regions, filled with incandescent molten lava, glowing and burning, with flames travelling to and fro over its surface, and scintillations scattering as from a wood fire, lighted by tongues of flickering flame which issued from cracks in the surrounding slopes. At intervals of about half-an-hour the volcano blew off steam, which rose in jets with great violence from the bottom of the crater and boiled over the lip, totally enveloping us.

Whymper was typical of a generation of mountaineers who, in the late 1800s and early 1900s, climbed many of the major peaks of the world, without oxygen, in pursuit of scientific knowledge and personal satisfaction. It is easy today to point to these climbers' deficiencies: their inadequate clothing and equipment, their lack of technical expertise, their callous treatment of animals, and (in most instances) their failure to see the people whose mountains they were climbing as anything other than somewhat tiresome beasts of burden. But it is more worthwhile to point to their virtues. They were pioneers: men who risked their lives to test, at high altitude, the limit of human endurance and to collect scientific data – as well as climbing the Andes, Whymper brought back a collection of lichens, insects and volcanic-dust-samples, a detailed comparison of aneroid and mercurial barometers and a wealth of information on altitude sickness. Above all they were men of courage: a courage encapsulated by the improbable vision of Whymper, his faithful guide hanging on to his legs, as he dangled wide-eyed with wonder over the crater of Cotopaxi.

A pioneer of a different sort who climbed in a different part of the Andes was Hiram Bingham.

Bingham is usually thought of today as an archaeologist, the man who discovered Machu Picchu. However, he first came to South America as a mountaineer, anxious to climb Mount Coropuna, the height of which an over-zealous railway engineer had calculated to be 22,684 feet – higher than Aconcagua. Coropuna is not, in fact, the highest mountain in Peru, let alone in the Andes. It is one of the many peaks of the Cordilleras Blanca and Occidental which between them offer climbers some of the most beautiful, spectacular and challenging ascents in the world: 'steep slopes, armoured with exotic ice-flutings, and summits defended by immense unstable cornices'. Among these magnificent peaks are Huascaran (the highest mountain in Peru), Alpamayo (claimed by many to be the most beautiful mountain in the world) and the desolate bastion of Coropuna.

Bingham and his three companions succeeded in climbing Coropuna – no mean feat. However, much to their chagrin, they found that their aneroids on the summit recorded not 22,684 feet but 21,161 feet. The view was spectacular: 'We were in the midst of a great volcanic desert; not an atom of green was to be seen anywhere; we were standing on top of a dead world.' It was, however, all too apparent that they were *not* standing on top of the highest point in the Americas. Bingham, a well-balanced and likeable character, put a brave face on it: 'If nothing else,' he wrote, 'at least we have climbed a thousand feet higher than the highest mountain in *North* America!'

He was to have better luck in the valleys than on the peaks.

Like most travellers in the Andes, Bingham had been deeply impressed by the magnificent Inca ruins that were so often found in the most inaccessible and apparently unlikely places. On an earlier visit to South America, as a member of the University of Yale archaeological expedition, he had visited some of the most spectacular of these ruins at Choqquequirau, an eyrie of palaces built into a rocky spur 5,000 feet above the Apurimac. Now, after the anticlimax of Coropuna, his thoughts turned from mountaineering to archaeology, stimulated by the discovery of an important Inca document, a letter written by Manco's son which contained references to the legendary city of Vilcabamba, the refuge from which the last of the Sun Gods had for so long defied the conquistadors. Like a good many other people, Bingham dreamed of discovering this lost city of the Incas.

His researches led him to the valley of the Urubamba, no more than a dozen miles from Cuzco. And as luck would have it, he arrived at a most fortuitous moment, when a new road had just been blasted through the gorges in order to provide an outlet for the produce of the Amazon (coca, sugar and rubber) for which there was now a growing demand. This road opened up a stretch of the Urubamba which for centuries had been bypassed by all travellers, including the conquistadors. Bingham was one of the first people to use it. He had been told that there were caves in the gorges where in the old days some of the Incas had hidden, and that farmers who had just moved into the area were cultivating great stone terraces built into the slopes of a nearby hill.

No one has ever described what happened next better than Bingham himself:

It was in July, 1911, that we first entered that marvelous canyon of the Urubamba, where the river escapes from the cold regions near Cuzco by tearing its way through gigantic mountains of granite. This is a land of matchless charm. I know of no other place in the world that can compare with it. Not only has it great snow peaks looming above the clouds more than two miles overhead, and gigantic precipices of many-colored granite rising sheer for thousands of feet above the foaming rapids; it has also, in striking contrast, orchids and tree ferns, the delectable beauty of luxurious vegetation and the mysterious witchery of the jungle. One is drawn irresistibly forward by ever-recurring surprises, through a deep winding gorge, turning and twisting past overhanging cliffs of incredible height.

On the morning of 24 July, together with one companion and an Indian guide, Bingham left the road, crawled over a frail and ramshackle bridge that spanned the Urubamba, and began to clamber up a little-used path through the rain forest. 'It was a hard climb, and for much of the distance we were on all fours. There were a lot of snakes. The humidity was great, and the heat excessive.' A little after midday they came to a grass-covered hut where two Indians, who had carved out a farm for themselves on the nearby terraces, gave them a most welcome drink of water and some sweet potatoes. The Indians said that there were ruins 'a little farther on'. Bingham, who had heard that story many times before, was not enamoured at the prospect of yet more climbing in the humid afternoon heat. However, with an Indian boy about ten years old to act as his guide, he set out; and almost at once, rounding a spur of the hillside, found himself looking up at what *per se* would have been an amazing discovery: a magnificent flight of stone agricultural terraces – roughly a hundred of them, each 10 feet in height and more than 300 feet in length – climbing for some thousand feet up the steeply sloping hillside. An even more amazing discovery was to come.

Crossing the terraces, I entered the untouched forest beyond, and suddenly found myself in a maze of the most beautiful granite houses! They were covered with trees and moss and the growth of centuries, but in the dense shadow, hiding in bamboo thickets and tangled vines, could be seen walls of white granite ashlars most carefully cut and exquisitely fitted together . . . The little boy showed me a cave, beautifully lined with the finest cut stone – it was evidently intended as a mausoleum. On top [of the cave] a semi-circular building had been constructed. Its walls followed the natural curvature of the rock and were keyed to it by one of the finest examples of masonry I have ever seen. These beautiful walls, made of carefully matched ashlars of pure white granite, were the work of a master artist. The exterior surface was simple and unadorned. The lower courses, of particularly large ashlars, gave it a look of solidarity. The upper courses, diminishing in size, gave it grace and delicacy. The flowing lines, the symmetrical arrangement and the gradual gradation of the courses, combined to produce an effect softer and more pleasing than the marble temples of the Old World. And owing to the absence of mortar, there are no ugly spaces between the rocks; they might have grown together. The elusive beauty of this building seems to me to be due to the fact that the walls must have been built under the eye of a master mason who knew not the straight edge, the plumb rule or the square. He had no instruments of precision, so he had to depend on his eye. He had a good eye, an artistic eye, and an eye for symmetry and beauty of form. His product had therefore none of the harshness of mechanical accuracy . . . Surprise followed surprised in bewildering succession. I climbed a marvelous stairway of granite blocks, walked along a pampa where the Indians had a small vegetable garden, and came to a clearing in which were two of the finest structures I have ever seen. Not only were they made of blocks of beautifully grained white granite, the ashlars were of Cyclopean size, some ten feet in length and higher than a man. I was spellbound. Each building had only three walls and was open on the side facing the clearing. One was lined with exquisitely made niches, below which was a rectangular block fourteen feet long, perhaps a sacrificial altar. The other had a wall in which were set three conspicuously large windows, beautifully made with the greatest care and solidarity . . . Further examination showed that I had found a huge and remote fastness, protected by natural bulwarks of which man had taken advantage to create the most impregnable stronghold in the Andes. It did not take an expert to realize that here were the most extraordinary ruins.

Bingham had discovered Machu Picchu, the most spectacular of the Inca temple-fortresses.

He and his team did little more that first year than start to map their discovery – a daunting task, with 'massive trees growing through the beautifully constructed buildings'. The following year and again in 1915 mapping and excavating continued. However, such was the difficulty of the terrain that Machu Picchu was not unveiled *in toto* until 1934, when the Peruvian archaeologist Luis Valcarcel cleared and investigated not only the main complex but its host of subsidiary shrines, agricultural terraces and lookout positions. Further work was carried out in 1940-1 by Paul Fejas, and between 1977 and 1982 by Ann Kendall, whose field-workers also helped to restore the Inca irrigation channels.

Machu Picchu today has been effectively cleared and exhaustively researched; it is one of the major tourist attractions of the world. Yet its aura of mystery and romance remains undiminished. Probably no other place on earth evokes so powerfully the link between human beings and the natural world.

Many of the myths that once surrounded this spectacular complex have now been dispelled. We know it was *not* Manco's Vilcabamba; that is was *not* 'a temple that provided shelter for the last Virgins of the Sun', and that it was *not* 'a fortress of almost unbelievable antiquity'. There is conclusive evidence that it was built by Pachacuti soon after his defeat of the Chancas (i.e. in about 1450); and it was certainly at too high an altitude, too cold and above all too close to Cuzco to have been the last Inca redoubt of Vilcabamba – this has been identified as Espiritu Pampa, in the lower, warmer and more heavily forested headwaters of the Amazon. Indeed it seems likely that within a hundred years of its first foundation stones being laid Machu Picchu was abandoned, and that it remained to all intents and purposes abandoned until Bingham fortuitously stumbled across it in 1911.

But in its heyday what a place it must have been to live in! By studying it we can learn a great deal about the people who built it. The Incas were a spiritual people and at the same time a down-to-earth people, and this duality is reflected in their masonry-work. Tied by religion and the practicalities of everyday life to their land, they created magnificent monuments in stone which blended into and mirrored the landscape in which they were set. It was as though they wanted to emphasize, by their hard work and artistry, that the god they worshipped was the god who had fashioned the spectacular and enduring contours of the Andes. They made their shrines in imitation of his. Edward Ranney, in *Monuments of the Incas*, makes this point very clearly:

The Incas' important religious sites are [often] situated on ridges that overlook the surrounding area, yet their structures are effectively integrated with the landscape. The temple-fortress of Sacsahuaman dominates the Cuzco valley, but its massive ramparts are related to the shapes of the hills behind it. The sun-temple of Ollantaytambo faces a hill whose powerful shape is abstracted in the rising and falling design of the temple monoliths. The aspiration for the union of heaven and earth, of spiritual and physical forces, is most strongly felt at Machu Picchu. At this unique sanctuary the buildings are fused with granite outcrops in a way that is more sculptural in feeling than architectural. Steep stairways lead one up, into and around enclosed religious and residential compounds, and on to small plazas with views precisely orientated to surrounding peaks and rock shrines. The altar on the highest pinnacle is open to the heavens, yet it [also] looks directly down to the Urumbamba two thousand feet below. The shapes of other altars clearly echo the forms of the landscape itself, and still others, like the awesome sacrificial condor stone, express the dark and terrifying forces of nature, which demanded continual attendance and propitiation.

It is impossible to visit this great temple-fortress without experiencing an almost overwhelming feeling of awe, for nowhere on earth is the union between flesh and spirit more powerfully symbolized than at Machu Picchu.

South of the Cordilleras Blanca and Occidental the Andes narrow to a jumble of great volcanic peaks, some of which lie a little to the east of the Chile-Argentine border and some a little to the west. Farther south again, the Andes coalesce to form a single range of snow-capped mountains, with the border running roughly along their spine. Here, outside of the Himalayas and the Karakoram, is the world's most magnificent array of 20,000-foot peaks: more than forty of them, dominated by the towering massif of Aconcagua.

The Aconcagua massif is bounded to the north by the Rio de los Patos, and to the south by the Pasco de la Cumbre – formerly known as the Uspallata Pass, the route by which the Andes were crossed in the last century by San Martin's patriot army and are crossed today by the Buenos Aires-to-Santiago railroad. This is desolate terrain; the distances are vast, the heights deceptive, the cold crippling, the wind debilitating, and there is a dryness in the air which makes breathing difficult, even at comparatively low altitudes. The Argentine government has now very wisely imposed the most stringent restrictions on those attempting to climb Aconcagua; for although the peak may appear to present few problems it has an alarming casualty rate. No one, with the possible exception of an unknown Inca and his guanaco, had succeeded in climbing it when in 1897 Edward FitzGerald arrived in South America. He had with him a team of five climbers, including the Alpine guide, Mattias Zurbriggen, and a disarming young Englishman, Stuart Vines, who, in his own words, 'only a year ago had had no more intention of climbing in the Andes than of making a trip to the moon'.

They decided to tackle Aconcagua via its south-eastern or Argentine face, and travelled by train from Buenos Aires to Punta de las Vacas, which in those days was the terminus of the as yet unfinished Transandine Railway. They were not impressed with Punta de las Vacas. 'It consists,' wrote FitzGerald, 'of only a few ramshackle railway sheds and a single *posada* [lodging-cum-drinking house], its rooms often six inches deep in water and its beds truckles of straw.' They established their own camp about half a mile from the railway terminus; and that first evening 'sat for a long time around a fire which burned brightly in the still mountain air. I shall never,' wrote FitzGerald, 'forget my first night in the Andes. The dark rocks towered above us into a cloudless sky. It was a magnificent evening, and Lightbody, who had brought a guitar with him, sang Spanish ballads until bedtime.' Next morning they suffered a rude awakening. A fierce wind came sweeping down from the mountains. Their tents, which had been pitched in sand, collapsed, and their tables and equipment were picked up bodily and deposited several hundred yards down-valley. Half choking in clouds of dust and sand, they searched for a better camp.

Although there had been several attempts to climb Aconcagua these were not well documented, and FitzGerald was uncertain which was the best route by which to approach the summit. Two rivers, the Vacas and the Horcones, cut in steep-sided gorges into the south face of the Aconcagua massif. FitzGerald decided to reconnoitre the Vacas first.

For three days, together with Zurbriggen and a posse of mules and *arrieros*, he ascended the valley, hoping to catch a glimpse of the summit which was hidden behind its southern buttresses. The valley became progressively steeper, narrower and more lunarlike. 'It struck us as about the most desolate spot imaginable; nothing but endless vistas of yellow-sand, with here and there a stunted bush, and a little withered grass peering through crevices in the stones and rocks.' The floor of the valley was strewn with huge bolders, which even the sure-footed Andean mules and ponies had difficulty negotiating. The river was swift, in many places unsuitable for drinking and prone to flash-floods; and they had to keep fording and re-fording it. At last, however, they were rewarded with a view of the summit, rising majestically over hills of terminal moraine at the head of the valley. FitzGerald and Zurbriggen both felt 'it did not look very accessible from this side'. The reconnaissance party therefore retraced their steps, and joined up with the rest of the expedition, who had been searching for a suitable site for their base-camp.

Punta dè las Vacas proved a wretched place in which to camp. It was at the junction of four valleys, and the winds were so strong that on each of the expedition's first three days there their tents were blown down; the water was bad – 'black as ink and full of sulphur' – and there was little grazing for their horses and mules. Vines, reconnoitring the approaches to the Horcones Valley, found a more suitable place, and by mid-December the expedition was established at 9,000 feet not far from Puente del Inca.

On 18 December Zurbriggen set out on what was to prove a vital reconnaissance.

Mattias Zurbriggen was one of that élite band of mountain guides who left their native European Alps to blaze new trails through the higher and more hazardous reaches of the Himalaya, Karakoram and Andes. Without the expertise of these tough and dedicated men the famous mountaineers of the late nineteenth and early twentieth centuries (Whymper, Conway, FitzGerald, Graham and the Duke of the Abruzzi) would never have achieved success. It is a reflection on the times that these guides were accorded in their lifetime little publicity and are today hardly known outside mountaineering circles; several of them would have died not only in obscurity but in poverty if the Royal Geographical Society had not awarded them pensions.

Certainly it was Zurbriggen rather than FitzGerald who was the key figure in the ascent of Aconcagua; and in his three-day climb up the Horcones Valley it was the Swiss guide who pioneered the route to the summit. On the strength of his reconnaissance, FitzGerald decided to attempt the peak without delay, and on 23 December an assault team set off up the Horcones Valley: FitzGerald, Zurbriggen, four porters, two horses and ten mules. The events of the next month are one of the minor epics in the history of mountaineering.

There was nothing technically difficult about the ascent of Aconcagua, although in places near the summit the rockface was to prove dangerously loose. The climbers' difficulties stemmed almost entirely from altitude sickness, brought about by lack of oxygen and exacererbated by the fact that the air was not only thin but exceptionally dry. On their first night, FitzGerald tells us: 'One of the Swiss porters, a tall, powerfully built man, Lochmatter by name, fell ill. He suffered from nausea and faintness, which it seemed impossible to check. We all thought that he was going to die.' On the second night it was FitzGerald's turn: 'I suffered acutely from nausea and inability to breathe. Sometimes I was obliged to cough, and this momentarily stopped my breathing and ended in a most unpleasant fit of choking.' Next day was Christmas Day, but there was nothing merry about it. They were by now so high (about 18,000 feet) that their fire was too starved of oxygen to heat their food – 'All we could do was melt the great frozen lumps of Irish stew in our mouths, then try to swallow them; the result was yet more violent fits of nausea.' When they tried to climb higher they discovered they were 'so weak at the knees we were obliged to pause every dozen or so steps to get back our breath; frequently we had to rest for as much as ten minutes before we were able to move on. That evening I was completely done up. We crept into our tent early, for the cold was unendurable – I have known strong men so overcome by it they have sat down and cried. At this altitude the nights are the worst. It is impossible to sleep for more than a few minutes without being awakened by a violent spasm of choking.' On 27 December FitzGerald decided, very prudently, to retreat: though only as far as their camp at 12,000 feet in the Horcones Valley.

On 30 December they tried again, and again they were forced back: this time not only by altitude sickness but by frostbite. They had set out at 5.45 a.m., with the summit looking so near they felt sure they could reach it by noon. The final slope, however, turned out to consist of steep, loose and crumbling rocks which they could cross only with the greatest care. After a while FitzGerald noticed that Zurbriggen, who as usual was in the lead, was climbing unusually fast. It was some time before the guide would admit why. He was so cold that he had lost all feeling in his feet. FitzGerald told him to dance up and down and kick the rocks. This he did, but could feel nothing. They took off his boots, and found to their horror that the circulation in his lower legs had to all intents and purposes stopped. They rubbed his feet alternately with melted snow and brandy, but still he could feel nothing. FitzGerald had visions of amputation, gangrene and all the horrors that loss of circulation can lead to. Then Zurbriggen went suddenly white as pain surged through his legs.

We hailed his pain with joy [wrote FitzGerald], for it meant that vitality was returning to the injured parts, and we renewed our efforts. The pain now came more strongly. He writhed and shouted and begged us to stop. Knowing, however, that this treatment was his only hope we continued to rub, literally holding him down, for his pain was so great that he could no longer contain himself and tried to fight us off . . . I gave him a strong dose of brandy, and with much difficulty got him to stand. We slipped on his boots, unlaced, and supporting him between two of us began slowly to get him down the mountain. After about an hour-and-a-half we reached our tent, where we took off his boots and continued the rubbing operations, during which he shouted in agony and cursed us volubly in about 7 languages! We then prepared some very hot soup and made him drink it, wrapped him up in all the blankets we could find and let him sleep in the afternoon sun . . . By evening he was able to walk about again; although he was still very much depressed and kept muttering that for 20 years he had been climbing mountains and never before had his party had to turn back because of weakness on his part. I narrate this incident as an example of what Aconcagua does to even the most hardy and experienced of mountaineers.

Incredible as it sounds, Zurbriggen declared next morning that he was fit for another attempt at the summit.

FitzGerald's account of the next few days brings out very clearly the utter physical and mental exhaustion experienced by the late-nineteenth century climbers who attempted the great peaks without proper acclimatization, equipment or food, and, above all, without oxygen.

Once more we set out to make the ascent, and headed directly for the summit . . . We soon reached the place where the day before we had turned back on account of Zurbriggen's frost-bite. The height of this spot was about 20,000 feet, and up to now we had advanced over great reefs of solid rock. But here conditions changed, and we came to a great and steep slope of loose, rolling stones. Looking at it from below, it had seemed the easiest kind of going. However, the first few steps we took caused us to look at one another in dismay. Every step we made, we slipped back sometimes the whole way, sometimes more and never less than halfway . . . Our breath got shorter and shorter as we struggled and fought with the rolling stones in a desperate attempt not to lose the ground we had gained. After a while the monotony began to have its effect on us. There was nothing on which we could fix our attention except those terrible, loose round stones, that kept roling down as if to engulf us. We became giddy, and it seemed as if the whole mountain was rolling down on top of us.

As they climbed higher the horizon widened, and soon they were looking down on the great expanse of the Pacific, glittering in the morning sunlight. They struggled on, continually slipping and bloodying their hands and knees on the loose stones. One of their porters, Louis Pollinger, turned 'a sickly green'; all colour left his lips, and he couldn't advance a step without being supported. Soon, to add to their discomfort, a fierce wind sprang up, ripping away myriads of tiny particles of rock and sand, which cut their faces and half blinded them. A little before midday they called a halt, huddling together for warmth in a crevice and trying to cook themselves some warm food. They failed, and were reduce to 'eating cold soup in the form of an almost frozen jelly'. In the afternoon the ascent steepened and the wind increased to a full hurricane: 'It seemed positively to blow the breath out of our bodies; we would gasp after each gust as a man does after plunging into ice-cold water.' It became obvious that they had little hope of reaching the summit. Again they retreated. Too exhausted that night to eat, they rolled themselves into their sleeping bags and closed the flap of their tent.

Realizing that in their weak and depressed condition it would be dangerous to remain at high altitude, they decided next morning to retreat. They were lucky with the weather: 'The sun shone all day,' wrote FitzGerald, 'and as we descended it became positively warm.' By noon they had reached their 14,000-foot camp in the Horcones Valley. Here Tomas Sosa, who had spotted them descending, was ready with horses and a hot meal. The latter did much to revive their spirits, and they decided, while the weather held, to descend all the way to their base-camp. As they set out they must have thought that their troubles, at least for the time being, were over. Yet Zurbriggen was soon to be even closer to death in Aconcagua's valleys than he had been on its arêtes.

It was the sun that so nearly proved his undoing. Not only did it warm the climbers, it melted enormous quantities of ice. The Horcones rose 10 feet in a couple of hours. And there were at least two places at which the river had to be forded.

When we reached the highest of the fords our arriero was the first to cross. The torrent was thundering down in immense volumes, and I could see that the passage was highly dangerous, for the water was passing completely over his horse so that at times the animal was practically swimming. I followed next and was fortunate to get across without an accident. Zurbriggen came next. He started well, mounted on one of the most powerful of our mules, but when he got to the middle of the river I was horrified to see him turn the mule's head downstream. This was fatal. The animal at once lost its balance and rolled over, precipitating Zurbriggen into the raging water. Both man and mule were swept rapidly downriver, turning over and over, so that one moment Zurbriggen was uppermost and next moment the mule. Even if he had been a strong swimmer it would not have availed him, such was the force of the water. Suddenly they both struck a boulder, Zurbriggen underneath. The force of the water held the mule tightly jammed against the rock, pinning its rider beneath it. In a moment I was alongside them, the arriero close behind, invoking all the saints to our assistance – though I noticed he was solely concerned with the fate of his animal; the fact that a man was drowning in front of his eyes seemed unimportant to him. It was necessary to move the mule before we could help Zurbriggen, so we plunged into the torrent, and tried to dislodge the unwieldy beast. Tomas wanted to haul him towards the bank. I wanted to shove him into midstream, for I saw this was easier to accomplish and would release Zurbriggen sooner. I seized him by the head, and tried to prise him away, while Thomas in a frenzy of excitement clung to his tail. The unfortunate creature was too terrified to move; so I got my back against the stone and pushed with all my strength. He gave way a few inches, and the water, rushing in between him and the rock with great violence, swept him away into midstream, Tomas being reluctantly compelled to let go of his tail. I at once grabbed Zurbriggen, and dragged him onto the bank. He was half-unconscious, and had swallowed considerably more water than was good for him. I laid him out on the grass, and with the help of first aid and a little brandy succeeded in restoring him to life. Tomas, meanwhile, had managed to throw his lasso round the mule's neck and bring it to shore, where it arrived in a most pitiable condition, trembling all over and covered in blood. While the arriero attended to his animal, I took off Zurbriggen's wet clothes, and wrapped him in dry ponchos. It was then that I saw he had seriously injured his shoulder. He was in great pain and much shaken.

They helped Zurbriggen on to another mule and again set off down-valley, anxious to reach their base-camp before it was dark. For a couple of hours all was well. However, it was not Zurbriggen's lucky day. His second mule also slipped, tumbling over a steep bank and catapulting the luckless guide on to his injured shoulder at the water's edge.

Zurbriggen, who had a premonition that he would meet his death by drowning, remarked mournfully: 'I knew it. Today I shall die!' And when they came to the last of the fords over the Horcones, it seemed that his fears might be well founded, for the river was 'in a very bad condition, deep and rushing white with foam'. Zurbriggen begged to be left behind. He would rather, he said, spend the night in the open and cross the river when frost had reduced the flow of water; but FitzGerald reckoned that in view of Zurbriggen's weakened and injured condition a night without a tent at 13,000 feet might be fatal. They cajoled him into the flood; and this time, in spite of his forebodings, the crossing was made without mishap.

The events of the next fortnight are an indication of how much the expedition depended on Zurbriggen. During his recuperation no major climbs were attempted. Instead FitzGerald started making a survey of the Aconcagua massif. This involved observations with theodolite and barometer by day, and astronomical observations by night. The map they eventually produced was both detailed and accurate, and formed the basis (in that area) for helping to settle the Chile/Argentine border dispute.

Meanwhile Zurbriggen, who must have had remarkable powers of resilience, took only ten days to make what was apparently a complete recovery – although reading between the lines, it seems that his shoulder probably gave him more pain than he was prepared to admit. One gets the impression that he reckoned he had a score to settle with Aconcagua: that he wasn't used to a mountain getting the better of him, and was determined to conquer it.

On 9 January FitzGerald and his team were heading yet again up the Horcones Valley.

During the surveying their porters had stocked Camp I with fresh food and kindling wood; so on their first night up the mountain the climbers were well fed and tolerably warm. The following day they were almost too warm! For once there was no wind, the sun blazed down out of a cloudless sky, and in the restricted confines of the valley the combination of heat, aridity and airlessness was almost overpowering. Towards evening, when they were nearing Camp II, clouds began to build up, and as the sun sank, the wind rose. They had a difficult night. 'Soon,' wrote FitzGerald, 'the sound of the men's breathing was silenced by the roar of a full hurricane as it shrieked and howled round our tent, threatening to rend in shreds the canvas which strained and tugged at the guy-ropes. We fastened the double-door, and lay panting and struggling for breath. The night passed slowly.' In the early hours of the morning the wind subsided and they were able to get a little rest – all except Zurbriggen, whose shoulder throbbed with an intensity that precluded sleep. FitzGerald offered to call the attempt off, 'but with the pluck and tenacity he always shows, Zurbriggen refused to give in.' Their thermometers next morning recorded 31° of frost; the wind, though light, had a cutting edge, and all day the sun lacked warmth; even in mid-afternoon the icicles on their leggings refused to thaw. They decided to spend a day resting at Camp II in an effort to acclimatize. This, however, was not a success. They continued to suffer from lethargy, nausea and shortness of breath, and felt weaker in the evening than they had felt in the morning. FitzGerald therefore decided to go for the summit the following day.

They set out in fair weather a little after 9.00 a.m.

Camp II had been pitched at 18,700 feet, which meant that to reach the summit they needed to climb (and descend) roughly 4,000 feet in a day: a task that was difficult but, since the slopes were gentle and there were no technical problems, not impossible. Right from the start, however, they had to contend with altitude sickness. 'I knew,' wrote FitzGerald, 'after the first quarter of an hour, that the attempt would be fruitless. I pushed on, hoping against hope that I might feel better; but I had barely reached 20,000 feet when I fell to the ground, overcome by acute pain and nausea.' Zurbriggen, in contrast, was still climbing strongly; and FitzGerald asked him to push on alone and search for a route that would circumvent the slope of loose stones which had proved such a bugbear on their previous attempt. He, meanwhile, crawled back to Camp II where he 'sat for the rest of the day, no more than half conscious . . . So feeble was I, both in brain and body that I lay in the shade and the wind, not having the wit or the energy to move some 20 yards into sunlight and shelter.' It was fortunate for him that Louis Pollinger, bringing up supplies, found him and gave him a hot meal and massaged the circulation back into his right hand in which he had lost all feeling.

In the afternoon FitzGerald and Pollinger scanned the upper reaches of the mountain with their field-glasses, searching anxiously for Zurbriggen. At last they spotted him. It was immediately obvious he was in trouble. 'He seemed able to take only a few steps at a time, then he would stumble and lie still for four or five minutes, before plodding on again . . . He did not reach us till well after sunset, by which time he was speechless with thirst and fatigue.' They helped him into the tent where, with rest and a hot drink, he gradually revived. He had, he told them, found a route to the summit: a route which lay over firm ground and was sheltered from the worst of the wind.

Next morning the sky was cloudless and the breeze gentle as they set out once again. At first they made good progress; but when they were at a little under 21,000 feet FitzGerald fell. 'I did not,' he wrote, 'hurt myself badly; but the fall seemed to shatter my confidence, and a few minutes later I was again desperately sick and unable to move.' Their porters were by now suffering from cold and loss of circulation, and mindful of the danger of frostbite, they agreed at midday to turn back. That evening, as they lay exhausted in Camp II, FitzGerald suggested that they tried to establish a higher camp at a little over 20,000 feet. The porters, however, 'were greatly afraid of the effect of sleeping at such a high altitude; they feared they might choke to death in the night from lack of oxygen'; and in deference to their fears FitzGerald agreed to launch one last assault from Camp II.

When they set out for the summit on 14 January they were very conscious of the fact that Aconcagua was wearing them down: they were now a great deal weaker than when they had first set foot on the mountain. This, they realized, might be the last attempt they were able to make.

There were four of them in the assault party: Zurbriggen, the porters Pollinger and Lanti, and FitzGerald himself. By 7.00 a.m. they had breakfasted, rested for an hour to give the meal time to digest, and were heading up the mountain, 'all in excellent spirits – so far as it is possible to be cheerful at 19,000 feet'. By 10.00 a.m. they had reached the slope of loose stones, and were heading up the alternative route reconnoitred by Zurbriggen. Moving slowly and carefully to conserve their energy, they picked their way between the great blocks of stone that covered the upper slopes of Aconcagua. At midday they halted, and with great difficulty lit a fire with kindling wood brought up by the porters and made themselves some hot soup. They were now within a thousand feet of the summit; there appeared to be no particular difficulties ahead, and success seemed virtually assured. Then once again FitzGerald succumbed to altitude sickness. Bitterly disappointed he let Zurbriggen attempt the summit alone.

From where they were resting FitzGerald and the porters watched the guide as, with painful slowness, he traversed the rockface which led to the saddle between the twin peaks. FitzGerald made a last effort to follow him. But once again, overcome by breathlessness and nausea, he was forced to admit defeat; with Lanti's help he began the painful descent to Camp II. It was a terrible journey, with his legs continually folding under him. By the time he reached the tents, he was unable to see and was barely conscious.

Zurbriggen arrived about an hour and a half later. He had, he told us, succeeded in gaining the summit, and had left an ice-axe there; but he was so weak and tired that he could scarcely talk, and lay quite stupified by fatigue. Though naturally elated by his triumph, he seemed for the moment not to care what happened to him ... That night we got little sleep, everyone making extraordinary noises during his short spells of unconsciousness – struggling, panting and choking. Next morning we closed up our camp and returned to the Inca.

Thus was Aconcagua conquered.

FitzGerald's expedition highlights the difficulties of climbing in this part of the Andes. The mountains, by and large, pose few technical challenges; but the peaks are higher than they look, the distances are vaster than they appear to be, the terrain is arid, wind is as injurious as cold, and in the higher reaches the air is not only thin but exceptionally dry. The expedition also highlights the enormous gulf that existed in those days between the 'gentleman' mountaineer and his porters; the latter were treated not as fellow-climbers but as servants. Few porters ever contributed more to the success of an expedition than Lanti and the Pollingers. They climbed to over 21,000 feet carrying heavy loads of food and kindling wood, on at least one occasion they saved FitzGerald's life; without them the expedition would have failed. Yet in FitzGerald's book *The Highest Andes* there is no mention of Lanti or the Pollingers in the index. All sorts of trivia are listed – 'Buzzards; Condiments, a popular; Penitent friars; Wine, an unfortunate breakage', while 'FitzGerald, Mr.' gets no less than three full columns of entries. But the men who climbed higher than the expedition-leader himself were not apparently thought worthy of mention – a reflection both on FitzGerald and the times he lived in.

To the south of Aconcagua lie the Andes of Patagonia, dubbed by the son of a missionary, Lucas Bridges, who spent most of his life there, as 'the uttermost part of the earth'. Within the span of only a few hundred miles the vast open reaches and treeless aridity of the cordillera of central Chile give way to a close-packed conglomeration of peaks sheathed in alternate swathes of forest, glacier and ice. Climbers in the Aconcagua massif and the Patagonian ice-cap might be on different planets.

Patagonia is neither a country nor a province; it is a name meaning 'land of the big feet' given by Magellan to the region around San Julian where he wintered during his first circumnavigation of the world; today it is loosely applied to the American mainland south of the 42nd parallel. Its Atlantic (Argentinian) side consists of undulating prairie, most of it arid and all of it covered in coarse grass and stunted scrub. Its Pacific (Chilean) side consists of the half-drowned spine of the Andes. This is a world of spectacular peaks, magnificent glaciers and dense forests; a world too of violent wind and torrential rain. The coastline is fragmented by fjords, which create a vast network of waterways and archipelagos stretching for more than 1,000 miles from Isla de Chiloe in the north to Cabo de Hornos in the south. This is one in the last wilderness areas of the world: a region sparsely populated and little known. As recently as 1958 Eric Shipton could write: 'most of this mountain region is still unexplored, and although sorties have been made into it few have achieved more than a very limited objective, and only one has penetrated inland from the Pacific coast. The reasons for this are the prevailing weather conditions – some of the roughest in the world – the fact that the range can be approached only by water, and the difficulty of penetrating the forests and the unusually broken glaciers.'

The two greatest explorer-climbers of these southern reaches of the Andes were Shipton himself and De Agostini.

Alberto De Agostini was born in Italy in November 1883, and trained as a Salesian – a Catholic Order founded by the Bishop of Sales. He was ordained in 1909, and a year later arrived in Patagonia as a missionary. It was a daunting first parish. The trees outnumbered the people by about a hundred thousand to one. To find, let alone get to know, his parishioners De Agostini had to be both explorer and mountaineer.

For more than forty-five years this gifted and remarkable man dedicated his life to Patagonia and its people. By the end of his mission he was respected by both Chileans and Argentinians; he was loved by the Indians (the Alacaluf and Ona) whose rights he never failed to champion; he had amassed during his travels a wealth of extremely accurate statistics on the region's geomorphology, geology, glaciology and climate; he had produced the first scientific map of the area; and he had surveyed and made the first ascent of a large number of its major peaks. A summary of the mountains he was first to set foot on reads like a Baedeker of Patagonia.

In 1910, only a few weeks after his arrival, he began to explore Tierra del Fuego, concentrating first on the Martial Mountains of Isla Grande, north of the Beagle Channel. The Martials, battered perennially by icy winds and skirted by fast-flowing Antarctic currents, are heavily glaciated, with steep-sided fjords penetrating almost to the heart of the massif. One of the first Europeans to sight the range was Darwin, who wrote in 1834 from his cabin in the *Beagle*: 'I was amazed that mountains only 4,000 feet high should have every valley filled with streams of ice descending to sea level . . . Great masses of ice frequently fall from these glaciers, and the crash reverberates like the broadside of a man-of-war through the lonely channels.' De Agostini made the first ascent of the highest peak in the Martials (4,590 feet), then turned his attention to the equally little-known Cordillera Darwin and Sierra Alvear. He also explored many of the smaller islands, including the remote Isla de los Estados – Le Maire's Staten Island which was for a time believed to be the tip of the mythical Great Southern Continent. He was, in the words of Jill Neate, 'the first to photograph and survey most of the mountain areas of Tierra del Fuego, and in many cases was the first human being to set foot on them'.

What makes these achievements the more remarkable is that the mountains of Tierra del Fuego afford, for their size, some of the most difficult climbs in the world. This is borne out by the many unsuccessful attempts on Mount Sarmiento.

Sarmiento (7,165 feet) is not the highest peak in Tierra del Fuego – that distinction belongs to Mount Shipton (8,100 feet) – it is, however, probably the best known, for its massive triangular bulk is a landmark to seamen rounding Cape Horn. It is surrounded on three sides by water, and is guarded by dense forests, spectacular glaciers and testing weather. It was first reconnoitred in 1881 by the geologist Domenico Lovisato, and the first attempt to climb it was made a few years later by Martin Conway, one of the foremost mountaineers of his generation who had several major Karakoram peaks to his credit. Conway landed on the shore of the Magdalena Channel, where he set up his base-camp. After an arduous trek through close-packed nothofagus forest, deep-cut ravines and slopes of crumbling moraine he at last emerged on to an open spur which appeared to lead to the summit. He soon discovered, however, that he was not on the main mountain but an outlier, and was separated from his objective by a formidable glacial trench. Before he could tackle this trench he was forced back to his base-camp by bad weather.

The next attempts were by De Agostini. In 1913 he made a thorough reconnaissance of the mountain by sea, discovering the great fjord that today bears his name. The weather, however, was too bad for climbing; during the whole of his expedition De Agostini only saw the summit twice, and then fleetingly. In 1915 he was back for another attempt, this time with the guides Guglieminetti and Piana. It is an indication of how much depended on the weather that the moment it cleared they set off for the summit – at 2.00 a.m.! They had little difficulty in reaching the subsidiary spur climbed by Conway, and descended in to the glacial trench. Here their progress was slowed by soft snow, unstable ice and mist. However, as they emerged from the trench the mist cleared. 'The view of Sarmiento,' writes Jill Neate, 'was magnificent but hardly encouraging. Two further mighty steps in the ridge led to a great crevasse at the base of the peak. The snow had softened in the brilliant sunshine, enormous cornices hung threateningly, and the ice-glazed rocks made every movement hazardous. Nevertheless De Agostini and the guides decided to persevere.' They managed to struggle to the top of the second step, which consisted of a great snow-dome, overhung by the summit – now less than 1,000 feet above them. A final assault, however, would have been suicide; for huge ice-blocks, melted by the heat of the midday sun, were breaking off in quick succession, and avalanching down the slopes. Reluctantly they turned back.

For forty years Sarmiento was considered 'unclimbable'. Several expeditions reconnoitred the peak; none managed to reach even the slopes that led to its summit. Then in 1956 the indomitable De Agostini, now aged seventy-three, was back again. He had assembled a team of Italy's most experienced climbers, who laid siege to the mountain in the approved Himalayan style. Several times they were forced by bad weather and avalances to retreat; but at last, after spending the night wedged into a crevice in the final ice-wall, Carlo Mauri and Clemente Maffei attained the east summit. The west summit has defied all efforts to climb it, although in 1972 another Italian expedition managed to struggle to within 130 feet of the top, only to be defeated by 'cauliflower' snow (big overhanging mounds of snow that look like cauliflowers).

In the 1920s and 1930s De Agostini turned his attention to the cordillera of the mainland, in particular to the Cerro Torre and Paine groups. These are remote, spectacular and technically difficult ranges: jagged, heavily eroded pinnacles of granite soaring to a height of more than 11,000 feet out of a storm-lashed canopy of ice – the largest ice-cap in the world outside the polar circles. One might have expected De Agostini to write of the harshness of this most daunting terrain; and it is true that as well as surveying it and photographing it, he did record the bitterness of the cold, the fury of the wind and the frequency of the blizzards. However, what he mentions most frequently is its beauty.

Another *aficionado* of these desolate regions was Eric Shipton, who was born in Ceylon in 1907, and is regarded by many as the greatest mountaineer of the twentieth century. Shipton's greatness lay not so much in the large number of major peaks that he climbed, nor in the fact that he pioneered the route by which Everest was first climbed, but in his peculiar ability to transform mountaineering into an adventure that was not only physical but spiritual. No one has described this quality better than his climbing companion, Sir Edmund Hillary:

To my eye, accustomed to the evergreen forests of New Zealand [the Himalayas] were almost unbelievable. It was like being in a new world. A world of crimson and gold, and above it the slender white purity of soaring ice and the deep dark blue of the sky. For ten days we climbed and explored in country that men had never seen. We crossed difficult passes and visited great glaciers. And at the end of it, it wasn't so much our achievements I remembered, exciting as they had been, but more the character of Eric Shipton: his ability to be calm and comfortable in any circumstances; his insatiable curiosity to know what lay over the next hill or round the next corner; and, above all, his remarkable power to transform the discomfort, pain and misery of high-altitude life into a great adventure.

As a young man in the 1930s Shipton had taken part in major climbs in the Himalayas. Most of these had been big, highly organized expeditions, with large numbers of climbers and porters laying siege to a mountain with the sole objective of attaining its summit. His personal preference, however, was for smaller, less formal and less competitive ventures, undertaken with a view to enjoying the mountains rather than conquering them; and late in his life he adopted this more relaxed approach while leading a number of climbs in the Andes of Patagonia.

Between 1958 and 1965 he explored the great lakes of the Chile/Argentine border, climbed extensively in the cordillera of Tierra del Fuego, searched for an elusive volcano – the 'Vulcan Viedma' – and made the first-ever crossing of both the northern and southern ice-caps. Perhaps the most important, and the most typical, of these journeys was his crossing of the southern ice-cap.

It was a four-man expedition which set out from Punta Arenas in December 1960: Shipton himself, Jack Ewer from the University of Chile, and two local mountaineers, Eduardo Garcia and Cedomir Marangunic. Their objective was to cross the ice-cap from north to south, from the Baker Channel to Lago Argentino, a distance of 150 miles over unexplored and exceptionally difficult terrain, where the weather was often a non-stop blizzard for days on end.

Although Shipton was a relaxed leader, his expeditions were most meticulously planned; on this occasion both his route and his equipment were chosen with the greatest care. They were taken to their starting point in the Baker Channel by a frigate of the Chilean Navy. For the first few days of their voyage they were enveloped in cloud and, although it was mid-summer, lashed by sleet – it had been sleeting nonstop, the captain of the frigate told them, for twenty-one days. However, the morning of 9 December was brilliantly clear, with the light and dark green of the forests and the white of the glaciers and snowfields mirrored with startling clarity in the still waters of the fjords. And it was fine a couple of mornings later as they were put ashore at the foot of a great glacier. 'It was,' wrote Shipton, 'a stimulating situation: left on a lonely shore, the way to the plateau unknown, 150 miles of rugged mountain travel ahead, and no ready means of retreat.'

They headed inland. They had with them 750 pounds of equipment and stores – most of it food for the sixty days they estimated it would take them to cross the ice-cap – and everything had to be shifted in three relays. This would have been tedious work were it not for their excitement at finding themselves in country which was not only unexplored but exceptionally beautiful. Ahead of them, the valley left by the retreating glacier contained a lake about 4 miles long, dotted with icebergs and geese; while to their right lay an unknown range, its upper slopes covered with snowfields, its lower with dense forest intersected by a mosaic of torrents, waterfalls and glaciers. At the head of the lake they came to a river far too deep to ford; so they assembled their fibreglass sledge, sealed its joints with paper and used it as a boat to ferry themselves and their baggage across: 'This was a somewhat delicate operation, but the sledge only capsized once and then luckily not with stores aboard but personnel.' As they headed up-glacier towards the plateau the sun disappeared behind an advancing battalion of cloud, and that was the last they saw of it for ten days.

Their climb on to the plateau and their subsequent crossing of it was not an epic of exploration. It was, however, a feat of considerable physical endurance; it opened up unknown territory, and it turned out to be an adventure which the participants themselves thoroughly enjoyed.

It took them almost a fortnight of hard climbing to haul their equipment from sea-level to the 5,000-foot ice-cap, initially via the glacier and then via a formidable icefall, whose chasms were bridged by newly fallen snow which trembled like illset blancmange as they hauled their sledges across it. By the end of December they had struggled on to the rim of the ice-cap, and saw ahead of them a featureless expanse of snow, flanked to the west by an unknown group of rockspires, their near-vertical sides plastered by the moisture-laden winds with a fantastic veneer of ice-cystals. It was an unknown and daunting world that they headed in to on the last day of 1960. In his account written for *The Alpine Journal* Shipton describes their experiences:

By now the weight of our baggage had been reduced to 600 lbs, which was about as much as we could drag on the sledges; for the snow was always soft and usually sticky. Though this was extremely heavy work, it was a welcome change from the tedious business of relaying. At first we found that we could only pull for ten minutes before stopping for a breather, but our performances gradually improved. The task of the leading man was the most exacting, for besides doing his share of the pulling, he had to make the trail in soft snow and concentrate on the compass . . . We maintained a regular routine. At 3.30 a.m. we started to prepare breakfast, which consisted of 'brose' (a mixture of oats, sugar, and powdered milk with boiling water added) followed by tea. The business of getting started was usually the most unpleasant of the day. Each morning we aimed at being ready by 7.30, but we rarely achieved this. What took time was digging away the drift-snow which had invariably half buried the tent during the night, and extracting the sledges and gear. This job sometimes took more than three hours. We usually stopped sledging at about 3 p.m. In pitching the tent we followed a carefully prepared drill to prevent it from being blown away. This usually took us rather more than an hour. We then prepared our evening meal which consisted of meat stew, thickened with potato powder and oats, followed by a cup of 'brose'. We were ready to turn in soon after 7.30 . . . In my previous experience of the ice-cap, precipitation had been mostly in the form of rain or sleet. This time, however, the snowstorms were heavy and continuous. This resulted in a far greater density of drift, which was particularly tiresome when we were striking or pitching camp, though it did have the advantage that badly crevassed areas remained well covered. Another novelty was the dense mist which persisted for days at a time and made navigation difficult . . . For the whole of the crossing the weather was atrocious; but as we gained confidence in our ability to survive the worst that it could do, we developed a stoicism which enabled us to derive a positive enjoyment from combating it.

On the rare occasions – usually counted in minutes rather than hours – when the snow eased off and the mist lifted, they caught glimpses of a world of haunting beauty:

We passed through a group of widely scattered rock peaks, rising like lofty islands out of the plateau. We rarely saw their summits but when they did appear, sheathed in glistening rime, looming out of the mist and swirling drift, they had the ethereal quality of a Chinese painting . . . All about us was an exotic statuary of ice, composed of delicate crystal flowers, huge mushrooms and jutting gargoyles sculptured in rime by the saturated wind. The most remarkable were on Cerro Murallon, a square block of granite, its vertical sides festooned with a fantastic ice drapery, its flat summit crowned by a line of ice minarets.

It took them fifty two days to cross the ice-cap, and in all that time, although it was midsummer, they saw the sun for less than twenty-four hours. Their last night was typical. They spent it on the Upsala Glacier, camped in a full blizzard, with the wind gusting to over 100 mph and snow streaming in continuous and near-horizontal cataracts over the ice. By the following afternoon they had left the glacier, and were walking through enchanted woodland, their world alive with colour, the song of birds and the fragrance of living things. 'It had,' wrote Shipton, 'been a stimulating experience . . . but I felt that I had scarcely begun to know this strange and beautiful land.'

Not everyone would call the Patagonian Andes 'beautiful'. Yet the two people who probably knew the area better than anyone – De Agostini and Shipton – both eulogize it; and it would probably be true to say both of the Patagonian Andes and the Andes as a whole that for those who find pleasure in the wonders of the natural world there are few more rewarding places to visit. Everything, however, depends on the attitude with which the mountains are approached. As Shipton wrote:

There are many ways of finding those moments of delight which come from a sense of complete harmony with wild surroundings. Some seek them through the mastery of difficult terrain or stormy seas. Others can discover the same magic in quieter pursuits . . . The springs of enchantment lie within ourselves: they arise from our sense of wonder, that most precious of gifts, the birthright of every child. Lose it and life becomes flat and colourless; keep it and

'all experience is an arch wherethro'
Gleams that untravell'd world, whose margin fades
For ever and for ever when I move.'

Few places evoke this primordial sense of wonder more powerfully than the Andes.

The Legacy of El Dorado

December: planting potatoes and quinoa.

'If it were possible,' wrote Bolivar, 'for any part of the world to revert to primordial chaos, South America would.' Some people believe that Bolivar's prediction is about to be fulfilled. They point to the torture that goes on in Chilean prisons, the spoliation of the rain forest, and the violence and corruption of the traffic in cocaine, and predict that the Andes will soon become as bitter a battlefield as El Salvador, Eritrea or Afghanistan.

This view strikes me as unduly pessimistic, for it fails to take into account the Andean peoples' innate sense of order and capacity for survival. There is, however, no doubt that the South American republics are currently in a state of flux and face difficult problems, the most intransigent being their lack of a sense of national identity, their tradition of being ruled by military juntas, the enormous gulf that still separates the rich from the poor, the question of land tenure (which is generally regarded as the key to almost everything in the Andes), and the perpetuation of the El Dorado syndrome.

The manner in which the republics came into being explains why a sense of national identity has not been easy to achieve. Of all the boundaries of the Andean republics only that between Chile and Argentina (running roughly along the spine of the Andes) makes geographical sense. The other boundaries approximate to the demarcation lines of the old Spanish *audiencias* and captaincies-general. That is to say they were drawn up by government officials in Spain some 450 years ago to subdivide the Inca Empire into convenient administrative districts; some represent little more than the limit of an individual conquistador's domain; they never were and never will be boundaries which take into account the needs and aspirations of the South American people. Inevitably those who live on one side of the border are very similar to those who live on the other; they share a common language, faith, background and way of life, and have common traditions, hopes and fears. The Indians, in particular, still think of themselves as people of the Andes rather than people of (say) Colombia, Bolivia or Peru. It would therefore seem that the republics might be better off without frontiers. A pan-Andean state without frontiers was the dream of San Martin and Bolivar; this is as worthy a desideratum today as it was some 160 years ago, and it may well be a pointer to the future that several of South America's most able politicians are currently canvassing support for the concept of federation. If Bolivar's dream *is* resuscitated, it may be no bad thing that in many of the Andean republics nationalism is still in embryo.

Each republic owed its existence in the first place to an army of liberation, the 'freedom-fighters' of the revolution. It is not therefore surprising that the army has always been an important part of the fabric of every Andean state, playing a more active role than it does in, say, the United States or western Europe. Initially the armed forces were popular and respected. However, as the republics fell one by one into the hands of dictators, their armies became used with increasing frequency to bolster up a succession of repressive regimes. While performing this role during the late nineteenth and early twentieth centuries the troops of the Andean republics acquired a reputation for brutality which, in our own day, is perpetuated by the atrocities of which they are not infrequently guilty. In the district of Puno, to the west of Lake Titicaca, the Peruvian army is currently waging a full-scale war against left-wing Sendero Luminoso guerrillas. The guerrillas claim that they are fighting to free the peasant-farmers from the incubus of working land that ought to be but isn't theirs; they make a point, they say, of handing over to them whatever land and livestock they capture. The army claim that the guerrillas are trying to bring down the government, and are more interested in politicizing the farm-workers than gaining them land. Whichever claim is justified, it is the luckless peasant-farmers who are the losers. In June 1986 a group of some sixty guerrillas enlisted the help of local farm-workers to attack a state-owned cooperative near Puno; in the fighting that followed seven cooperative officials were killed. Next day the army arrived with a list of farm-workers believed to have taken part in the raid; the latter were arrested and beaten up and their homes burned. A few weeks later the guerrillas made another attack and afterwards tried to hand over captured livestock to the farm-workers; when the latter refused to accept the livestock for fear of reprisals, they were again beaten up, this time by the guerrillas, who likewise set fire to their houses. One of the farm-workers, Fernando Cala, was 'persuaded' to accept a number of vicuñas. He was arrested by the army, and subsequently found naked on the hillside above his village. Round his neck was a label on which was written: 'This is how we deal with you peasants'. His teeth, tongue and eyes had been gouged out.

The guerrillas, it needs to be said, are equally guilty of atrocities. In one city (Lima) in one season (the summer of 1986) they dynamited three hotels, four restaurants, five embassies, six factories, fifteen shopping centres, seventeen government offices and fifty banks, causing the death of over 500 Peruvians. It could be partly because of such attacks that in some republics the army has recently developed an increasing empathy with the people. In the past the armed forces tended to sire and support dictatorships; in the last couple of decades they have tended to sire and support democracies, helping on at least two occasions (in Peru and Paraguay) to replace a dictatorial junta with a freely elected constitutional government. As Weber Johnson puts it: 'In the Andes the armed forces have become facts of national life.' Their influence is unlikely to diminish.

The first thing a visitor to the republics is most likely to notice is the gulf between rich and poor; in few other parts of the world does one find such luxury, opulence and elegance existing cheek-by-jowl with such squalor, poverty and ugliness. A number of enlightened governments have realized that unless a middle class is created not only is this division going to continue but the rich are likely to get richer and the poor poorer. Determined attempts have therefore been made to nurture a middle class by encouraging industrialization and the redistribution of land.

Industrialization has been a difficult goal for the republics to achieve. What happened in Peru is typical. In the late 1960s a radical military government expropriated the landowners' haciendas and gave them in return bonds which could be exchanged for shares in industrial enterprises, the idea being to transform a traditional rural élite into industrial capitalists. However, the Peruvians soon discovered that they lacked some of the essentials on which industrial prosperity is based. Having no prosperous middle class with excess purchasing power, they lacked a home market for the goods they manufactured; and because they lacked both the capital and the expertise to run major manufacturing industries, most projects only got off the ground with the help of foreign loans. These loans were taken out in the expectation that economic growth would be capable of covering them. However, the majority were negotiated at a time when the price of raw materials such as oil, tin and copper were high, and the economic prospects for the Andean states which exported these raw materials looked roseate. The world recession of the late seventies and eighties brought about the collapse of oil and metal prices, with the result that the republics found themselves saddled with debts which they were unable to meet and which, in the last decade, have been a millstone round their necks. Of the world's ten largest debtors, four – Chile, Peru, Colombia and Venzuela – are countries of the Andes.

It is proving almost as difficult to redistribute land as to stimulate industry. Yet this is a vital issue, for land reform is widely believed to be the key to the future of the Andes – a recent confederation of aid agencies went on record as saying that 'land tenure lies at the root of rural instability and malnutrition, and until it is solved political unrest and migration to the cities is likely to increase'.

The ownership of land is a complex and emotive issue. Does it belong to the *hacendado* who (particularly in Chile) still farms it with feudal authority, or to the state-run cooperative which supervises the planting of this or that crop, or to the peasant-farmers resettled on it under the aegis of some government enterprise, or to the speculator who has bought the land-rights, or does it belong to the indigenous people whose ancestors lived in it long before the first European set foot in the Andes?

In the broadest possible terms land in the Andes falls into two basic categories: areas already under cultivation, principally haciendas; and virgin territory, principally rain forest.

The South American revolution swept away the fabric of colonial government but left intact those bastions of colonial society, the haciendas. These great agricultural complexes dominated South American life for more than a century; 'at one time,' writes Lynch, 'many of the republics looked like little more than agglomerations of haciendas'. It is easy to condemn them: to point out that the *hacendados* ruled their domains with the arrogance of medieval barons, that their family feuding led to caucuses and to the cycle of *coups d'état* which for long bedevilled the republics, that they were a barrier to change and helped perpetuate inequality. All this is undeniable. Yet there was another side to them. Many *hacendados* cared deeply not only for their land but for the people who worked it. A well-run hacienda under a caring owner was like a close-knit clan under a patriarch who concerned himself with every aspect of his extended family's welfare – their birth, education, material comfort, health, marriage, old age and burial – while at the same time enabling them to follow their traditional (agricultural) way of life. They were at the same time an anachronism and a stabilizing factor, and the testimony of those who worked on them suggests that labourers on some haciendas led happier lives than their children lead today as they search in vain for work in the slums of La Paz or Lima.

Each republic has handled the problem of how to break up its haciendas in its own way. Ecuador has done little. No more tha 1¼ million hectares of land have been redistributed, and 60 per cent of the land under cultivation is still owned by only 1.5 per cent of the landowners. Agriculture today flourishes in Ecuador, and is coming increasingly under government control; but the profits still go to a small agricultural-cum-commercial élite. To be Indian is to be poor, and to be poor is to be very poor indeed, with 30 per cent of the rural population eking out a precarious existence below the recognized subsistence level.

The problem of land tenure in this part of the Andes has been shelved not solved.

Chile went to the opposite extreme. Allende's Marxist government expropriated over 19 million hectares, and gave the land to individual peasant-farmers, most of whom ended up with less than a single hectare. The result was economic disaster. The *hacendados* drove their cattle and sheep over the border into Argentina; uncertainty over land-titles put an end to agricultural investment; the land deteriorated; output plummeted, and the resulting food shortages, allied to American 'diplomacy', brought about a violent end to Allende's regime. When the haciendas were given back to the big landowners, production again increased – although, significantly, the increase was not in much-needed basic foodstuffs, but in the luxury fruit, vegetables and wine which earned their growers the most profit.

In Bolivia the *hacendados* were fairly compensated, and their land parcelled out in a way that was both socially acceptable and economically viable. Selected colonists were given 10-12 hectare plots, each plot being part of a nucleated structure: i.e., a carefully thought-out communal project, soundly financed and with a captive market – the shanty towns that encircle La Paz. Initially the resettled 'colonists' were Aymara Indians. When it was seen that the Aymara were becoming not only self-sufficient but prosperous, similar projects were initiated by groups of Mennonites, Italians and Japanese, all adhering to the basic concept of a manageable-sized 'clan' tied to a specific patch of land and working it communally. If the idea sounds familiar, this is hardly surprising, for it is 3,000 years old. The wheel has turned full circle; the Andes once again are being cultivated by people working in *ayllus*.

No one can doubt that the republics have a right to handle their land-already-under-cultivation without interference. However, some people believe that virgin land is another matter; that the manner in which the rain forest is handled is of international as well as national concern.

It is easy for people in the First World to point in horror to the spoliation of the rain forest, to cry 'rape' and to condemn the South American governments for failing to protect the world's richest ecosystem. However, it is not so much the governments who are to blame as the frontier riff-raff: the horde of on-the-make land speculators, cattlemen, loggers and easily bribed officials who are currently turning the South American frontier into as volatile a trouble spot as was the North American frontier 150 years ago.

In the 1960s Brazil moved its capital from Rio de Janeiro to Brasilia, a volte-face which symbolized the nation's shift from dependence on its coast to dependence on its interior; highways thin as laser-beams – and as lethal – began to probe the virgin territory of the Mato Grosso. This move was greeted with international approval and international loans, which is hardly surprising, since the idea of transforming Brazil's out-of-work and overcrowded urban poor into gainfully employed rural labourers was not *per se* an unworthy one. However, the transformation was inadequately thought out; it was pushed through far too quickly, and it soon got out of control. Thousands of would-be Arcadians found themselves dumped at the side of some advancing highway, pitiably ill-equipped to survive let alone prosper in an alien environment. They had no capital to buy fertilizers, herbicides or machinery, and above all they lacked the know-how which had enabled the Indians to make the rain forest a home. They hacked down the great trees and planted a crop (sugar, tea, coffee or simply grass-seed for pasture). In their first season they got a reasonable yield; in their second season they found to their dismay that their crops were sickly and sparse; and in their third season they found to their horror that nothing would grow, that the soil, utterly impoverished, had degenerated to dust. They had failed to appreciate the basic principle on which the vegetation of Amazonia has, for millennia, survived.

Looking at the great trees of the rain forest and the riot of ferns and epiphytes that festoons them, one might imagine them to be rooted in soil both nutritious and deep. This is not so. The soil of Amazonia is poor and thin. The rain forest owes its lushness entirely to its own detritus – 'a frenetic recycling of nutrients from the forest floor back into the trees. Once the trees are taken down, the whole system collapses. The soil soon shrivels in the sun and is blown or washed away.' (*The Times*, 29 April 1989). Several decades ago scientists gave a clear warning that this is what would happen if the forest was destroyed. In the 1960s the Royal Geographical Society sent an expedition to the Mato Grosso which swiftly published its findings:

The low fertility of the predominant dystrophic soil will be a limiting factor to agricultral development. Not only is the reserve of nutrients low, it is concentrated in the organic fraction of the soil . . . Agricultural use requires the felling and burning of the vegetation, and this will allow a brief period in which crops can be sustained by the released nutrients. However, the rapid mineralization of soil humus following clearing will result in a sharp fall in the capacity of the soil to retain nutrient ions, and the leaching released by mineralization will result in extremely low nutrient levels within one or two years of the burn. Continued crop production will then be impossible.

This warning was not heeded. Indeed the Brazilian government, conscious of the fact that its rehabilitation programme was running into difficulties, increased the financial incentives it offered to those who made 'productive use' of new land. It was a case of good intentions paving the road to hell. For during the last decade land speculators – often, it is alleged, with forged documents – have been buying up huge tracts of virgin forest. If a road is built near their land this is likely to increase its value by anything up to a hundred-fold. If there is no road, they can still make a handsome profit by claiming the government's financial bonuses for bringing new land into use. This they do by simply burning the forest down and turning loose into its charred remains a few head of cattle. Thus within the span of three or at the most four years a rich and varied ecosystem is transformed into a barren wilderness which, the experts say, will take centuries to recover, if indeed it recovers at all.

Supporters of Brazil's development programme used to claim that the end would justify the means; that the Mato Grosso would be transformed into one of the great cattle-pastures of the world. This is not happening. For, in spite of the millions of hectares of forest which have been burned down, Amazonia today still imports more beef than it exports. The truth is that in one of the most criminal land scams of all times the rain forest is being destroyed not to feed the hungry but to line the pockets of the speculators.

Two things about this land scam are particularly terrifying: its scale and its ruthlessness.

Estimates vary, but it seems probable that since the end of World War II about 50 per cent of the Earth's rain forest has been destroyed, the main areas of spoliation being the Philippines, Indonesia and Amazonia. In Amazonia some of the largest fires in recorded history have been set alight; areas the size of an English county have, in a single burn, been deliberately incinerated, and eyewitness accounts tell of huge walls of flame whose heat can be felt 20 miles away, and which create their own thunder, lightning and mini-tornadoes. According to even the most conservative estimates trees are disappearing at the rate of something like 1 trillion a year, and by the end of the century there will be little rain forest left apart from the relatively small areas set aside as National Parks. Since rain forests are our planet's principal generator of oxygen, the effect on the world's climate may be catastrophic. Small wonder it is not only conservation groups like Greenpeace and Friends of the Earth who are now crying 'enough'; this cry is being echoed world-wide by all those with common sense.

It is, however, easier to condemn the rape of the rain forest than to prevent it, as thousands of men, women and children in Amazonia are finding to their cost; for they are paying for their efforts to save the forest with their lives.

It would be comforting to believe that some of the atrocity-stories emanating from South America are indeed no more than stories, with the truth distorted by those grinding some political or ecological axe. Can it *really* be true that an Indian tribe who refused to leave their forest homes were sent blankets impregnated with smallpox virus? Can it *really* be true that over the last few years there have been more than 1,100 murders on the Brazilian frontier over issues of land tenure? Unhappily, these are well documented and proven facts. Another proven fact is that deforestation is *not* being caused by Third World subsistence farmers destroying their own forest by refusing to give up traditional methods of 'slash and burn' agriculture. This is a falsehood spread by loggers and cattlemen in an effort to divert attention from their own misdemeanours. The truth is that so-called 'primitive' people, who have lived in the rain forest for millennia, understand it too well and are too dependent on it to be foolish enought to harm it, let alone destroy it. The destroyers are the speculators and their 'hit men', who, even as international aid programmes fund conservation and replanting projects, are biting ever deeper and more ruthlessly into virgin territory. The 'little' people who try to stand up to them die. The story of one such person, Francisco 'Chico' Mendes, is the story of them all.

Chico was born on 15 December 1944 not far from Xapuri, at a spot where the borders of Peru, Brazil and Bolivia converge in what is virtually the geographical heart of South America. Like most of Xapuri's inhabitants he became a rubber-tapper, extracting and then smoking the milky fluid from the rain forest's *Hevea brasiliensis*, which are the world's primary source of natural rubber. It was a difficult and demanding calling; this was partly because throughout the twentieth century the market for plantation-rubber from Malaysia gradually superseded the market for natural rubber from Amazonia, and partly because the rubber-tappers had no land-rights to the forests they worked in, and found themselves exploited by middlemen. When Chico was eighteen he made contact with the Brazilian revolutionary Euclides Tavora, who was then in hiding from government troops in the rain forest. Tavora taught him to read and imbued him with political awareness, and slowly over the next decade Chico managed to persuade the rubber-tappers to stand up for themselves. He formed them into a union, the Partido dos Trabalhadores, which spoke out against the near-slavery conditions of their trade, and by 1980 his members had established their rights to work the rain forest; what is more they had eliminated the middleman who for more than a century had kept them in a state of near-permanent indebtedness. Schools and medical centres were set up, and it seemed that the rubber-tappers might be entering an era of comparative prosperity. Then came the road.

For some years the terminus of Highway BR 364 had been Porto Velho, 370 miles to the north-east of Xapuri; however, in 1980 it was decided to extend the highway through Xapuri and up to the Bolivian frontier. This brought Chico and his rubber-tappers to the attention of the land developers. In particular it brought them to the attention of the Uniao Democratico Rural, an oligarchy run by a small rural élite who between them own 96 million head of cattle and over 100 million acres of land. The UDR has always been fiercely determined on deforestation. This is partly because deforestation was, until recently, not only government policy but was also the desideratum of most Brazilians who saw their rain forest not as a heritage to be preserved but as a source of wealth to be exploited, a panacea for their nation's economic ills. Not all land-developers were rogues and vagabonds, and, especially in the early days, many started to clear the forest with high hopes and high ideals. It was not long, however, before the rogues and vagabonds began to outnumber the honest men; for as the frontier extended westward it attracted a scum of speculators, con-men and opportunists, all eager to make a quick profit. It became standard practice for a developer to buy up a patch of land, burn off the forest, claim the government's financial bonus, then move on to another patch and do the same. Anyone who stood in their way was eliminated.

Chico Mendes stood in their way.

His rubber-tappers' union developed a tactic known as *empate* – a draw in chess, but better translated in this context as a stalemate. When they learned that a certain area of forest was about to be cleared, they would bring together the families who lived in it and get them to form a human wall round the threatened area, so that the bulldozers and chainsaw crews couldn't enter. Chico would put the women and children in front so that the *pistoleiros* (the UDR's hit men) didn't dare shoot, and would walk up and down the line saying, 'Don't be afraid. Nothing is going to happen.' And nothing did happen. It was *empate*. Chico had never heard of Gandhi or Martin Luther King, but he had come up intuitively with the same formula of passive resistance. It has been estimated that in thirteen years he organized forty-five *empates*, and saved more than 3 million acres of forest from destruction.

From the moment he organized his first act of passive resistance he was a marked man, and the wonder is not that he was eventually gunned down but that he survived for as long as he did. In 1979 he was beaten up and left for dead by four hooded men. In 1980 his friend, the leader of the rubber-tappers' union, was murdered. During the next eight years there were five attempts on Chico's life. Initially he survived partly by good fortune and partly by acting on the warnings of his multitudinous friends. Subsequently he survived because he found himself an internationally known figure, and was accorded police protection. His championship of the rain forest and its people brought him to the attention of world-famous conservationists like the anthropologist Mary Allegretti, the film-maker Adrian Cowell and the pop star Sting. He was invited to plead his cause in major American cities – Brasilia, Rio de Janeiro and Miami. He was awarded the freedom of Rio. He won accolades from the Better World Society and the United Nations – 'for outstanding practical achievements in the protection of the environment'. He suddenly found himself the champion not of a few thousand rubber-tappers in a remote corner of Amazonia, but of those millions of ordinary people throughout the world who were becoming increasingly appalled at the devastation of the planet. He began to achieve not minor but major successes. The international banks withdrew their funding for Highway BR 364. 'Extractive reserves' were created – 'areas of virgin forest in which renewable resources can be extracted without destroying the habitat'; and the Brazilian government found itself obliged by pressure of public opinion to rethink its policy.

This was not to the liking of the UDR and the frontier riff-raff whose tentacles embraced not only the frontier but the corridors of power in Brasilia. Incredible as it sounds, they persuaded the government to create a vast new state, Tocantins, which was handed over to them to do as they liked with; when it was pointed out that the Caxinaua Indians lived in Tocantins, the agency supposed to protect the Indians' rights (FUNAI) was persuaded to issue 'negative certificates' to say that they didn't exist; murders in connection with land-tenure trebled, and Chico was declared *anunciado* – he was sent the equivalent of a Mafia death sentence. He knew it was a sentence from which, in Amazonia, there would be no escape. 'I shall not live,' he told his wife and two young children, 'to see the New Year.' And he was right. Alex Shoumatoff in *The Times* wrote his 'obituary'.

Three days before Christmas, Mendes came home after a trip to the town of Sena Madureira, where he had brought 500 more tappers into the union's fold. He played dominoes with the men guarding him, then went in for supper. The family were watching a television soap opera called 'Anthing Goes'. Chico wasn't interested in 'Anything Goes', and throwing a towel over his shoulder, he went to take a shower. The shower was in an outbuilding in the back yard. He had opened the kitchen door about two-thirds of the way and was about to step outside when a blast from a long-barrelled shotgun caught him on the right side of his chest and shoulder. Chico staggered back into the kitchen, crashed against the table, reeled into the bedroom and died on the floor.

It is now 20 years since an earlier martyr, Che Guevera, died in a hail of bullets in the rain forest and became a legend to his generation. Chico died for a nobler cause. He will, however, have died in vain if we don't face the fact that when a forest giant falls to the logger's saw or the speculator's flames it is no good telling ourselves that another will rise phoenixlike from its ashes. That is wishful thinking. Once the forest is gone it is gone if not for ever at least for the forseeable future.

In the eastern Andes the question of land tenure has been complicated by the fact that, quite apart from the rain forest, the area is now known to contain two of the world's most marketable products: oil and coca.

The republics today are becoming increasingly anxious to exploit the 'empty' east-facing slopes of the Andes; for this, it is believed, will lead to increased agricultural productivity, new sources of revenue, and relief from urban overcrowding. With such high stakes it is not surprising that the rights of the few thousand Indians who live in the area are accorded low priority. What has happened to the Mapuche is typical. When the first white men arrived in the Andes these fiercely independent people, who were never conquered by either the Incas or the Spaniards, held 31 million hectares of land; today they hold less that ⅓ million hectares, and even this last remnant of their forest home is under threat of expropriation, because oil – President Garcia's 'suitcase full of cash' – has been found in their territory. Oil production and Indian rights are uneasy bedfellows, and there is little doubt which will go by the board.

The controversy over coca production is more complex. Coca (*Erythroxylon coca*) is a small bush which grows in the hot and humid east-facing slopes of the Andes, usually between heights of 2,000 and 7,000 feet. Its leaves have been described as 'the oldest stimulant known to man'. Chinese opium-smokers would probably dispute this; nevertheless it is true that partially chewed quids of coca found in Peruvian middens have been dated *circa* 2,100 BC, and that the faces of carved Colombian idols with the extended cheeks of coca-chewers have been dated *circa* 1,500 BC. Under the Incas the use of coca was a privilege of the élite – the priestly hierarchy, senior officers, doctors, scholars and road-runners – and the plant featured in many of the Sun God's religious rituals. With the collapse of the Incas' rule of law, coco-chewing (like alcohol addiction) became the solace of a defeated people; and although the practice is now thought to be on the wane it has been estimated (in *The Cocaine Wars*) that at least eight million South Americans still regularly chew coca; *mate de coca* (coca tea) is still sold in virtually every supermarket, and coca leaves are still given as good luck symbols to the parents of Indian brides and are placed under the cornerstones of new houses.

It is therefore not surprising that the people of the Andes don't take kindly to foreigners telling them they shouldn't grow coca. Much less do they take kindly to the simplistic view that the way to deal with the cocaine trade is to defoliate the coca fields. This is like telling a Frenchman that the way to curb alcohol abuse is to dig up his vineyards – it is no more wrong to grow coca than to grow grapes. Wrongdoing stems from the refining of the coca leaves into cocaine-hydrochloride, a paste converted by further treatment into the 'crack' which is today selling in the United States and Europe at $US 40,000 a kilo. This, ethically, is a problem not for the Andean republics, but for the United States and Europe. However, as has happened so often in South American history, the people of the Andes are finding themselves subjected to misery and violence not of their making; for the greed of the cocaine-traffickers has transformed at least one of the republics into a battlefield.

It is difficult to say exactly how many people die each year in Colombia in drugs-related violence, for drug-trafficking is often bound up with disputes over land tenure, politics and Indian rights; however, the number is certainly in four figures not three. To quote a recent researcher:

Guerrilla groups and death squads operate openly throughout the country, often with semi-official blessing, and life has become precarious for those who try to stand up to the powerful interests that contravene the law . . . The leading figure in the Medallin drugs-cartel, Jorge Luis Ochoa, is said to have spent over three-and-a-half-million U.S. dollars to avoid extradition, and the Attorney General investigating his case was murdered, his body being found with horrific mutilations and a warning from the drugs mafia that anyone else who stood in their way would get similar treatment . . . The lengths to which these mafia are prepared to go is shown in their efforts to kill Enrique Paredo, the former minister of justice; when Paredo was appointed ambassador to Hungary, gunmen tried to murder him in Budapest . . . In 1987 Colombia's minister of the interior acknowledged that there were over 130 illegal paramilitary groups operating in his country, but admitted he was making no attempt to curb them. After a spate of killings in Medallin, a number of trade unionists, students, university professors, lawyers and human rights activists organized a "march for freedom" through the city. Within a fortnight every one of the march-organizers was dead, including a senator who was gunned down in front of his family after the door of his home had been rammed and broken open by a Jeep.

Medallin today has similarities to Cuzco yesterday; it is a city where foreign predators exploit the wealth of the local people. For today's drug barons are the counterpart of yesterday's conquistadors: men imbued with the same ruthlessness, the same social airs and graces, and the same determination to extract as much as possible from the Andes while giving nothing in return.

This is perhaps the most deep-rooted of all the problems that face the Andean republics. The search for El Dorado – albeit with a different crock of gold at the rainbow's end – is still going on: the rest of the world still regards South America as an untapped treasure-trove awaiting exploitation. The metal from Andean mines, the timber from Andean forests, the beef from Andean pastures and the drugs derived from Andean crops are being used to increase the wealth not of the indigenous people but of outsiders.

If this was the end of the story the future would be bleak indeed. However, at the same time as some people are trying to exploit the Andes, others are trying to protect the mountains and restore to their people the sort of prosperity they enjoyed in the days of the Incas. One such person is Dr Ann Kendall.

It is now more than twenty years since Ann first brought a small team to the valley of the Cusichaca (not far from Machu Picchu) to study Inca and pre-Inca remains. Initially there were no more than half-a-dozen archaeologists crammed into a couple of tents; but as the importance of their work became apparent, Ann found herself in charge of a succession of large and highly organized expeditions which often consisted of nearly 100 archaeologists, scientists, students and volunteers among whom were an increasing number of Peruvians. These expeditions, coming to the Cusichaca year after year, have not only added enormously to our knowledge of the Incas, they have brought hope and a new purpose in life to the people of the valley.

The Cusichaca is not a major river, but in its 12-mile descent from the snowfields of Mount Salcantay to its junction with the jungle-lined Urubamba, it embraces a wide variety of ecological zones in which it is possible to grow a wide variety of crops. When Ann first arrived here in the summer of 1968 the valley was practically deserted. Only fifteen families lived in it. There was no obvious sign of the network of roads, canals and terraces which – we now know – once made Cusichaca one of the most prosperous farming areas of the Inca empire; for in the harsh climate of the Andes it doesn't take long for nature virtually to eradicate all evidence of the tenancy of man. 'Virtually eradicate,' yet not completely eradicate; for as Ann and her co-workers quickly found, for those who were prepared to search and to dig, the Cusichaca Valley contained abundant proof of the splendours of the past.

There are few jobs more rewarding than that of the archaeologist who is lucky (or skilful) enough to work a rich and virgin site. The scholar who discovers a rare manuscript must always wonder if it records the truth; the botanist or entomologist who mounts a new specimen must often wonder if his find will add much to human knowledge; but the archaeologist's every find can, with the help of modern techniques such as carbon dating, help us to piece together a picture of the past. And how many finds Cusichaca yielded! To quote the expedition report of 1986: 'The number of Inca and pre-Inca sites to be described and registered has now risen to 90 in the valley and 200 in the surrounding hills . . . [while] over half-a-million artefacts of pottery, bone, lithic, metal and shell have been discovered, described, identified and documented.' From this cornucopia it has been possible to deduce what life must have been like in the valley 500 years ago.

It was densely populated; for the first and most basic of the archaeologists' discoveries were the remains of 175 houses and 36 large barrack-type buildings, the latter almost certainly used to house itinerant agricultural labourers. Assuming that each house had 6 inhabitants (2-3 adults, plus 2-4 children), this would represent a resident population of 1,050; and assuming that each barrack housed 15 workers, this would give a transient population of 540. The archaeologists also unearthed the remains of a fort, a number of observation posts and a cluster of residences on the opposite bank of the Urubamba, all of which were clearly part of the same community. The valley and its immediate environs must therefore have had a population of at least 1,800. It was obvious from their artefacts that most of these people were farmers, and the archaeologists' next step was to evaluate the extent, variety and yield of their crops. As Ann and her co-workers uncovered mile after mile of terracing and mile after mile of irrigation-channel it became increasingly evident that farming in the valley had been highly intensive. It is difficult to arrive at exact figures, but it would seem there were at least 390 hectares of terraced cultivation, 226 hectares of irrigated cultivation, and 164 hectares set aside for growing maize; in addition, in the dry upper reaches of the valley, some 677 hectares were used for growing potatoes and root crops – this last figure, however, has to be reduced by 70 per cent, because the Incas are known to have followed a system whereby three successive years of root-crop cultivation were followed by seven years during which the land was allowed to lie fallow. So during the regime of the Incas almost a thousand hectares were under cultivation each year in the Cusichaca Valley. Since two crops annually were the norm rather than the exception, it is clear that the yield from such a large area must have greatly exceeded the needs of the local (residential) population – indeed to quote Ann Kendall: 'even if we accept the lowest estimate of agricultural production, it would have supported a local population of 1,800 and would have left *a surplus that would have supported four times this number of people elsewhere.*' The layout of the nearby Inca roads suggests where this surplus went to. One road leads to Cuzco, and the nearby Inca capital was an obvious market for Cusichaca's produce; another leads to Machu Picchu, and from this it is possible to make several deductions. Since Machu Picchu is known to have been not so much a city as a ceremonial centre, it can never have had a large permanent population, and its own system of agricultural terracing would have been well able to support its small number of inhabitants. On the other hand the *building* of Machu Picchu would have been a gargantuan undertaking, involving tens of thousands of artisans over several decades, and it seems highly probable that Cusichaca was developed as an intensely cultivated area in order to supply this labour force with food – an assumption strengthened by the fact that carbon dating indicates the terraces of the valley and the altars of the temple-fortress were laid at much the same time: *circa* AD 1450.

Here is evidence to support the claim that the Incas were an efficient poeple, well able to organize on the grand scale; evidence too to support Prescott's contention that in their empire 'the mountains and uplands [were indeed] whitened with flocks, the valleys teeming with the fruits of a scientific husbandry . . . [and] the whole land rejoicing in its abundance'. In the absence of written records it is important that claims of Inca puissance can be corroborated by archaeological evidence, and it has been not the least of Ann Kendall's achievements that her team has provided abundant, tangible and irrefutable evidence of the Incas' agricultural expertise.

As the achievements of the past were progressively unveiled, the archaeologists began to ask themselves if it might not be possible to restore to Cusichaca at least a degree of its former prosperity. This idea became, for many of the expedition, a compulsive desideratum as they gradually made friends with the people of the valley. This was never easy, for the deep-rooted mistruct of centuries cannot be expected to vanish overnight. However, the team managed over the years not only to build up an excellent working relationship with the people of Cusichaca but to rekindle in them their love affair with the land. To quote the expedition's most recent report:

Our work has not been without a practical end. Our understanding of past achievements has enabled us to make a special contribution to finding ways of helping the local people to help themselves, and has formed the basis of a successful pilot rehabilitation scheme . . . The Incas spared no man-power expenses in reclaiming valley bottoms from meandering rivers and hillsides from erosion, and the cost of now restoring these existing systems is small compared to the cost of building new ones . . . In our programme of canal and agricultural rehabilitation, four pre-Hispanic canals have been repaired and consolidated, and 52 hectares of ancient agricultural terraces have been brought under year-round irrigation and hence cultivation. Also a blacksmithy, a rotary seed capital and a medical centre have been established.

This, in the long term, may be the most important aspect of Ann Kendall's work: that she and her team have proved, in the most practical manner possible, that if the people of the Andes are given half a chance they can restore their mountain world to its former prosperity. For in the 20 years since the archaeologists first set foot in the Cusichaca Valley the population has more than doubled, agricultural production has more than trebled, and the rate of infant mortality (of children under 5) has dropped from 30 per cent to 10 per cent.

Ann Kendall and her team are typical of the small but growing number of people who are currently fighting to preserve in the Andes things that are very much worthwhile – like the right of the indigenous population to follow their traditional way of life. Most ordinary people can't be expected to go and work in the Andes like Ann Kendall, much less to die in the mountains like Chico Mendes; they can, however, on issues such as the spoliation of the rain forest, stand up and be counted.

Four hundred and fifty years ago conquistadors in search of El Dorado plunged half a continent into misery and chaos in their lust for gold. Today land speculators and drug barons, in search of other El Dorados, are repeating the pillage. It is an old story, given a new and sinister twist by the fact that the rapacity of the current spoliators may affect not merely half a continent but the whole world. For if the flames which create a pall over the rain forest are not extinguished today, they may create a shroud which will envelope all of us tomorrow.

Acknowledgements

The library of the Royal Geographical Society has been my principal source for research, and I should like to say a personal 'thank you' to the Society's librarian, David Wileman, and his assistants. Even when I inadvertently went home with the keys of their rare books archives in my pocket, their kindness never wavered!

My best thanks are also due to the London Library who managed to produce almost every book – no matter how esoteric – that I asked for.

In the text I acknowledge with thanks permission to quote from the following sources:

The Alpine Journal, vol. LXVII (1962), by permission of *The Journal* and the estate of Eric Shipton

The Amazon, The World's Wild Places, 1978 Time-Life Books

The Andean Republics, Life World Library, 1966 Time-Life Books

The Ancient Civilizations of Peru by permission of Penguin Books and the estate of J. Alden Mason

The Conquest of the Incas by permission of John Hemming and Macmillan London Ltd

Darwin's Moon by permission of the estate of Amabel Williams-Ellis

The Geographical Journal, vol. 149 (1983), a paper entitled 'Water Resources and Irrigation Agriculture in Pre-Hispanic Peru' by Chris C. Park

The Highest Andes by permission of the estate of E.A. FitzGerald and Methuen and Co

The History of the Conquest of Peru by William H. Prescott by permission of Unwin Hyman ltd

High Adventure by Edmund Hillary by permission of Hodder and Stoughton Ltd

Inca Land by Hiram Bingham by permission of Houghton Mifflin & Co

The Liberators by Irene Nicholson by permission of Faber and Faber Ltd

Mountaineering in the Andes: a source book for climbers by Jill Neate, Expedition Advisory Centre at the Royal Geographical Society, 1988

Monuments of Civilization: the Andes by Enrico Guidoni and Roberto Magni by permission of Macmillan Inc

Pathways to the Gods by Tony Morrison by permission of Michael Russell (Publishing) Ltd

The New Conquistadors by Jan Read by permission of Unwin Hyman Ltd

The Spanish American Revolutions by John Lynch by permission of Weidenfeld and Nicholson

Royal Commentaries of the Incas by Garcilaso de la Vega el Inca translated by H.V. Livermore (1966) by permission of the University of Texas Press

The Search for El Dorado by John Hemming by permission of Michael Joseph Ltd

Travels Amongst the Great Andes of the Equator by Edward Whymper by permission of John Murray

My best thanks are also due to Anthony Lambert and Marcus Colchester for help and research with the final chapter.

Select Bibliography

CHAPTER ONE

Cocks, L. R. M., *The Evolving Earth* (Cambridge: Cambridge University Press, 1981).

Darwin, C., *Narrative of the Surveying Voyage of HMS 'Adventure' and 'Beagle', 1826-36*, vol. III (London: Henry Colburn, 1839).

Heather, D. C., *Plate Tectonics* (London: Edward Arnold, 1979).

King, L. C., *Wandering Continents and Spreading Sea Floors on an Expanding Earth* (New York: John Wiley & Sons, 1983).

Moorehead, A., *Darwin and the Beagle* (London: Hamish Hamilton, 1969).

Ogilvie, A. G., *Geography of the Central Andes* (New York: The American Geographical Society, 1923).

Press, F., (ed.), *Planet Earth* (San Francisco: Scientific American/W.H. Freeman & Co., 1975).

Skinner, B. J., (ed.), *Earth's History, Structure and Materials* (Los Altos, California: American Scientist/William Kaufmann Inc., 1982).

Sullivan, W., *Continents in Motion* (London: Macmillan, 1977).

Wegener, A., *The Origins of Continents and Oceans* (London: Methuen, 1966).

CHAPTER TWO

Barraclough, C., (ed.) *The Times Atlas of World History* (London: Times Books, 1981).

Bates, M., and the Editors of Life, *The Land and Wildlife of South America* (New York: Time-Life International, 1965).

Garcilaso de la Vega el Inca, *Royal Commentaries of the Incas* (Austin: University of Texas Press, 1966).

Howell, F. C., and the Editors of Life, *Early Man* (New York: Time-Life International, 1966).

Osborne, H., *Indians of the Andes* (London: Routledge & Kegan Paul, 1952).

Tax, S., (ed.) *Indian Tribes of Aboriginal America* (New York: Selected Papers of the XXIX International Congress of Amercanists, Cooper Square Publishers Inc., 1967).

CHAPTER THREE

Aveni, A. F., *The Lines of Nazca* (Oklahoma: Oklahoma Press, 1987).

Bird, J. and Bellinger, L., *Paracas Fabrics and Nazca Needlework* (Washington, D.C.: The Textile Museum, 1954).

Bushnell, G. H. S., *Ancient Arts of the Americas* (London: Thames and Hudson, 1967).

D'Harcourt, R., (ed.), *Textiles of Ancient Peru and their Techniques*, trans. S. Brown (Seattle: University of Washington Press, 1962).

Farrington, I.S., *The Archaeology of Irrigation Canals with special reference to Peru*, World Archaeology II (London: Routledge & Kegan Paul, 1980).

Garcilaso de la Vega el Inca, *Royal Commentaries of the Incas* (Austin: University of Texas Press, 1966).

Guidoni, E. and Magni, R., *Monuments of Civilization: the Andes* (London: Cassell, 1977).

Hawkins, G. S., *Ancient Lines on the Peruvian Desert* (Cambridge, Mass.: Smithsonian Institute, 1969).

—*Beyond Stonehenge* (London: Harper & Row, 1973).

Karsten, R., *The Civilization of the South American Indians* (London: Kegan Paul, 1926).

Kus, J. S., *Irrigation and Urbanization in Pre-Hispanic Peru*, Association of Pacific Coast Geographers' Yearbook (Oregon: Cornwallis, 1972).

Mason, J. A., *The Ancient Civilizations of Peru* (Harmondsworth: Penguin, 1957).

Means, P. A., *Ancient Civilizations of the Andes* (New York: Scribners, 1931).

Morrison, T., *Pathways to the Gods* (Salisbury: Michael Russell, 1978).

—*The Mystery of the Nasca Lines* (Woodbridge: Nonesuch Expeditions Ltd., 1987).

Park, C. C. 'Water Resources and Irrigation in Pre-Hispanic Peru', *Geographical Journal*, vol. 149, part II (1983) pp.153-66.

Reiche, M., *Peruvian Ground Drawings* (Munich: Kunstraum, 1974).

Willey, G. R. *Prehistoric Settlement Patterns in the Viru Valley, Peru* (Washington, D.C.: Smithsonian Institute, Bureau of American Ethnology, 1953).

CHAPTERS FOUR, FIVE AND SIX

Acosta, José de, *Historia Natural y Moral de las Indias* (Seville, 1590); trans. C. R. Markham, vols. 60-1, 1st series (London: Hakluyt Society, 1880).

Andrade, J. C., 'The Royal Highway of the Incas' *Unesco Courier* 22 (1969) pp. 71-3.

Bethell, L., (ed.)., *The Cambridge History of Latin America* vols. I and II (Cambridge: Cambridge University Press, 1984).

Cieza de Léon, Pedro, *The Travels of Pedro Cieza de Leon*, trans, C. R. Markham, vol. 33, 1st series (London: Hakluyt Society, 1864).

Cobo, B. *Historia de Nuevo Mundo*, ed., L.A. Pardo (Cuzco. 1956).

Garcilaso de la Vega el Inca, *Royal Commentaries of the Incas* (Austin: University of Texas Press, 1966).

Hagen, V.W. von, *Highway of the Sun* (London: Thames & Hudson, 1957).

—*The Ancient Sun Kingdoms of the Americas* (London: Thames & Hudson, 1963).

Hemming, John, *The Conquest of the Incas* (Macmillan, 1970).

—*The Search for El Dorado* (London, Michael Joseph, 1978).

Hemming, J., and Ranney, E., *Monuments of the Incas* (Boston: Little, Brown & Co., 1982).

Innes, Hammond, *The Conquistadors* (London: Collins, 1969).

Kendall, A., *Everyday Life of the Incas* (London: Batsford, 1973).

Kirkpatrick, F. A., *The Spanish Conquistadors* (London: A & C Black, 1934).

Markham, C. R., *History of the Incas* (Hakluyt Society, 1907).

Mason, J. A., *The Ancient Civilizations of Peru* (Harmondsworth: Penguin, 1957).

Means, P. A., *Ancient Civilizations of the Andes* (New York: Scribners, 1931).

Pizarro, Pedro, *Relation of the Discovery and Conquest of Peru*, trans. P. A. Means (New York: Cortes Society, 1921).

Prescott, W. H., *The Conquest of Peru*, many editions; revised von Hagen (New York: New York American Library, 1961).

Rowe, J. H., *Inca Culture at the Time of the Spanish Conquest: Handbook of South American Indians* (Washington, D.C.: Smithsonian Institute, Bureau of American Ethnology, 1946).

Sancho, P., *Relacion de lo sucedido en la conquista y pacification de . . . Neuva Castilla*, trans. P.A. Means (New York: Cortes Society, 1917).

Squier, E. G., *Peru: Incidents of Travel and Exploration in the Land of the Incas* (London: Macmillan, 1877).

Zimmerman, A. F., *Francisco de Toledo, Fifth Viceroy of Peru* (Idaho: Caldwell, 1938).

CHAPTER SEVEN

Bates, H. W., *The Naturalist on the River Amazons* (London: Dent, 1969).

Botting, D., *Humboldt and the Cosmos* (London: Michael Joseph, 1973).

Darwin, C., *Narrative of the Surveying Voyage of HMS 'Adventure' and 'Beagle', 1826-36,* vol. III (London: Henry Colburn, 1839).

—*The Origin of the Species* (Bromley: John Murray, 1859).

Hagen, V. W. von, *South America Called Them* (New York: Knopf, 1945).

Hamy, E. J., (ed.), *Joseph Dombey, médicin, naturaliste* (Paris: Guilmato, 1905).

Humboldt, A. von, *Personal Narrative of Travels to the Equinoctial Regions of the New Continent, 1797-1804,* trans. H. M. Williams (7 vols., London: Longman Hurst, 1814).

—*View of Nature,* trans. E. C. Olte and H. Bohn (London: Bohn, 1850).

Juan, G. and De Ulloa, A., *A Voyage to South America,* trans. John Adams (London: John Stockdale, 1806).

Karsten, R., *The Civilization of the South American Indians* (London: Kegan Paul, 1926).

La Condamine, C. M., de, *Relation abrégée d'un voyage fait dans l'interieur de l'Amerique meridionale* (Paris, 1745). Trans: *A Succinct Abridgement of a Voyage Made Within the Inland Parts of South America* (London: Withers & Woodfall, 1747).

—*Mesure des trois premiers degrés du Meridien* (Paris, 1751).

Moorehead, A., *Darwin and the Beagle,* (London: Hamish Hamilton, 1969).

Mutis, J. C., *Diario de Observaces . . .* (Madrid: Editorial Minerva, 1958).

Richards, P. W., *The Tropical Rain Forest* (Cambridge: Cambridge University Press, 1952).

Ruiz, L. H., *Travels of Ruiz, Pavon and Dombey in Peru and Chile, 1777-78* (Madrid, 1794). *Flora Peruvianae et Chilensis prodromus . . .* (Madrid, 1794).

Spruce, R., *Notes of a Botanist on the Amazon and Andes,* (London: Macmillan, 1908).

Steele, A. R., *Flowers for the King* (Durham, N. Carolina: Duke University Press, 1964).

Sterling, T. and the Editors of Time-Life, *The Amazon* (Amsterdam: Time-Life Books, 1973).

Wallace, A. R., *Narrative of Travels on the Amazon and Rio Negro* (London: Reeve, 1853).

—*The Malay Archipelago* (London: Reeve, 1869).

Williams-Ellis. A., *Darwin's Moon* (Glasgow: Blackie, 1966).

Woodcock, G., *Henry Walter Bates* (London: Faber & Faber, 1969).

CHAPTER EIGHT

An Officer of the Colombian Navy, *Recollections of a Service of Three Years During the War of Extermination* (London: published privately, 1828).

Bealunde, V. A., *Bolivar and the Political Thought of the Spanish American Revolution* (Oxford: Oxford University Press, 1938).

Bolivar, S., *Decretos de Libertador* (3 vols., Caracas: Sociedad Bolivariana de Venezuela, Imprenta Nacional, 1961).

Brown, Captain C., *Narrative of the Expedition to South America for the Service of the Spanish Patriots* (London: John Booth, 1819).

Collier, S., *Ideas and Politics of Chilean Independence* (Cambridge: Cambridge University Press, 1967).

Dundonald, Thomas Cochrane, Tenth Earl of, *Autobiography of a Seaman* (London: Richard Bentley, 1859).

—*Narrative of Services in the Liberation of Chile, Peru and Brazil* (London: James Ridgway, 1860).

Graham, G. S. and Humphreys, R.A., (eds), *The Navy and South America* (London: Navy Records Society, 1962).

Hall, B., *Extracts from a Journal written on the coasts of Chile, Peru and Mexico* (2 vols., Edinburgh: Constable & Co., 1824).

Hanke, L., *The Spanish Struggle for Justice in the Conquest of America* (Cambridge, Mass: University Press, 1945).

Herring, H., *A History of Latin America* (New York: Knopf, 1961).

Lecuna, V., (ed). *Cartas del Libertador* (10 vols., Caracas: Venezuelan Government Press, 1929-30).

—*Simon Bolivar, Selected Writings* (New York: Colonial Press Inc., 1951).

Lynch, J., *The Spanish American Revolutions, 1808-1826* (London: Weidenfeld & Nicholson, 1973).

Madariaga, Salvador de, *Bolivar* (USA: Hollis & Carter, 1952).

Miller, J., *Memoirs of General Miller in the Service of the Republic of Peru* (2 vols., London: 1828).

Mitre, B., *Historia de San Martin y de la emancipacion sud-americana* (4 vols., Buenos Aires, 1890). Translated and abridged as *The Emancipation of South America* by W. Pilling (London: Chapman & Hall, 1893).

Nicholson, I., *The Liberators* (London: Faber & Faber, 1969).

Paez, J. A., *Autobiografia* (Caracas: Venezuelan Ministry of Education, 1946).

Read, J., *The New Conquistadors* (Evans, 1980).

Robertson, W. S., *Life of Miranda* (2 vols., Chapel Hill: University of North Carolina Press, 1929).

Rourke, T., *Simon Bolivar* (London: Michael Joseph, 1940).

CHAPTER NINE

Beaud, P., *The Peruvian Andes* (Leicester: Cordee, 1988).

Bingham, H., *Inca Land: Exploration in the Highlands of Peru* (Boston: Houghton Mifflin, 1922).

—'Ascent of Coropuna', *Harper's Magazine* 124 (1912).

Bonington, C., 'Central Tower of Paine', *Alpine Journal* 68 (1963).

Conway, M., *Aconcagua and Tierra del Fuego* (London: Cassell, 1902).

De Agostini, A., *Andes Patagonicos* (Milan: published by the author, 1945).

—*Ai limite del Mondo* (Milan: Alpinismo Italiano del Mondo, 1953).

—*Trent anni nella Terra del Fuoco* (Turin: Societa Editrice Internazional, 1955).

Echevarria, E., 'The South American Indian as a pioneer alpinist'. *Alpine Journal* 73, (1968) pp. 81-8.

—'The Cordillera Blanca of Peru as a National Park', *Alpine Journal* 85 (1980).

Fanton, M., 'Some Notes on the history of Aconcagua', *Alpine Journal* 71 (1966).

FitzGerald, E., 'Expedition to Aconcagua', *Alpine Journal* 19 (1898).

—*The Highest Andes* (London: Methuen, 1899).

Hausser, G., *White Mountain, Tawny Plain* (London: Allen & Unwin, 1961).

Keenlyside, F., *Peaks and Pioneers* (London: Elek, 1975).

Maestri, C., *La conquista del Cerro Torre* (La Montana, 1969).

Morrison, A., *Land Above the Clouds* (London: Deutsch, 1974).

—*The Andes* (Time-Life Books, 1975).

Neate, J., *Mountaineering in the Andes* (London: Expedition Advisory Centre, Royal Geographical Society, 1987).
Peck, A., *Search for the Apex of America* (New York: Dodd Mead, 1911).
Portway, C., *Journey Along the Spine of the Andes* (Oxford: Oxford University Press, 1984).
Rudolph, W., 'Licancabur, mountain of the Atacamenos', *Geographical Review* (1956).
—*Vanishing Trails of the Atacama* (New York: American Geographical Society, Research Series, 1963).
Shipton, E., 'Explorations in Patagonia', *Geographical Magazine* 32 (1960) pp. 493-505.
—'Journey over the Patagonian ice cap', *Alpine Journal* 67 (1962) pp. 259-68.
—*Land of Tempest* (London: Hodder & Stoughton, 1963).
—*That Untravelled World* (London: Hodder & Stoughton, 1969).
—*Tierra del Fuego* (London: Charles Knight, 1973).
Terray, L., *Conquistadors of the Useless* (London: Gollancz, 1963).
Vines, S., 'Ascent of Aconcagua and Tupunqato', *Alpine Journal* 19 (1899) pp. 565-78.
Whymper, E., *Travels Amongst the Great Andes of the Equator* (London: John Murray, 1891).
Zurbriggen, M., *From the Alps to the Andes* (London: Fisher Unwin, 1899).

EPILOGUE

Blakemore, H. and Smith, C. J., (eds.), *Latin America* (London: Methuen, 1971).
Cubitt, T., *Latin American Society* (London: Longman, 1988).
Eddy, P. with Sabogal, H. and Walden, S., *The Cocaine Wars* (London: Century, 1988).
Morris, A. S., *South America* (London: Hodder & Stoughton, 1979).
Odell, P. R. and Preston, D., *Economics and Societies in Latin America* (London: John Wiley, 1975).
Preston, D., (ed.), *Latin American Development* (London: Longman, 1987).
Taylor, N., *Plant Drugs that Changed the World* (London: Allen & Unwin, 1966).

Relevant issues of Anmesty International reports
Andean Group reports
The Cusichaca Project reports
Geographical Journal
Geographical Magazine
The Times

Illustration Acknowledgements

The author and publishers would like to thank the following for supplying photographs and illustrations.

Black and white chapter openers of the Inca agricultural year by the Chronicler Guaman Poma: South American Pictures.

Photographs between text pages 40 and 41: South American Pictures.

Photographs between text pages 88 and 89: page i (top) South American Pictures, (right) J. Allan Cash Ltd; pages ii and iii J. Allan Cash Ltd; page iv Manuel Romero.

Photographs between text pages 136 and 137: pages i-iii South American Pictures; page iv (top left and right) Manuel Romero, (bottom) Victoria and Albert Museum.

Photographs between text pages 168 and 169: page i *Real Jardin Botanico* – Madrid (taken from the Ruiz and Pavón Collection); pages ii-iv South American Pictures.

Index